ZAGAT SURVEY

AMERICA'S TOP RESTAURANTS

Published and Distributed by

ZAGAT SURVEY
4 Columbus Circle
New York, N.Y. 10019
212-977-6000

Second Printing

©1992 Eugene H. Zagat, Jr., and Nina S. Zagat
ISBN 0-943421-67-5

ACKNOWLEDGMENTS

Our special thanks to the thousands of surveyors who have shared their views with us and made this nationwide *Survey* possible. We would also like to thank our editors in each city: Karen Berk, Sally Bernstein, Anthony Dias Blue, Olga Boikess, Robert Bone, Teresa Byrne-Dodge, Paul A. Camp, Millard Cohen, Cass Davies, Pat Denechaud, Audrey Farolino, Hal Foster, Jocelyn Fujii, Randall Gates, Kay Goldstein, Norma Gottlieb, Valerie Hart, Sam Hughes, Leslie James, Elin Jeffords, Bill Kent, Michael Klein, Carole Kotkin, Corby Kummer, Jane Heald Lavine, Joan Lang, Christiane Lauterbach, Freddie and Myrtle Lee, Sharon Litwin, Charles Malody, Carolyn McGuire, Kitty Morgan, Todd Persons, Joe Pollack, Ron Ruggless, Susan Safronoff, Merrill Shindler, Art Siemering, Elaine Tait, Paul Uhlmann III, Jack Weiner and Mary C. Wright.

TO ORDER

ZAGAT U.S. HOTEL, RESORT, SPA SURVEY

ZAGAT SURVEY: AMERICA'S TOP RESTAURANTS

ZAGAT SURVEY: AMERICA'S BEST VALUE RESTAURANTS

ZAGAT RESTAURANT SURVEYS
Atlanta; Atlantic City; Boston; Chicago; Dallas–Fort Worth; Hawaii; Houston; Kansas City; London; Los Angeles–Southern California; Miami–Southern Florida; Montreal; New Orleans; New York City; Orlando–Central Florida; Pacific Northwest; Philadelphia; San Francisco; Southwest; St. Louis; Tri-State–CT/NJ/NY; Washington, D.C.–Baltimore

ZAGAT NYC MARKETPLACE SURVEY
covering food, wine and entertaining sources

ZAGAT/AXXIS CityGuides™
for desktop, notebook and handheld computers. Comprehensive mapping software fully integrated with Zagat restaurant and hotel ratings; available by city on disk or nationwide on CD-ROM.

Call (212) 977-6000 • (800) 333-3421

or Write to:

Zagat Survey
4 Columbus Circle
New York, New York 10019

Regarding Corporate Gifts and Deluxe Editions, call (212) 977-6000 or (800) 333-3421

CONTENTS

Introduction	6
Foreword	7
Explanation of Ratings and Symbols	9
ALPHABETICAL DIRECTORY,	
RATINGS AND REVIEWS	
• Atlanta	12
• Atlantic City	21
• Baltimore	26
• Boston	33
• Chicago	43
• Dallas	54
• Fort Lauderdale	63
• Fort Worth	71
• Honolulu	76
• Houston	84
• Kansas City	94
• Los Angeles	103
• Miami	113
• Milwaukee	122
• New Orleans	125
• New York City	135
• Orange County, CA	144
• Orlando	149
• Palm Beach	156
• Philadelphia	161
• Phoenix–Scottsdale	170
• Portland, OR	178
• San Diego	183
• San Francisco	188
• Santa Fe	197
• Seattle	201
• St. Louis	208
• Tampa Bay–St. Petersburg	217
• Washington, D.C.	222
Types of Cuisine	233
Alphabetical Page Index	244
Wine Chart	252

INTRODUCTION

Here are the results of our first *Zagat Survey of America's Top Restaurants*, covering 1,010 restaurants in 29 U.S. cities. This book represents a compilation of the best restaurants selected by thousands of local *Survey* participants. Though the cities covered were chosen mainly because they are leading culinary centers, this is still a "work in progress" in the sense that there are some areas that we have yet to cover. For example, we are now publishing our first *Survey* in five Rocky Mountain states and another covering Ohio. The Carolinas and Virginia will follow.

By surveying large numbers of local restaurant-goers, we think we have achieved a uniquely reliable guide. We hope you agree. On the assumption that most people want a "quick fix" on the places at which they wish to eat, we've tried to be concise.

Knowing that the quality of this *Survey* is the direct result of their voting and commentary, we sincerely thank each participant. They include numerous professionals, business executives and just plain folks – food lovers all. We also thank our local editors. It was they who helped us choose the restaurants to be surveyed, and then edited the *Survey* results.

We invite you to be a reviewer in our city *Restaurant Surveys* or in our nationwide *Travel Survey*. So that we can contact you at the time of the next *Survey*, send a stamped, self-addressed, business-size envelope to ZAGAT SURVEY, 4 Columbus Circle, New York, N.Y. 10019 indicating which *Survey* interests you. If you want to participate in more than one *Survey*, e.g. your home-town *Restaurant Survey* and our *National Hotel Survey*, please write on the envelope "NYC Restaurant" or "U.S. Hotel", or both. Each participant will receive a free copy of the resulting *Survey* when it's published.

Your comments, suggestions and criticisms of this *Survey* are also solicited. There is always room for improvement – with your help!

New York, New York　　　　　　Nina and Tim Zagat
December 1, 1992

FOREWORD

Twenty years ago, if you asked any gourmet which country in the world had the best restaurants, the answer would have been a near unanimous "France." Today most sophisticated diners would agree that the answer would be the USA. What explains this fundamental change?

The answer has to do with many complex factors: First, the job of chef, which a generation ago was viewed by many as servile, has become highly respected; second, the enormous growth of America's cooking schools, led by the Culinary Institute of America provides the U.S. with a constant flow of skilled young chefs; third, America's fields and waters provide the best and most varied sources of ingredients in the world; fourth, our unique mix of people – we are still a nation of immigrants – provides America with the most varied cuisines of any nation on earth; and fifth, there has been a fundamental change in our nation's dining habits.

The change began with the rise in the number of women in the work force. This has meant that fewer women have the time to shop and prepare dinners. Indeed, working mothers at the end of the day want to either eat out or order in. Simultaneously, the growth of white-collar jobs with long hours has meant that more and more workers of both sexes, especially in big cities, must eat out – at both lunch and dinner. Thus, "dining-out", once restricted to Saturday nights and holidays, is now a way of life, with 10-year-olds regularly making restaurant selections for their families – pizza or Chinese tonight?

Given all of this eating out, consumers are more educated than ever before. Thanks to the jet age, Americans more than ever have been traveling and trying good restaurants, both here and abroad. We can also thank the food educators –

in particular James Beard, Julia Child and Craig Claiborne – for bringing culinary sophistication to America's homes.

In the course of the last generation, there has also been a revolution in what a "top restaurant" is supposed to look like. Back in the '60s, the best restaurant in a city was usually a carpeted room with sparkling chandeliers, gilded Louis XVI chairs, starched table linens, gleaming crystal stemware and food exquisitely arranged on every plate by a veteran French chef. Today it may be found anywhere – a wooded lodge clinging to timeworn cliffs with ocean surf pounding the rocks below...or in a stark, spare former factory with a bare-wood floor, white walls hung with museum posters and food served casually out of an open kitchen whose chef embraces mix-and-match of cuisines, e.g. Wolfgang Puck's Chinois on Main.

In the following city-by-city guide, you will find our surveyors' "Top Restaurants" in descending order of food ratings. Anyone tapping into these lists can be assured of restaurants that offer the finest food in their locality. We've also included a category of "Other Top Places" that covers popular local restaurants and landmarks. Some of these don't-miss spots are longer on atmosphere than they are on taste; some places are part of the lore and attraction of their region. For example, New York's Tavern on the Green would never make the top food ratings list, but is too important a restaurant not to mention. All of these "Other Top Places" came in as the leaders in one or more categories of our reviewers' voting.

In sum, there is quality food for every taste, almost without exception, and not all of it is expensive. Most important, this compendium represents the absolute tops in eating-out experiences: beautiful places, superlative food and service on a level suggesting that the diner in search of excellence can do no better than here in America.

New York, New York	Nina and Tim Zagat
December 1, 1992	

EXPLANATION OF RATINGS AND SYMBOLS

Our **TOP RESTAURANTS** lists are based on each restaurant's food rating, starting with the highest rating. Our lists of "Other Top Places" not only reflect food quality but also consider outstanding popularity, decor and service.

FOOD, DECOR and **SERVICE** are each rated on a scale of 0 to 30 in columns marked **F, D** and **S:**

> 0–9 = poor to fair
> 10–19 = good to very good
> 20–25 = very good to excellent
> 26–30 = extraordinary to perfection

The **COST** column, headed by a **C**, reflects the estimated price of a dinner with one drink and tip. As a rule of thumb, lunch will cost 25 percent less.

An **Asterisk (*)** after a restaurant's name means the number of persons who voted on the restaurant is too low to be statistically reliable; an **L** after a restaurant's name means that the restaurant serves after 11 PM; **S** and **M** means it is open on Sunday and Monday, respectively; **X** means no credit cards are accepted.

By way of **Commentary**, we attempt to summarize the comments of our *Survey* participants. The prefix **U** means comments were uniform; **M** means they were mixed.

If we do not show ratings on a restaurant, it is either an important **newcomer** or a popular **write-in**; however, comments are included and the estimated cost, including one drink and tip, is indicated by the following symbols:

> **I** = below $15
> **M** = $15 to $30
> **E** = $30 to $50
> **VE** = $50 or above

ALPHABETICAL DIRECTORY OF RESTAURANTS

ATLANTA

TOP 30 RESTAURANTS
(In order of food rating)

Restaurant	Cuisine Type
28 – Dining Rm., Ritz/Buck.	Amer. Contemp.
27 – La Grotta	Northern Italian
26 – Pano's and Paul's	Amer. Tradition.
103 West	Continental
25 – Hedgerose Hts. Inn	Continental
Restaurant, Ritz/Atl.	French Classic
Chefs' Cafe	Californian
24 – Bone's	Steakhouse
Nikolai's Roof	Continental
Cafe, Ritz/Atlanta	Amer. Contemp.
Cafe, Ritz/Buckhead	Amer. Tradition.
Chops	Steakhouse
Honto	Chinese
Chopstix	Chinese
La Grotta (Roswell)	Northern Italian
23 – House of Chan	Chinese
Buckhead Diner	Amer. Contemp.
A Taste of New Orleans	Creole
Burton's Grill	Soul Food
Indigo	Eclectic
Mah Jong	Chinese
Ho Ho	Chinese
22 – Janousek's	Continental
Delectables	Amer. Contemp.
Dessert Place	Desserts
Pleasant Peasant	Amer. Contemp.
First China	Chinese
Hsu's	Chinese
Partners Morningside	Amer. Contemp.
21 – Haveli	Indian

OTHER TOP PLACES
(In alphabetical order)

Abruzzi	N/S Italian
Azalea	Californian/Eclectic
Carbo's Cafe	Continental
City Grill	Nouvelle French
Coach and Six	Amer. Tradition.
Indian Delights	Indian
Murphy's	American
Pricci	Italian
Veni Vidi Vici	N/S Italian

ATLANTA

| F | D | S | C |

Abruzzi Ristorante
| – | – | – | E |

Peachtree Battle Shopping Ctr., 2355 Peachtree Rd. (Peachtree Battle Ave.), 404-261-8186
This New York–style Italian newcomer in the old Brass Key location in Peachtree Battle is winning a heavy-hitting clientele with waiters "who actually speak Italian and serve dishes that can actually be found in Italy"; the food (pasta and dessert especially) is as tasteful and conservative as the decor.

A Taste of New Orleans/S
| 23 | 15 | 20 | $23 |

889 W. Peachtree St. (bet. 7th & 8th Sts.), 404-874-5535
M – *It must be the "excellent seasoning" on the crab cakes, or the gumbo, or the oyster-stuffed chicken, because it's certainly not the Midtown location, sometimes "snooty service" or "awful" decor that inspires the passionate devotion of most of our reviewers; take flowers – some "wish to be buried there."*

Azalea/S
| – | – | – | M |

3167 Peachtree Rd. (Grandview Ave.), 404-237-9939
Master chef Thomas Catherall and partner Todd Kane are wowing Atlantans with their flashy LA-style Buckhead restaurant, enjoying a celebrity clientele and accolades aplenty for their chic, generously portioned and fairly priced fusion cuisine, a mix of Asian, Mediterranean and regional American dishes; a terrific team in the kitchen and high intensity in the dining room have propelled this restaurant to star rank within its first year.

Bone's/S
| 24 | 20 | 23 | $34 |

3130 Piedmont Rd. (Peachtree Rd.), 404-237-2663
U – *In the heart of Buckhead, this "ultranoisy steakhouse" for the good ol' boys' power network serves "superb steaks" and "lobsters bigger than you are"; though somewhat "clique-ish", confident efficient service, a relaxed dress code and many famous guests make this one of Atlanta's "must" restaurants; its new Southern focus broadens the appeal and the menu.*

Buckhead Diner/S
| 23 | 26 | 22 | $22 |

3073 Piedmont Rd. (E. Paces Ferry Rd.), 404-262-3336
U – *"Noisy and congested", this multimillion-dollar glamour diner serving contemporary renditions of classic American favorites is immensely popular, but also provokes some clientele who "can't stand" the no-reservations policy and the lines; most people would do almost anything to soak up the "fabulous decor" and the outstanding "grazing menu" and rich desserts by star-chef Gerry Klaskala; trendy, trendy, but extraordinarily good.*

ATLANTA

| | F | D | S | C |

Burton's Grill/X | 23 | 9 | 16 | $6 |
1029 Edgewood Ave. (Hurt St., near the Inman Park MARTA station), 404-525-3415
U – "Soul Food supreme" in a hole-in-the-wall in Inman Park; run by an octagenarian with a heart of gold, Burton's has served "Atlanta's definitive fried chicken" for nearly half a century; ever popular with politicos and cops, this place remains unspoiled by success, with prices so low they're hard to believe; breakfast and lunch only, usually closed in August.

Cafe, The/LS | 24 | 26 | 24 | $31 |
Ritz-Carlton Atlanta, 181 Peachtree St. (Ellis St.), 404-659-0400
U – "Perfect for a business lunch", this stylish eclectic cafe racks up high scores across the board – for its first-rate Contemporary American food, interesting low-cal specials, handsome polished decor and professionally attentive service; truly one of Downtown's most useful spots – even on weekends.

Cafe, The/LS | 24 | 26 | 25 | $30 |
Ritz-Carlton Buckhead, 3034 Peachtree Rd. (across from Lenox Sq.), 404-237-2700
U – It is hard to imagine a more "civilized place" to dine than at this elegant Buckhead hotel cafe; whether you're looking for a simply "superb breakfast", "Atlanta's only power brunch" or great spa specials for lunch and dinner, this sophisticated American kitchen does it well and with flair.

Carbo's Cafe/S | 20 | 22 | 20 | $37 |
3717 Roswell Rd. (north of Piedmont Rd.), 404-231-4433
M – Comments about this classy, Buckhead Continental with piano bar, supper club and mover-and-shaker clientele range from "lovely romantic spot" to "most pretentious"; loyal followers like the tasty cuisine bourgeoise and "excellent wine list", but others find it "overpriced" and "spotty" and have mixed feelings about the staff as well.

Chefs' Cafe/S | 25 | 18 | 21 | $25 |
La Quinta Motel, 2115-A Piedmont Rd. (I-85), 404-872-2284
U – Thanks to a "unique" menu including many Californian specialties and innovative dishes prepared with a fresh light touch, this unpretentious San Francisco import has beaten the odds of its awkward location in a budget motel almost under I-85; prices have gone up and down, but the cheerful modern decor has been upgraded to create more intimacy; "super" staff, great wine list and "the best Intown brunch" have won Atlanta's heart.

ATLANTA | F | D | S | C |

Chops | 24 | 25 | 21 | $36 |
70 W. Paces Ferry Rd. (Peachtree Rd.), 404-262-2675
U – Pano's and Paul's power steakhouse in Buckhead rocks the industry with new standards of luxury and is priced accordingly; a "super addition" to the restaurant scene and "everything a steakhouse should be", this is a rich man's idea of a Traditional American meat palace with sumptuous decor by Patrick Kuleto; "fumbly" at first, the service is finding its stride.

Chopstix/S | 24 | 20 | 22 | $23 |
Chastain Sq., 4279 Roswell Rd. (2 blocks south of Wieuca Rd.), 404-255-4868
U – Sleek Hong Kong cafe that has emerged as the most successful among Atlanta's Chinese gourmet restaurants, thanks to snazzy decor and a first-rate "Eclectic, Westernized" menu; this place is a big hit with trendy Buckhead clientele who praise its freshness and creativity, concluding that the restaurant is "outstanding"; a few dissidents rate service borderline snobbish.

City Grill/S | 19 | 27 | 18 | $37 |
55 Hurt Plaza (Edgewood Ave.), 404-524-2489
The grand old dining room in the recently renovated Hurt Building Downtown has made dramatic progress with its lavish French menu, especially strong on seafood dishes and fancy desserts; since the restaurant was last surveyed, the food has improved dramatically from the ratings above.

Coach and Six, The/S | 20 | 19 | 19 | $34 |
1776 Peachtree St. (26th St.), 404-872-6666
M – "Old-line Atlanta" all the way in this pricey steak-and-lobster, Traditional American restaurant south of Buckhead; 25 years of taking better care of regulars than ordinary Joes have produced widely differing opinions about food and service: critics hope the new owner "will revitalize" the place, while others are nervous about any changes at their "longtime favorite."

Delectables/X | 22 | 16 | 16 | $10 |
Atlanta-Fulton Public Library, 1 Margaret Mitchell Sq. (Carnegie Way), 404-681-2909
U – Power luncheonette with an attractive, sunny patio and dining room at the Atlanta-Fulton Public Library; acknowledged as "one of the best lunches Downtown", this is a gourmet cafeteria with sophisticated, pretty salads and sandwiches, outstanding homemade desserts and real silverware, but pace yourself or "you can be shocked at the cash register."

ATLANTA

| F | D | S | C |

Dessert Place, The/LX | 22 | 16 | 16 | $8 |

1100 Virginia Ave. (N. Highland Ave.), 404-892-8921
279 E. Paces Ferry Rd. (near Peachtree St.),
404-233-2331
Underground Atlanta, 110 Lower Alabama St. (Old Pryor St.), 404-577-5565
Macy's Downtown, 180 Peachtree St. (Ellis St.),
404-221-7931

M – "The name says it all" at these "sticky, gooey heavens for chocolate lovers" with three attractive locations and one counter inside Macy's Downtown; "a little pricey for a piece of cake and coffee buffet-style", but the goodies are homemade ("celestial" Quaker oatmeal cake, apple pie "to die for", spectacular cookies); even among the chocoholics there are critics – personnel "consistently snippy", food "too, too sweet."

Dining Room, The | 28 | 28 | 27 | $49 |

Ritz-Carlton Buckhead, 3434 Peachtree Rd. (across from Lenox Sq.), 404-237-2700

U – This luxury restaurant is rated "superlative on all counts" ranking No. 1 for food in Atlanta; chef Guenter Seeger, a national figure, has taken the city by storm, elevating the status of The Dining Room to "Best in the Southeast" with his cutting-edge American cuisine, making a meal here a "world-class experience"; refined surroundings reminiscent of a private club and a "relaxed", "caring" staff complete the winning combination.

First China/S | 22 | 13 | 20 | $14 |

5295 Buford Hwy. (1/2 mile inside I-285),
404-457-6788

U – Excellently run, affordable but somewhat plain Cantonese especially famous for "exquisite" family-style dishes in a special section of the menu that includes hand-rolled noodles and steamed chicken with black mushrooms; our surveyors report that this is a natural for banquets or low-key business gatherings and that the small but selective dim sum menu is a winner.

Haveli/S | 21 | 17 | 17 | $16 |

2706 Cobb Pkwy. (1/2 mile north of Cumberland Mall), Smyrna, 404-955-4525

U – Ambitious decor and above-average quality set this Cobb County Indian restaurant apart from the competition; people praise its atmosphere ("the best") and food ("spicy, wonderful") and feel they are getting their money's worth for the "great lunch buffet"; Vegetarian dishes are particularly good, and the management is "friendly."

ATLANTA

| F | D | S | C |

Hedgerose Heights Inn, The | 25 | 25 | 22 | $41 |
490 E. Paces Ferry Rd. (Maple Dr.), 404-233-7673
U – "Luxurious, romantic decor with a classic Continental menu" gives this European-style Buckhead charmer an edge on the competition as "the place to go for that special meal"; Swiss-born chef Heinz Schwab produces a uniformly winning menu – his sole and dessert soufflés are "unbeatable"; drawbacks are minimal – the two-seatings system "messes up the evening" for some, others criticize "poor arrangement" of closely placed tables and "haughty, stuffy" service.

Ho Ho/S | 23 | 7 | 18 | $12 |
3683 Clairmont Rd. (Buford Hwy.), Chamblee, 404-451-7240
U – Nothing to laugh at, this very authentic Chamblee Chinese "hole-in-the-wall" was one of the first to serve the ethnic community and "remains a favorite" for inexpensive no-frills meals, including "unusual" items such as oyster pancakes, marinated pig's nose and many seafood specialties from the coastal provinces of China; expect "grotty" decor, but friendly management.

Honto/S | 24 | 7 | 14 | $14 |
3295 Chamblee-Dunwoody Rd. (Buford Hwy.), Chamblee, 404-458-8088
U – Best-known and largest of the Chinese restaurants in Chamblee serving an excellent (mainly seafood) menu that gets top ratings among Atlanta's Chinese; some call the service "definitely Third World" and the surroundings "unappetizing", but the food "can be extraordinary"; try steamed Thai fish, salt-and-pepper shrimp, green mussels and more; "cleanliness is improving" and weekend dim sum is a must.

House of Chan/S | 23 | 10 | 19 | $15 |
2469 Cobb Pkwy. (across from Loehman's Plaza), Smyrna, 404-955-9444
U – Hong Kong comes to Cobb County with "consistently excellent food" that's a "close runner-up for best Chinese", according to the locals; it's not much from the decor standpoint, but don't be fooled – the food is unusually sophisticated from pine nut snapper to potato baskets filled with seafood; "warm and friendly", it's sometimes too crowded.

Hsu's | 21 | 20 | 21 | $21 |
Tower Place, 3340 Peachtree Rd. (Piedmont Rd.), 404-233-3891
U – "Beautiful presentations" and "outstanding", sophisticated Hong Kong cuisine are to be had at this upscale Chinese with a refined and classy interior near the Tower Place Cinemas; the owner is "a gracious host" and can be trusted to help with menu choices; the elegant formal service is in keeping with the "expensive" – for Chinese food – prices.

ATLANTA

| F | D | S | C |

Indian Delights/SX | – | – | – | I |
1707 Scott Blvd. (Church St.), Decatur, 404-296-2965
Trust the name and go the distance: there's no better Indian food at no better prices than what's offered at this tiny Vegetarian cafe; the unfamiliar dishes from Southern India will open new horizons to those willing to do without comfort or ambiance (service is at the counter only).

Indigo/S | 23 | 18 | 21 | $21 |
1397 N. Highland Ave. (University Ave.), 404-876-0676
U – "Fun" is the word most people mention first about this casual grill that draws big crowds to Morningside with "beachy chic" and "zippy seafood specialties"; the upbeat menu includes all sorts of fish, tequila oysters and a "great Key lime pie"; bland is banned from the kitchen, the jukebox plays funky tunes and the staff is as cute as the customers.

Janousek's | 22 | 16 | 21 | $23 |
1475 Holcomb Bridge Rd. (next to King's Market), Roswell, 404-587-2075
U – Run by a Czech family, this Roswell Continental is considered "a well-kept secret" by the locals who use it more for pleasure than business; the high price is "a shocker" by neighborhood dining standards, but the regulars appreciate the "high quality in every detail."

La Grotta | 27 | 23 | 24 | $36 |
2637 Peachtree Rd. (W. Wesley Dr.), 404-231-1368
U – Near the top of everyone's list, this excellent Northern Italian classic located in the basement of a Buckhead office building has been a popular favorite since the mid '70s; its recently redecorated dining room finally matches the "warm, friendly, wonderful" service orchestrated by owner-maitre d' Sergio Favalli, a top professional who "makes all the difference"; his partner in the kitchen, Antonio Pecondon, admirably takes care of a large, traditional menu and some adventurous specials.

La Grotta(Roswell) | 24 | 20 | 22 | $31 |
647 Atlanta St. (north of Upper Roswell St.), Roswell, 404-998-0645
M – "Just not the same as Buckhead", sigh those who find the Roswell outpost of Atlanta's favorite Northern Italian "stuffy, heavy, not worth the money"; most others stay away from comparison and, as their ratings indicate, simply enjoy the "intimate" setting, "personalized service" and "very impressive" food.

ATLANTA

| F | D | S | C |

Mah Jong/S | 23 | 21 | 22 | $22 |
Brookwood Sq., 2140 Peachtree Rd. (Lindbergh Rd.),
404-352-8339
*U – "Chinese chic" sums up this handsome, upscale
South Buckhead Hong Kong restaurant where "the maitre
d' makes a limited menu speak volumes"; from alligator
to rabbit and black pepper oysters, you will find many
"exotic, elegant" dishes in a glossy, streamlined setting.*

Murphy's 'Round the Corner/S | 19 | 14 | 16 | $13 |
1019 Los Angeles Ave. (N. Highland Ave.), 404-872-0904
*U – "Cozy", "charming", "comfortable", "casual" are the
adjectives for this American spot (deli, desserts, "great
breakfasts") that the Virginia-Highland crowd treats as a
second home, be it in the cute "cramped" dining room, at
the counter or on the covered patio; the "varied menu"
is good and cheap enough that "there is always a wait."*

Nikolai's Roof/S | 24 | 25 | 26 | $49 |
Atlanta Hilton & Towers, 255 Courtland St. (Harris St.),
404-659-3282
*M – Ten years ago this pricey "pseudo-Russian"–
Continental in the Hilton was the one and only spot in
Atlanta for "elegant and fine dining"; though many still rate
it "near the top" and find it "very impressive", part of the
clientele feels "someone has forgotten to tell them that
Atlanta has grown"; still, the fixed-price menu, beautiful
view of Downtown and fancy service keep the two
seatings ("one too early, the other too late") usually full.*

103 West | 26 | 24 | 24 | $40 |
103 W. Paces Ferry Rd. (off Peachtree Rd.), 404-233-5993
*U – "First-class all the way", the most Continental
among Pano's and Paul's restaurants is "a hoi polloi
palace" of fancy European cuisine and sensory overload,
including "too good" service by hovering waiters; its
flamboyant, borderline "gaudy" decor seems "overdone"
to some, but all agree that this place has excellent
facilities for fancy parties ("they do it right") and is a
wonderful spot to knock someone's socks off; if the
excellent entrees don't do it, the desserts and wine list will.*

Pano's and Paul's | 26 | 24 | 25 | $39 |
1232 W. Paces Ferry Rd. (Northside Pkwy.), 404-261-3662
*U – By now a culinary landmark, this extravagantly
decorated and priced American in a North Buckhead
shopping-strip mall is, according to its many fans who
vote it the city's most popular restaurant, "single-
handedly responsible for leading Atlanta out
of the surf-and-turf woods"; lobster tails and pasta
specialties are generally acknowledged to be wonderful;
Pano Karatassos and Paul Albrecht cater to special
requests and pampering service is a trademark, but
some grumble that reservations are "meaningless"
and you may have to do time at the romantic bar.*

ATLANTA

| F | D | S | C |

Partners Morningside Cafe | 21 | 16 | 19 | $22 |
1399 N. Highland Ave. (University Dr.), 404-875-0202
U – "Fun, funky, festive" Morningside/Virginia–Highland neighborhood cafe with a casual, "innovative" American menu jazzed up by exotic spices; relaxing and chic with a good blend of local customers, its "great pasta appetizers", the "best blackened tenderloin", stimulating wine list and free-flowing creativity are all part of the success formula that has also caused its chief problems – "too little space" and long waits.

Pleasant Peasant/LS | 22 | 20 | 22 | $22 |
555 Peachtree St. (Linden Ave.), 404-874-3223
U – The first link in what has become an immensely successful chain started as Country French, but has become more American over the years; nonetheless, it remains a favorite of Atlantans who remember the Peasant's role in the reclaiming of Midtown in the early '70s and who recommend that this old romantic spot "be made into a shrine."

Pricci/S | – | – | – | M |
3018 Maple Dr. (Pharr Rd.), 404-237-2941
This Buckhead stunner (a recycled, dramatically redesigned Capriccio) is the restaurant everyone has been waiting for; clad in a new, brilliant-white facade and decorated in glamorous style, this restaurant offers up-to-the-minute Italian, plus a fresh-pasta counter and fabulous in-house retail bakery; Sunday "family night" is a special treat.

Restaurant, The/S | 25 | 27 | 26 | $42 |
Ritz-Carlton Atlanta, 181 Peachtree St. (Ellis St.), 404-659-0400
U – "An excellent elegant restaurant", this Downtown location is a convenient option for "fine dining" and a great place to do business or "be discreet"; it gets top marks for atmosphere ("they define elegance"), French food ("classy") and service, running neck-and-neck with its sibling The Dining Room at the Ritz Buckhead; weekend brunch is a deluxe experience.

Veni Vidi Vici/S | – | – | – | E |
IBM Pk. Garage, 41 14th St. (W. Peachtree St.), 404-875-8424
At the bottom of the IBM Tower in Midtown, this stunning Italian is a revelation to Atlanta; inspired by Italian cooking doyenne Marcella Hazan's gutsy authentic regional recipes and opened as a team effort (and prototype) with her husband and son, the restaurant has excellent pasta and a breezy, chic atmosphere.

ATLANTIC CITY

TOP 10 RESTAURANTS
(In order of food rating)

Restaurant	Cuisine Type
26 – Le Palais	Continental
25 – Prime Place	Steakhouse
White House	Sandwiches
Meadows	French
24 – Ivana's	Continental
Capriccio	Italian
23 – Oaks	Seafood/Steakhouse
Il Verdi	Northern Italian
Tre Figlio	N/S Italian
22 – By-The-Sea	N/S Italian

OTHER TOP PLACES
(In alphabetical order)

Caruso's	N/S Italian
Castle Steakhouse	Steakhouse
Harbor View	Seafood
Hyakumi	Japanese
Max's Steakhouse	Steakhouse
Peking Duck House	Chinese
Pier 7 Restaurant	Seafood
Portofino	Southern Italian
Ram's Head Inn	Amer. Tradition.
Roberto's	N/S Italian

F	D	S	C

By-The-Sea/L | 22 | 21 | 19 | $36 |
Bally's Park Place Hotel and Casino, Park Pl. & The Boardwalk, 609-340-2000
M – A "favorite" of many, this "nice, quiet" casino restaurant at the best spot on the Monopoly board offers "generous servings" of "excellent" seafood and "tasty, well-seasoned" Italian food; despite a few complainers who think the food is "inconsistent" and overpriced, it's still packed with happy eaters.

Capriccio/S | 24 | 23 | 22 | $37 |
Merv Griffin's Resorts & Hotels, North Carolina Ave. & The Boardwalk, 609-340-7836
M – This highly rated Northern and Southern Italian serves convincingly "authentic" food, according to its many fans; however, dissenters say the fare is "mass-produced" and predict that "you've had better"; in either case, the spacious room has a wonderful view of the Atlantic and a "pleasant atmosphere."

ATLANTIC CITY | F | D | S | C |

Caruso's/LS | 22 | 23 | 22 | $39 |

Bally's Grand Casino Hotel, Boston & Pacific Aves., 609-347-7111

M – A worthy choice "before or after a show", this "exquisite room" in Bally's Grand serves regional Italian food that has many admirers who also like the "quick" service; critics think that even with all this "elegance", the food "used to be much better" and it's pretty pricey.

Castle Steakhouse | 21 | 23 | 22 | $39 |

Trump Castle Casino Resort, Huron Ave. & Brigantine Blvd., 609-441-2000

M – For steaks that are "thick, juicy and tasty", this western-style steakhouse in the Trump Castle is a "big surprise – it's good for a casino restaurant"; critics report that it's "not wonderful" and the staff doesn't pay enough attention to nongambling customers.

Harbor View/LS | 20 | 24 | 21 | $33 |

Trump Castle Casino & Resort, Huron Ave. & Brigantine Blvd., 609-441-2000

M – The "beautiful view of the marina and the Atlantic City skyline" from every seat makes this seafood restaurant in the Trump Castle a "wonderful sunset spot" as well as a good place for a "leisurely lunch" or a "beautiful Sunday brunch"; some think the food is "great", but others say it's "undistinguished."

Hyakumi* | 23 | 24 | 24 | $33 |

Caesars Atlantic City, Arkansas Ave. & The Boardwalk, 609-348-4411

U – The "fun" of this "excellent" Japanese restaurant in Caesars makes it "more than a meal" to its fans, who enjoy the teppanyaki cooking; sure, Benihana has done it before, but it's still an interesting dining experience, especially watching the samurai chefs slice and dice your meal; "too bad there's no sushi on the menu."

Il Verdi/S | 23 | 22 | 22 | $42 |

Tropworld Casino & Entertainment Resort, Brighton Ave. & The Boardwalk (Pacific Ave.), 609-340-4000

M – Some think the Northern Italian food at this attractive dinner house is the "best casino Italian" in Atlantic City, "good even if you're not on a comp"; others think it's "not all that great" and say it goes downhill after the waiter asks, "what'll youse have?"

ATLANTIC CITY

| F | D | S | C |

Ivana's/S
| 24 | 24 | 23 | $44 |

Trump Plaza Hotel & Casino, Mississippi Ave. & The Boardwalk, 609-441-6000
M – The "excellent Continental cuisine" and "elegant, romantic atmosphere" of this posh Trump Plaza spot (named after The Donald's ex) makes it the "nicest place in AC" for some, who praise its "great food" ("delish" soufflés and "rich sauces") and "snappy service"; others say the food's "a little heavy" and "not worth it" – unless someone else is paying.

Le Palais
| 26 | 25 | 26 | $49 |

Merv Griffin's Resorts & Hotels, North Carolina Ave. & The Boardwalk, 609-344-6000
U – The "romantic" red-bedecked setting and "excellent", "well-prepared" Continental food make this "fine spot" in the Resorts "the best in Atlantic City" in the eyes of most of our surveyors, who give it top honors for food and service, and second place for decor; yes, it's expensive, but for special occasions it's the ne plus ultra in this town.

Max's Steakhouse*/S
| 25 | 25 | 23 | $38 |

Trump Plaza Hotel and Casino, Mississippi Ave. & The Boardwalk, 609-441-6000
U – Although this steakhouse in the Trump Plaza will cost you, fans say it's "a great special-occasion place" – if you like the "men's-club feeling" – with "good steaks" and seafood and "incredible" service to boot.

Meadows, The
| 25 | 24 | 24 | $46 |

Harrah's Atlantic City, Brigantine Blvd. & the Bay, 609-441-5000
U – Retreat to a "quiet corner" of Harrah's for some of "the best French at the Shore" at this "beautiful", "intimate" casino restaurant, which also has a "nice view at sunset" and service that's "tough to beat."

Oaks, The/L
| 23 | 24 | 23 | $39 |

Bally's Grand Casino Hotel, Boston & Pacific Aves., 609-347-7111
M – This "beautiful" steak-and-seafood room in Bally's Grand is a "great place" for "excellent steaks", an "awesome salad bar" and "good service"; others say the "food has deteriorated" and are appalled by the prices.

Peking Duck House/S
| 22 | 20 | 20 | $29 |

2801 Atlantic Ave. (Iowa Ave.), 609-344-9090
M – Possibly "the best Chinese in the area", this handsome contemporary spot has a "great host", "the best service ever" and an "unusual selection of exceptional dishes", including "excellent" Peking duck; critics rebut: "too expensive" for "little better than average."

ATLANTIC CITY

| F | D | S | C |

Pier 7 Restaurant*/S | 22 | 21 | 25 | $29 |
Tropworld Casino and Entertainment Resort, Brighton Ave. & The Boardwalk, 609-340-4000, x4936
U – This "very comfortable" Fisherman's Wharf–style seafooder serves "excellent" fresh fish, much of it grilled over mesquite; it's a "good value" and a worthwhile break from the gambling hustle-bustle; try the "hot rock" appetizer: bite-size seafood that you cook on a slab of heated pumice, then dip into a variety of sauces.

Portofino/S | 22 | 24 | 23 | $35 |
Trump Castle Casino Resort, Huron Ave. & Brigantine Blvd., 609-441-2000
M – Fans say this "beautiful", "elegant" Italian spot serves "gourmet Italian specialties" and "beats many others" in its class; critics think it's a "big disappointment" and has "slipped badly"; friend or foe, our reviewers are unanimous in praising the view.

Prime Place/S | 25 | 23 | 25 | $41 |
Bally's Park Place Hotel and Casino, Park Pl. & The Boardwalk, 609-340-2000
U – "Real good steaks" and a "great salad bar" are the main attractions of this handsome clubby spot, which is highly rated by our surveyors as a "quality casino restaurant"; though fans say the service is "always courteous", others get the feeling that paying customers take second place to casino guests.

Ram's Head Inn, The/S | 21 | 25 | 22 | $35 |
9 W. White Horse Pike (Rte. 30 & Garden State Pkwy.), Absecon, 609-652-1700
M – The "very charming atmosphere" and "gracious" service at this colonial inn just off the Garden State Parkway has made it a "landmark" and a "favorite" for fans who praise its "A-1" American food; however, one naysayer recommends it as "a beautiful place – to drive right past"; N.B. "ask for the Garden Room."

Roberto's*/S | 24 | 25 | 24 | $39 |
Trump Plaza Hotel and Casino, Mississippi Ave. & The Boardwalk, 609-441-6000
M – This "romantic room" in the Trump Plaza has a "great view", though the less amorously inclined among our surveyors think there are "too many cherubs with bunches of grapes"; fans say the Italian food is good – even "excellent" on occasion – but inconsistency can make it a bit of "a gamble."

ATLANTIC CITY

| F | D | S | C |

Tre Figlio/S | 23 | 19 | 21 | $35 |
500 White Horse Pike (bet. Pomona Ave. & Tilton Rd.),
Pomona, 609-965-3303
M – Often "mobbed, and rightfully so", this "gourmet Italian" is a winner in an area with precious few decent restaurants; don't let the roadhouse exterior throw you off – inside, there's a convivial, witty trattoria setting and food that can be "outstanding", with "excellent pasta dishes"; a few think it's "overpriced" and grumble that "everything has tomato sauce on it."

White House, The/LSX | 25 | 9 | 15 | $11 |
2301 Arctic St. (Mississippi Ave.), 609-345-1564
U – Quite a controversy on this one: "best hoagies in the tri-state area" vs. "best hoagies on the East Coast" vs. "best hoagies in the world"; it's a matter of opinion, but almost everyone agrees that the "mouth-watering" subs and cheesesteaks from "this ultimate hoagie shop" are "worth risking your life for" and a "must in AC."

BALTIMORE

TOP 20 RESTAURANTS
(In order of food rating)

Restaurant	Cuisine Type
27 – Prime Rib	Amer. Tradition.
Milton Inn	Continental
26 – Hamptons	Amer. Contemp.
Conservatory	French Classic
Tio Pepe	Spanish
Linwood's Cafe Grille	Amer. Contemp.
Pierpoint	Amer. Cont./Seafood
25 – L'Auberge	French Classic
Rudys' 2900	Continental
Polo Grill	Seafood/Steakhouse
24 – Tersiguel's	French Bistro
Pavilion at the Walters	American/Eclectic
23 – Puffin's	Amer. Contemp.
Brass Elephant	Northern Italian
Bombay Grill	Indian
Trattoria Alberto	Northern Italian
Jeannier's	French Classic
Martick's	French/Indochine
22 – Tabrizi's	Mediteranean
Tony Cheng's	Chinese

OTHER TOP PLACES
(In alphabetical order)

Chiapparelli's	Italian
Haussner's	German/Seafood
Hersh's Orchard Inn	Continental
Ikaros	Greek
Josef's Country Inn	German
Kawasaki	Japanese
Kings Contrivance	Continental
Obrycki's	Seafood
Peerce's Plantation	Continental/Seafood
Waterside	American

F	D	S	C

Bombay Grill/S | 23 | 19 | 21 | $21 |
2 E. Madison St. (bet. Read & Monument Sts.),
410-837-2973
U – Most consider this "nifty" Mt. Vernon storefront the best Indian in town with "flavorful", subtly spiced food, a decorative ambiance "if you sit in the front room" and, above all, the owners' attentiveness; patrons report being ushered through a pleasantly exotic evening.

BALTIMORE

| F | D | S | C |

Brass Elephant, The/S | 23 | 25 | 22 | $32 |
924 N. Charles St. (bet. Read & Eager Sts.), 410-547-8480
M – The Edwardian opulence of this "great old merchant house" is the tone for one of the "best dining experiences in town"; fine North Italian food and wines complement the setting, while a slight "seediness" and a well-intentioned "effort at good service" simply add to its charm; the $7 prix fixe lunch and $15.95 pre-theater menus afford elegance on the cheap.

Chiapparelli's/S | 19 | 15 | 19 | $23 |
237 S. High St. (Fawn St.), 410-837-0309
M – The veal may be "kind of tough", pasta soggy and sauces "bland", and it's loud, crowded and disorganized; however, none of this discourages yearly pilgrimages to "one of Little Italy's most beloved restaurants"; it has the biggest, "best-tasting house salad anywhere" and plenty of tradition.

Conservatory, The | 26 | 28 | 25 | $50 |
Latham Hotel, 612 Cathedral St. (Monument St.), 410-727-7101
U – When "everything goes right", a dressed-up dinner at this "elegant" and "expensive" French Classic aerie is "perfection"; even when the kitchen slips and the pace slows (changing chefs can take their toll), watching the city lights spread out below "makes up for lapses"; N.B. at press time this restaurant was scheduled to close on March 1, 1993.

Hamptons/S | 26 | 28 | 27 | $48 |
Harbor Court Hotel, 550 Light St. (bet. Conway & Lee Sts.), 410-234-0550
U – Our reviewers find practically nothing wrong with this "formal" hotel dining room; ranking it No. 3 for food in Baltimore, they rave about its "elegant" appointments, "dazzling" Inner Harbor views, "superb" Contemporary American food and "excellent wines"; if anything, there may be "too much" of its top-rated service; only the fact that it's "pricey" may give one pause.

Haussner's | 19 | 24 | 21 | $24 |
3242 Eastern Ave. (Clinton St.), 410-327-8365
U – A fabled art collection lines every square inch of this "Baltimore landmark's" vast dining halls, and the menu covers every German and Old Maryland culinary base from crab cakes to hasenpfeffer; the Haussners don't believe less is more and neither do their legions of fans and tourists who "must see" this Highlandtown institution described as "overwhelming"; P.S. don't miss the strawberry shortcake.

BALTIMORE

| F | D | S | C |

Hersh's Orchard Inn/S | 21 | 19 | 22 | $30 |
1528 E. Joppa Rd. (½ mile west of Loch Raven Blvd.),
Towson, 410-823-0384
M – This suave Suburbanite with ample seating has a solid menu of "simple, properly cooked" steaks, seafood and Continental fare; its popularity especially reflects proprietor Hersh Pachino's savvy handling of the Towson business crowd; however, some say the one constant here is that "reservations are ignored always" and wonder how it got ranked as No. 1 by Baltimore Magazine.

Ikaros/S | 22 | 15 | 20 | $18 |
4805 Eastern Ave. (bet. Oldham & Ponca Sts.),
410-633-3750
M – Greektown's "best Greek" restaurant is as popular for a favorable portion/price ratio as for the succulence of its lamb; the neighborhood trade and "quantity buffs", who look for lots of hearty peasant food and few amenities, keep it "going strong": regulars recommend the appetizers and lamb dishes.

Jeannier's | 23 | 19 | 21 | $29 |
Broadview Apts., 105 W. 39th St. (bet. University Pkwy. & Charles St.), 410-889-3303
U – Just because it's "Mother's favorite place" is no reason to shrug off this excellent French restaurant; its bourgeois "food is a lot livelier than the arsenic and old-lace atmosphere" in its shabby, Uptown residence; its service is fine and the "price is fair", particularly the pre-theater $14.75 dinner.

Josef's Country Inn*/S | 22 | 18 | 20 | $28 |
2410 Pleasantville Rd. (Rte. 152), Fallston,
410-877-7800
U – Drive to this bit of Bavaria in the Fallston countryside when you crave schnitzel, spaetzle and "mit schlag" desserts – the food is "excellent", but be prepared for a wait; there are often more travelers than tables in the kitsch-trimmed old farmhouse, and whoever promises reservations hasn't learned to say no.

Kawasaki/L | 21 | 17 | 20 | $22 |
413 N. Charles St. (bet. Mulberry & Franklin Sts.),
410-659-7600
U – "First-rate sushi" and "consistently great sashimi" star at this "simple", "subtle", "anxious-to-please" Downtowner; its raw fish choices are so "fresh and tasty" that some diners never investigate its delicious, well-priced tempura, teriyaki and noodle-based casseroles.

BALTIMORE

| F | D | S | C |

Kings Contrivance/S | 21 | 24 | 20 | $35 |
10150 Shaker Dr. (off Rte. 29 or Rte. 32), Columbia, 410-995-0500
M – A "civilized" dinner at this "landmark" country mansion near Columbia is a good way to rekindle a romance or reward a special account; the Continental fare falls short of the "lovely setting", but is "still worth doing"; try to go mid-week when the kitchen and the servers aren't too pressed, or arrange for a private party; critics say it's "pretentious", "overrated" and "expensive."

L'Auberge | 25 | 23 | 24 | $35 |
505 S. Broadway (bet. Eastern Ave. & Fleet St.), 410-732-1151
U – Hidden above the Broadway Market in Fells Point is what may be the "finest and most consistent French restaurant in Baltimore" as well as a "best buy" with a "wonderful five-course lunch for under $25"; an enticing Country French interior harmonizes with its culinary style and air of "quiet quality"; Francophiles sigh "c'est magnifique."

Linwood's Cafe Grille/S | 26 | 25 | 23 | $33 |
25 Crossroads Dr. (Reistertown & McDonough Rds.), 410-356-3030
U – This smash hit in Owings Mills supplies a smart, sophisticated backdrop for suburban business and pleasure; its skillful treatments of "luminously" fresh seafood, produce and meats cause skeptics to change their minds about Contemporary American cuisine; service, supposedly its "weakest link", is usually "excellent"; just don't expect the waitress to call you "hon" – not at these prices.

Martick's | 23 | 16 | 18 | $24 |
214 W. Mulberry St. (bet. Park Ave. & Howard St.), 410-752-5155
M – Literally a hole-in-the-wall – with no sign, light or doorknob, this East Baltimore testimonial to its owner's eccentricity offers a "most unique", vaguely French-Indochine, dining experience; respondents find it, off and on, "weird and wonderful" – go if you're in an adventurous mood.

Milton Inn/S | 27 | 26 | 25 | $41 |
14833 York Rd. (bet. Hunt Valley Mall & Belfast Rd.), Sparks, 410-771-4366
U – A jump in ratings – it's now No. 2 for food in Baltimore – rewards the past several years' work of updating this "romantic" "country inn", modernizing its Continental menu, selecting wonderful wines and recruiting an effective staff; even the drive is "relaxing" to this wonderful, if "pricey", place to celebrate.

BALTIMORE | F | D | S | C |

Obrycki's/S | 21 | 14 | 18 | $24 |
1727 E. Pratt St. (bet. Broadway & Register St.),
410-732-6399
M – Smashing steamed hard crabs at this Fells Point institution is de rigueur after "at least one" baseball game each season; many consider their peppery seasoning "the best"; old-timers grumble that the "noisy, sloppy" dimly lit dining "arena" is too fancy – "you're paying for the ferns."

Pavilion at the Walters, The | 24 | 23 | 22 | $24 |
600 N. Charles St. (bet. W. Monument & Centre Sts.),
410-727-2233
U – A lovely marriage of art and dining is realized at the Walters Gallery Art Museum; diners find the imaginative, eclectically American food "totally unexpected" in a museum setting; connoisseurs are quick to recognize "masters of the art of brunch"; occasional service snags should unravel "as the place matures" – with an early verdict of "outstanding."

Peerce's Plantation/S | 22 | 22 | 20 | $32 |
12450 Dulaney Valley Rd. (Loch Raven Dr.), Phoenix,
410-252-3100
U – This picturesquely situated country restaurant overlooking Loch Raven Reservoir serves up "solid" Continental and Maryland seafood specialties and southern hospitality that suit its special-occasion clientele; first-timers are advised to try the brunch, "eat alfresco" and remember that "service suffers on Saturday night."

Pierpoint/S | 26 | 17 | 21 | $29 |
1822 Aliceanna St. (bet. Ann & Wolfe Sts.), 410-675-2080
U – Nancy Longo is one of the most accomplished young chefs in our region; her easygoing creativity pervades her busy Fells Point bistro; the "always winning" food she serves starts with the freshest local ingredients and is inspired by her Italian and Old Maryland culinary heritage; it's hardly surprising that her small place is cramped, "crowded", "cozy" and "fun."

Polo Grill, The/S | 24 | 25 | 21 | $36 |
The Inn at the Colonnade, 4 W. University Pkwy. (bet. Canterbury & Charles Sts.), 410-235-8200
U – From breakfast on, this handsome, easily reached restaurant is the proscenium for a major power/social scene; its producers, Gail and Lenny Kaplan, have transposed the traditional Baltimore seafood-steak-Continental menu into the likes of fried lobster, mod sandwiches, pastas and heart-healthy grills; despite trendy (i.e. "unshaven") waiters, the Grill is playing to an SRO audience with mostly rave reviews.

BALTIMORE | F | D | S | C |

Prime Rib, The/S | 27 | 25 | 26 | $39 |
Horizon House, 1101 N. Calvert St. (Chase St.), 410-539-1804
U – Sweeping up first-place honors for food, this "sensuous" Downtown supper club combines some of the best qualities of a NY steakhouse (i.e. top-notch beef, bonhomie and booze) with delicious Old Maryland seafood, a black lacquered art deco look and "special attention" to its well-heeled clientele; for its many loyal customers, there's "no place else like it."

Puffin's/S | 23 | 17 | 21 | $24 |
1000 Reisterstown Rd. (Sherwood Ave.), Pikesville, 410-486-8811
U – Who would have "thought healthy dining could taste" so good is the mantra of this new age American; it's smoke-free, red meat-free, caffeine- and liquor-free, yet its food is flavorful, attractively plated and considerately priced; the unexpected "La Cage aux Folles decor" in a Pikesville shopping-strip storefront apparently adds to the "fun" for most diners.

Rudys' 2900/S | 25 | 20 | 23 | $33 |
2900 Baltimore Blvd. (off Rtes. 91 & 140), Finksburg, 410-833-5777
U – Classic Continental and regional dishes always develop a wonderful edge in meisterchef Rudy Speckamp's kitchen; but some of its fine seafood, "marvelous" lobster bisque, "remarkable" rabbit, smoked salmon and wines come at a price – there's the drive to Westminster, a charmless interior with "too many tables" and contrasting reports of a "relaxing" ambiance; one diner spells the restaurant's name "rude."

Tabrizi's | 22 | 19 | 19 | $24 |
1026 S. Charles St. (bet. Cross & Hamburg Sts.), 410-752-3810
U – This Federal Hill cafe quickly found its niche turning Middle Eastern basics into a fashionable, healthy "Mediterranean" cuisine; its "intriguing", relatively inexpensive menu, atrium-brightened interior, appealing patio and helpfulness have many fans and an occasional nonfan – only "fair to me."

Tersiguel's/S | 24 | 23 | 24 | $36 |
8293 Main St. (Old Columbia Pike), Ellicott City, 410-465-4004
U – High numbers across the board reflect Baltimore's satisfaction that Ferdinand Tersiguel "still works his magic" at this yearling bistro; his inimitable "personal attention", a "really pleasant" countrified setting and most of all his seasonal specialties provide a "wonderful excuse for an excursion" to Ellicot City.

BALTIMORE | F | D | S | C |

Tio Pepe/S | 26 | 22 | 22 | $34 |
10 E. Franklin St. (bet. Charles & St. Paul Sts.),
410-539-4675
M – Perennially Baltimore's most popular restaurant, this festive Spanish Downtown stalwart remains "the place" to go for rich-tasting dishes – particularly if you fancy dining in "underground caves"; it's "deafening", "claustrophobic", "slow" and "stuffy" yet it's "crowded with who's who" and considered "worth the trip" by legions of out-of-towners; go early for dinner – "like a doctor's appointment, a reservation guarantees nothing."

Tony Cheng's Szechuan/S | 22 | 20 | 18 | $22 |
801 N. Charles St. (Madison St.), 410-539-6666
M – Surveyors consider this classy Szechuan the "best undiscovered restaurant in Baltimore", citing its "great" food in an "elegant" townhouse with a "nice view of Baltimore's Washington monument"; locals fault service slips and "high (for Baltimore) prices."

Trattoria Alberto | 23 | 18 | 20 | $35 |
1660 Crain Hwy. (bet. Hospital Dr. & Aqua Heart St.),
Glen Burnie, 410-761-0922
U – If Baltimore's No. 2 Italian was housed in "nicer quarters" than a Glen Burnie "truck-stop", it would have "everything one would wish for"; as is, settling for delicious North Italian pastas and the "best veal chop around" in an elegantly appointed storefront makes sense; if the waiters were less "pushy", it would be even nicer.

Waterside/S | 22 | 22 | 20 | $28 |
The Columbia Inn, 10207 Wincopin Circle (Rte. 175),
Columbia, 410-730-3900
U – A "superior" hotel dining room in Columbia where the lovely setting is matched by "consistently good American food", this is one restaurant where the wide-angle water views enhance, rather than eclipse, a delicious meal; service is much improved.

BOSTON

TOP 30 RESTAURANTS
(In order of food rating)

Restaurant / **Cuisine Type**

- 27 – Olives — No. Italian/Mediterranean
- L'Espalier — French Nouvelle
- 26 – Hamersley's Bistro — Eclectic/French Bistro
- Jasper's — Seafood
- Seasons — Eclectic
- Aujourd'hui — Continental
- Julien — French Nouvelle
- 25 – Biba — Eclectic
- Chez Nous — French Nouvelle
- Harvard Street Grill — Eclectic/French
- 24 – Gyuhama — Japanese
- Cornucopia — Amer. Contemp.
- Ristorante Toscano — Northern Italian
- Giacomo's — N/S Italian
- East Coast Grill — BBQ/Caribbean
- Morton's of Chicago — Steakhouse
- Icarus — Amer. Contemp.
- Davide — Northern Italian
- Five Seasons — Vegetarian
- Michela's — Nuova Cucina Italian
- Takeshima — Japanese
- Upstairs at the Pudding — Nuova Cucina Italian
- Le Bocage — French Classic
- Dali — Spanish
- 23 – Legal Sea Foods — Seafood
- Green Street Grill — Caribbean
- Oasis Cafe — Amer. Tradition.
- Rarities — Amer. Contemp.
- Plaza Dining Room — Continental
- Chau Chow — Chinese

OTHER TOP PLACES
(In alphabetical order)

- Blue Room — Eclectic
- Davio's — Nuova Cucina Italian
- Elephant Walk — Cambodian/French
- Grill 23 — Steakhouse
- Il Capriccio — Northern Italian
- Locke-Ober Cafe — Amer. Tradition.
- Maison Robert — French Classic
- Parker's — Amer. Tradition.
- Ritz Dining Room — Continental
- St. Cloud — Amer. Contemp.

BOSTON | F | D | S | C |

Aujourd'Hui/SM | 26 | 27 | 26 | $48 |
Four Seasons Hotel, 200 Boylston St. (across from Public Garden), 617-338-4400
U – In just a few years, this "beautiful" redecorated room overlooking the Public Garden has established itself as one of Boston's favorites for its "elegant" Nouvelle Continental kitchen – recently taken over by rising-star–chef Michael Kornick – and service that makes you feel "pampered"; the Sunday brunch and weekday breakfasts are very popular, and there's an "alternative" low-fat menu, but remember to "bring serious money"; the change of chefs and decor may bring even higher ratings.

Biba/LS | 25 | 25 | 17 | $41 |
272 Boylston St. (bet. Arlington St. & Haddassah Way), 617-426-7878
M – This Eclectic stunner, overlooking the Public Garden, is among Boston's most popular restaurants, owing to the bold originality of chef-owner Lydia Shire and the "dynamite decor" of designer Adam Tihany; a "must for foodies" since it opened, comments are nonetheless mixed – the "wild food" that draws on India, Asia and many other places is "beautifully prepared and intriguing" to most, but a "puzzle" to some; praise of the always-hopping bar downstairs, with its "great hors d'oeuvres", is mixed with complaints of "spotty" service and noise.

Blue Room, The | – | – | – | E |
1 Kendall Sq. (Prospect St.), Cambridge, 617-494-9034
This chic Cambridge newcomer is free 'n' easy with a fun-loving but competent staff; however, owners Stan Frankenthaler (the chef), Chris Schlesinger and Carrie Wheaton (of Cambridge's ever-popular East Coast Grill) are very serious about their ever-changing fresh and delicious International fare that's cooked on an open fire in an open-to-view kitchen; this is a great spot to eat tapas-style, but watch out – the tab adds up.

Chau Chow/SX | 23 | 4 | 14 | $14 |
52 Beach St. (bet. Harrison Ave. & Kneeland St.), 617-426-6266
U – This bargain Chinatown Cantonese was a foodie's secret until it was reviewed; it's still top-notch, with the soups and seafood (salt-baked shrimp, fried squid) especially praised, but as you might expect, lines can be long; some say the "waiters have an attitude" and there's no denying that the surroundings are "grim."

BOSTON | F | D | S | C |

Chez Nous | 25 | 20 | 24 | $39 |
147 Huron Ave. (Concord Ave.), Cambridge,
617-864-6670
U – This French Nouvelle in a Cambridge storefront is "one of the few places left for a good, quiet meal"; chef Elizabeth Fischer has attracted a devoted following for her "simple, light" fare in an "intimate and romantic" setting; not cheap, but worth the price for a first-class, well-served meal.

Cornucopia | 24 | 22 | 21 | $31 |
15 West St. (bet. Tremont & Washington Sts.),
617-338-4600
U – The "imaginative", "well-prepared" Contemporary American menu executed by chef Stuart Cameron at this Downtown restaurant in a historic building has won a delighted following that enjoys "dining, not eating"; there's a carefully selected wine list and many wines by the glass; it's good "with a new friend" or for lunch while shopping; N.B. *they plan to move in early '93.*

Dali | 24 | 21 | 21 | $24 |
415 Washington St. (near Beacon St.), 617-661-3254
U – This Cambridge tapas bar near Inman Square caught on immediately for its festive atmosphere, "genuinely warm and friendly" staff and "wonderful" tapas "for garlic lovers"; the sangria and extensive Spanish wine list are also much admired; even if the entrees are less memorable, it "fills a huge void for good Spanish food in Boston."

Davide/SM | 24 | 20 | 22 | $34 |
326 Commercial Ave. (across from Union Wharf),
617-227-5745
U – Though this fancy Northern Italian is just a little outside the North End, it's far above it in terms of ambition and delivery; although a vocal minority find it "pretentious" and pricey, most admire its "elegance", exemplary service and "dependable", excellent food.

Davio's/SM | 23 | 19 | 20 | $28 |
269 Newbury St. (bet. Fairfield & Gloucester Sts.),
617-262-4810
Hotel Sonesta, 5 Cambridge Pkwy. (across from Cambridgeside Galleria), Cambridge, 617-661-4810
204 Washington St. (off Rte. 9), Brookline, 617-738-4810
U – An extremely popular chain of Nuova Cucina Italians in Back Bay and Brookline Village with a new addition in Cambridge, these siblings win praise for their consistency and "classy settings"; most diners prefer the Brookline location, but recommend the upstairs cafe on Newbury Street for good, quick pizzas at moderate prices; service can be slow.

BOSTON

| F | D | S | C |

East Coast Grill/SM | 24 | 16 | 19 | $24 |
1271 Cambridge St. (near Prospect St.), Cambridge, 617-491-6568
U – This elemental Inman Square storefront "delivers exactly what it promises" – "the best BBQ in Boston" and "fantastic", Caribbean-influenced dishes, all served by chef-owner Chris Schlesinger and an "exceptionally friendly staff"; the no-reservations policy often means waiting for a long time in close, noisy quarters; but whether you're in "black-tie or jeans", this place is "the greatest"; P.S. the restaurant has a "perfect" takeout, Jake & Earl's, next door.

Elephant Walk | – | – | – | I |
70 Union Sq. (Washington St.), Somerville, 617-623-9939
Bostonians aren't walking but running to this Somerville French-Cambodian that gets a trunks-up for its flavorful, delightful, delicate fare at bargain prices, welcoming staff and modestly attractive atmosphere (the outdoor cafe is a bonus); hurry up and visit because elephantine lines are forming.

Five Seasons/S | 24 | 16 | 20 | $22 |
669A Centre St. (bet. Severns Ave. & Green St.), Jamaica Plain, 617-524-9016
U – For "homey, healthy Vegetarian" food, turn to this Jamaica Plain storefront with wooden tables and long lines; even though prices can be higher than you'd expect, the portions are big, and regulars "love this kooky place."

Giacomo's/S | 24 | 16 | 22 | $22 |
355 Hanover St. (bet. Little Prince & Fleet Sts.), 617-523-9026
U – Those who know this North End eatery with its open kitchen and both Northern and Southern Italian dishes are crazy about the "excellent" and moderately priced seafood, as well as the "excellent, schmaltzy" (though sometimes "rushed") service; it's "small and fun", but often crowded.

Green Street Grill/S | 23 | 11 | 18 | $21 |
280 Green St. (bet. Magazine & Pearl Sts.), Cambridge, 617-876-1655
U – This "great dive" behind Central Square has "innovative", "spectacularly well-prepared" Caribbean food, especially the sausages so hot they can "make your eyes water"; however, most love the burn as much as they do chef John Levins, who is a "sorcerer"; all in all, "the best dump in Cambridge."

BOSTON

| F | D | S | C |

Grill 23/SM
| 22 | 21 | 21 | $36 |

161 Berkeley St. (Stuart St.), 617-542-2255
U – The "best steak in town" to some is served in this clubby, "masculine" Back Bay room; the people-watching's great, even if the high ceilings make it so noisy that it's "like eating inside a drum"; despite complaints about prices – a new downpriced premium wine list should alleviate complaints – the staff is "well-trained" and you "can't go wrong taking a client or your boss."

Gyuhama/LSM
| 24 | 18 | 19 | $24 |

827 Boylston St. (bet. Gloucester & Fairfield Sts.), 617-437-0188
U – Boston's Top Japanese specializes in the "best sushi" and "freshest sashimi" in town; the decor at this Back Bay basement is functional, if less than exceptional, and the service is "sometimes not attentive", but that doesn't concern the sushi addicts who come in droves; the "in" spot for late-night sushi and rock 'n' roll.

Hamersley's Bistro/SM
| 26 | 18 | 22 | $36 |

578 Tremont St. (bet. Clarendon & Dartmouth Sts.), 617-267-6068
U – "Really sensational" Eclectic food on a French base has made this South End storefront "as close to a real bistro as you can get in Boston"; chef Gordon Hamersley "gets better all the time without being pretentious about his food"; no matter what, he keeps the lemon-garlic roasted chicken, many people's favorite dish, on the menu; some "wish it were cheaper", but customers generally feel they get their money's worth; the early '93 move may affect the above ratings.

Harvard Street Grill/L
| 25 | 17 | 22 | $32 |

398 Harvard St. (bet. Naples & Fuller Sts.), Brookline, 617-734-9834
U – "One of the best-kept secrets" in town, this Brookline storefront offers nearly "perfect" Eclectic food with a French accent, cooked by chef-owner John Vyhanek, with lamb chops and desserts especially outstanding; the plain-Jane room isn't up to the cooking, and the prices are too high for regulars to be as regular as they'd like, but reviewers say "this spot never disappoints" and hope it isn't "too good to last."

Icarus/S
| 24 | 24 | 22 | $37 |

3 Appleton St. (bet. Arlington & Berkeley Sts.), 617-426-1790
U – An elegant South End secret, this New American garners many raves for its "delicious, imaginative" food, its tastefully eclectic dining room and its "friendly", professional service – all in all, a restaurant ripe for discovery; a handful of critics find it "disappointing" and "overpriced."

BOSTON | F | D | S | C |

Il Capriccio | 25 | 16 | 22 | $37 |
53 Prospect St. (bet. Vermont & Charles Sts.), Waltham, 617-894-2234
U – "The chef really takes pride in the food, and it shows" at this "always enjoyable" Northern Italian; not that there aren't quibbles – the "small space" is a problem and the staff, while "personable", tends to "play up to regulars" – but the "A+ food" and wine list go a long way toward justifying the expense; the decor rating may change due to the face-lift by George Germon of Al Forno.

Jasper's/M | 26 | 23 | 25 | $48 |
240 Commercial St. (Atlantic Ave., across from Lewis Wharf), 617-523-1126
U – Chef-owner Jasper White has been the king of Boston chefs for a decade; maintaining his touch for "outstanding" updated New England food, especially impeccable seafood; he has brought down his prices – they're now lower than the Survey reflects, which qualifies this as an authentic dining bargain; he's also redecorated, and the bold new colors are striking.

Julien/M | 26 | 26 | 25 | $47 |
Hotel Meridien, 250 Franklin St. (Pearl St.), 617-451-1900
U – This French Nouvelle with new chef Andre Chouvin strikes the great majority as "total class" and the "most elegant in Boston"; agreeing that it's "impressive", our respondents hail the room with its soaring ceiling; the speedy and well-priced business lunches are popular, and at night it's an "excellent choice for a special celebration" that's "worth the money"; the adjoining bar, with 1920s murals and piano music, is often called the "best" in town.

Le Bocage/M | 24 | 19 | 22 | $38 |
72 Bigelow Ave. (off Mt. Auburn St.), Watertown, 617-923-1210
M – "They try and most often succeed" at this Watertown storefront French with "well-prepared, traditional, fresh food" and an "attentive, knowledgeable staff"; however, there is the occasional "disappointed" respondent who finds the ambiance "self-conscious", the prix fixe menu "outdated" and the prices unwarranted; perhaps the new ownership will be an improvement.

Legal Sea Foods/SM | 23 | 15 | 17 | $24 |
Park Plaza Hotel, 35 Columbus Ave. (Park Sq.), 617-426-4444
100 Huntington Ave. (Copley Pl., bet. Dartmouth & Exeter Sts.), 617-266-7775
5 Cambridge Center (Kendall Sq.), Cambridge, 617-864-3400
43 Boylston St. (bet. Hammond St. & Hammond Pond Pkwy.), Chestnut Hill, 617-277-7300
Burlington Mall, 1131 Middlesex Tpke. (Rte. 128), Burlington, 617-270-9700

BOSTON | F | D | S | C |

Legal Sea Foods (Cont.)
1 Exchange Pl. (across from The Centrum), Worcester,
617-792-1600
1400 Worcester Rd. (across from Shoppers World),
Natick, 508-820-1115
*M – Once again, this seafood chain drew the most
comment of any restaurant in the Survey, so it's not
surprising that so many complain of "annoyingly
overcrowded" and clamorous conditions at its many
branches; as for the food, the majority still find it
"consistently excellent", "always fresh" and "perfectly
prepared"; locals recommend Kendall Square as the
best (and calmest) overall; the Copley Square branch is
"surprisingly pretty."*

L'Espalier/M | 27 | 26 | 25 | $56 |
30 Gloucester St. (bet. Newbury St. & Commonwealth
Ave.), 617-262-3023
*M – For a restaurant with ratings this spectacular, this
Back Bay French Nouvelle gets surprisingly mixed reviews
from our surveyors; few disagree that "when money is
no object, it's heaven", with the "exquisite", "artfully
presented" food of Frank McClelland, a "lovely setting"
and "very formal" service – in short, the "fanciest in
Boston"; however, "haughty" waiters can make you feel
"like the village idiot", and though it's arguably "the top in
Boston", for many it's "too expensive for what you get."*

Locke-Ober Cafe/SM | 21 | 22 | 22 | $39 |
3 Winter Pl. (bet. Tremont & Washington Sts.),
617-542-1340
*M – This "last bastion of Brahmin Boston" is simply "on a
different level" from every other restaurant in town, for
better or worse; if your tastes run to "utterly dependable"
American food, "gentlemanly quarters" heavy on the "dark
wood" and "waiters who are waiters, not friends", you'll
find it "magically charming"; uncharmed diners object to
the "boring New England cuisine", "tired and grumpy" staff
and an "atmosphere of testosterone."*

Maison Robert/M | 23 | 22 | 22 | $40 |
45 School St. (bet. Tremont & Washington Sts.),
617-227-3370
*M – With "gracious dining in a historic setting" in the Old
City Hall, this French Classic delivers the goods, even if
its "staid and respectable" air doesn't appeal to all; the
food is "wonderful" to some, though to others it "could
be more creative"; similar mixed reactions greet the
service and decor, which elicit responses from "top-notch"
to "atrocious, '70s-style"; most raters agree, however,
that it's at its best at lunch in the cafe.*

BOSTON

| F | D | S | C |

Michela's
| 24 | 21 | 21 | $36 |

1 Athenaeum St. (bet. 1st & 2nd Sts.), Cambridge, 617-225-2121

M – This Italian trendsetter, led by the stylish Michela Larson, is "hot, hot, hot" and since chef Jody Adams (ex Hamersley's) moved to Cambridge, it's sizzling; the "Spartan" decor and noise bother some, and so do the prices in the dining room, but many reviewers call its atrium cafe "one of the best deals in the city", and everyone swoons over the delicious food and "great bread."

Morton's of Chicago/M
| 24 | 17 | 21 | $37 |

1 Exeter Place (bet. Exeter & Dartmouth Sts.), 617-266-5858

U – "Leave your vegetarian friends at home" when you enter this ineffably "macho" Back Bay steakhouse; it bases its reputation on "lotsa meat" of very high quality, and many say it has the "best steaks in Boston", though less carnivorous sorts proclaim it "big, beefy and boring"; watch out for "too many add-ons", or you'll find you could "eat twice elsewhere for less."

Oasis Cafe
| 23 | 18 | 20 | $16 |

176 Endicott St. (bet. N. Washington & Thatcher Sts.), 617-523-9274

U – Devotees go for the "great old-fashioned American food and Ella Fitzgerald on the jukebox" at this North Ender that, for once, isn't Italian; a few come away "disappointed", but most like the "good value", "huge portions" and casual atmosphere.

Olives
| 27 | 18 | 20 | $32 |

10 City Sq., Charlestown, 617-242-1999

M – The good news is that this foodie favorite in yuppie-invaded Charlestown is "the hottest spot in town", with "phenomenal" Northern Italian–Mediterranean cooking under the direction of Todd English, and "affordable, too"; the problem is, "they make it as difficult as possible to eat here" – it's cramped and "full of commotion", and the no-reservations policy for groups of fewer than six often results in long waits.

Parker's/SM
| 23 | 24 | 24 | $37 |

Omni Parker House, 60 School St. (Tremont St.), 617-227-8600, x1600

U – This is a "real Old Boston" bastion of "hearty" fare, stately and "attentive" service and "unabashed elegance" – a "classic in every sense"; go for the unequivocally "civilized brunch" to see it at its best.

BOSTON

| F | D | S | C |

Plaza Dining Room
| 23 | 25 | 23 | $49 |

(aka Cafe Plaza)
Copley Plaza Hotel, 138 St. James St. (Dartmouth St. at Copley Sq.), 617-267-5300
M – Is one of Boston's most expensive spots "worth the coin?" – most respondents think so, citing the "Victorian splendor" of the turn-of-the-century room, the "excellent Continental food" and "exquisite service" that "makes the food even better"; a few, while conceding that it's "a great place to impress someone", consider the cost excessive.

Rarities/SM
| 23 | 24 | 23 | $46 |

Charles Hotel, 1 Bennett St. (Eliot St.), Cambridge, 617-864-1200, x1214
M – This "beautiful" Nouvelle American "just misses the top rank"; "sometimes precious, but mostly exquisite", there's always "something inspired" on its "creative menu", and the service and wine list both win high praise; what keeps it from greatness, our surveyors suspect, is its way of "trying too hard."

Ristorante Toscano/SM
| 24 | 19 | 21 | $34 |

41 Charles St. (bet. Mt. Vernon & Chestnut Sts.), 617-723-4090
M – The "only authentic Northern Italian in Boston", this Beacon Hill class-act has become a "local favorite" with its "wonderful menu" and "wonderful flavors"; a small number find it "correct but rather boring", but they're outvoted by those who say it's "absolutely fabulous."

Roka/S
| 23 | 19 | 19 | $23 |

1001 Mass. Ave. (bet. Harvard & Central Sqs.), Cambridge, 617-661-0344
U – Since reopening after a fire, "the food has vastly improved" at this "pleasant", "dependable" Cambridge Japanese; critics are of two minds toward the "ultramoody" setting, but "sublime" sushi and "excellent, fresh Japanese dishes" win them over.

Seasons/SM
| 26 | 25 | 26 | $46 |

Bostonian Hotel, 9 Blackstone St. N. (bet. North & Blackstone Sts.), 617-523-3600
U – This finishing school for great Boston chefs – Jasper White, Lydia Shire, Bill Poirer and now the very talented Tony Ambrose – remains "consistently better than others in its price category"; though a few voters detect "signs of fatigue", the great majority contends that the mix of "inventive" food, "great surroundings", "super wine list" and "pampering service" add up to dining that "doesn't get any better"; a major redo should raise the decor ratings even higher when it's finished.

BOSTON

| F | D | S | C |

St. Cloud/LSM | 22 | 21 | 20 | $31 |
557 Tremont St. (Clarendon St.), 617-353-0202
U – The chef "does it right" at this Nouvelle American with "interesting food" and "terrific Sunday brunch"; still holding on to its "glittery crowd", this newly remodeled hot spot could easily be in NYC; the main drawback is that "Suburbanites have discovered it."

Takeshima | 24 | 17 | 22 | $20 |
308 Harvard St. (Babcock St.), Brookline, 617-566-0200
U – Most everyone goes for the "consistently wonderful and fresh" sushi at this "clean, attractive" Brookline Japanese; despite a few qualms about the service, a great majority of respondents praise the variety of the menu and "would hate to have all of Boston know about it – it's already tough enough to get in."

Upstairs at the Pudding | 24 | 19 | 21 | $42 |
10 Holyoke St. (bet. Mass. Ave. & Holyoke Ctr., Harvard Sq.), Cambridge, 617-864-1933
U – A recent changing of the guard may affect ratings at this "slightly too Harvardy" "special-occasion place"; the "excellent" and "very innovative" Continental–Northern Italian fare, though "overpriced", helps make it "a great spot to entertain people"; your appreciation of things Ivy will determine whether you find the atmosphere "lovely" or "shabby", the service "terrific" or "atrocious."

CHICAGO

TOP 30 RESTAURANTS
(In order of food rating)

Restaurant	Cuisine Type
29 – Le Francais	French Classic
28 – Carlos'	French Classic
Ambria	French Nouvelle
27 – Jimmy's Place	French/Japanese
Tallgrass	French Nouvelle
Dining Room	French Classic
Everest Room	French Classic
Yoshi's Cafe	French/Japanese
Jackie's	French Nouvelle
Cafe Provencal	French Bistro
Charlie Trotter's	Amer. Contemp.
26 – Le Titi de Paris	French Classic
Montparnasse	French Classic
Emilio's Tapas Bar	Spanish
Frontera Grill	Mexican
Seasons	Amer. Tradition.
Cottage	American/Continental
Morton's of Chicago	Steakhouse
Meson Sabika	Spanish
25 – Gordon	Amer. Contemp.
La Tour	French Classic
Greenery	Cajun/Creole
Topolobampo	Mexican
Printer's Row	Amer. Contemp.
Arun's	Thai
302 West	Californian
Le Vichyssois	French Bistro
Va Pensiero	N/S Italian
24 – Bird	Chinese
Franco's Ristorante	N/S Italian

OTHER TOP PLACES
(In alphabetical order)

Berghoff	German
Bistro Banlieue	French Bistro
Entre Nous	Seafood
Gene & Georgetti	N/S Italian/Steakhouse
Hatsuhana	Japanese
Le Mikado	Eurasian
95th	Amer. Tradition.
Pizzeria Uno & Due	Pizza
Pump Room	Amer. Contemp.
Shaw's Crab House	Seafood
Spiaggia	N/S Italian
Trattoria No. 10	N/S Italian
Un Grand Cafe	French Bistro
Vivere	N/S Italian
Walker Bros.	Amer. Tradition.

CHICAGO

| F | D | S | C |

Ambria
| 28 | 27 | 27 | $54 |

2300 N. Lincoln Park W. (Belden Ave.), 312-472-5959
U – "Always one of the best", this "exquisite" French Nouvelle in tony Lincoln Park is No. 3 for food in our Chicago Survey; "sophisticated" wood-paneled "elegance" makes a "gorgeous setting" for "consistently marvelous" food that is "so beautiful you don't want to disturb your plate", and the tuxedo-clad staff is always "well orchestrated"; despite scattered complaints of stuffiness, inconsistency and high prices, for the great majority, Ambria "approaches perfection"; N.B. try the degustation menu.

Arun's/S
| 25 | 23 | 23 | $30 |

4156 N. Kedzie Ave. (Berteau Ave.), 312-539-1909
U – "The best-kept secret in Chicago", this top-rated Thai pleases with its "delicious, unusual" "haute cuisine" and "elegant setting", "lavishly decorated" with native artwork; though some complain of "microscopic portions" and contend that this is the "Thai-food version of the emperor's new clothes", most say it's a "class act" all the way.

Berghoff
| 20 | 19 | 19 | $16 |

17 W. Adams St. (bet. State & Dearborn Sts.), 312-427-3170
M – A Loop tradition since 1898, this affordable German still reaps raves for its "old-world ambiance and food that's "much heavier than the average daily allowance" including "legendary creamed spinach" and delicious rye bread; critics say beware of tourists, lines and "bad food."

Bird, The/X
| 24 | 13 | 20 | $21 |

1119 N. 25th Ave. (5½ blocks south of Kostner Ave.), Melrose Park, 708-681-0414
U – Champions of this "out-of-the-way" Chinese point to "landmark chef" Ben Moy's "unusual" European-accented food and "outstanding quality and presentation", especially the seafood and vegetarian dishes, but a few note that there's "no ambiance" and no liquor – but you can BYO.

Bistro Banlieue/S
| 24 | 19 | 22 | $24 |

44 Yorktown Convenience Ctr. (bet. Butterfield Rd. & Highland Ave.), Lombard, 708-629-6560
U – "Hard to believe" – a truly "excellent" restaurant that thrives in the Western 'burbs; this "cozy" "oasis" is a "gem in a mall", where the "French food is fantastique" and "you're only a stranger once"; attractive "contemporary decor", "personal" service and "creative" food make this spot a favorite in a "crazy location."

CHICAGO | F | D | S | C |

Cafe Provencal | 27 | 26 | 26 | $49 |
1625 Hinman Ave. (bet. Davis & Church Sts.), Evanston, 708-475-2233
U – Leslee Reis's "legacy lives on" at this "romantic" Country French cafe that most consider "one of the benchmark" dining experiences in the Chicago area; the "cozy", "relaxing" ambiance and "knowledgeable staff" provide the perfect setting for an ever-changing selection of "wonderful", "beautifully presented" food that is "a nice mix of creative and classic"; P.S. it's pricey.

Carlos'/S | 28 | 25 | 27 | $57 |
429 Temple Ave. (1½ blocks east of Green Bay Rd.), Highland Park, 708-432-0770
U – "For a truly special occasion", it's hard to beat this "top-notch", "expensive" French Classic, which gets nearly unanimous accolades from Chicagoans who gladly drive to Highland Park for "food as an art form": "incredible" cooking, "awesome presentation", "helpful" service and a "super wine list" – only the "cramped quarters keep this from being the best of the best"; if one big eater reports "portions so small" he had to "buy a Snickers bar afterward", for the great majority it's "always a culinary delight."

Charlie Trotter's | 27 | 25 | 26 | $62 |
816 W. Armitage Ave. (Halsted St.), 312-248-6228
U – The "cutting edge for Chicago", this "outstanding" De Paul/Lincoln Park Contemporary American awes with "daring", "intriguing" food and presentation, a stylish townhouse setting and "superb" service; isolated complaints of "egotistical" service and "small portions" for which you have to "take out a second mortgage" don't deter the vast majority, who say it's "truly a unique experience, worth every penny"; N.B. reserve the table for six in the kitchen or try the "killer" tasting menus – "what a way to die."

Cottage, The | 26 | 23 | 23 | $36 |
525 Torrence Ave. (Sibley Blvd.), Calumet City, 708-891-3900
U – After nearly a year spent traveling the world to recharge her batteries, chef Carolyn Buster has reopened this well-liked American-Continental; customers are flocking back for the new lighter menu, "lower prices" and casual, airy atmosphere.

CHICAGO

	F	D	S	C

Dining Room, The/S | 27 | 27 | 27 | $52 |

Ritz-Carlton Hotel, 160 E. Pearson St., 12th fl. (Michigan Ave.), 312-266-1000
U – This "elegant", "charming" Classic French sets a new standard for hotel dining with what many believe is the "highest-quality food and service in the city" – "refined, not pretentious"; add a "spectacular Sunday brunch" and "fabulous" wine list, and you have "civilized dining" at its best; none of this comes as a surprise since the Four Season chain, which anonymously and anomalously owns the hotel, is known for its fine restaurants.

Emilio's Tapas Bar & Restaurant/S | 26 | 21 | 22 | $23 |

4100 W. Roosevelt Rd. (Mannheim Rd.), Hillside, 708-547-7177
U – Ex–Cafe-Ba-Ba-Reeba! chef Emilio Gervilla is becoming "the Mediterranean Melman of the suburbs", starting with the opening of this "crowded", colorful, "neighborly", "deliciously different" tapas restaurant; it wins raves for quality and value, which at times produces "lengthy" waits.

Entre Nous/S | 23 | 24 | 23 | $39 |

Fairmont Hotel, Illinois Ctr., 200 N. Columbus Dr. (Wacker Dr.), 312-565-7997
U – A harpist sets the tone for this very "romantic", "elegant", "très serene" hotel dining room that wins high marks for its "innovative" seafood, served with a "civility" rarely found on today's dining circuit – "a sleeper."

Everest Room, The | 27 | 27 | 27 | $58 |

The LaSalle Club, 440 S. LaSalle St., 40th fl. (bet. Congress Pkwy. & Van Buren St.), 312-663-8920
U – For a "peak dining experience", few other restaurants scale the heights of this Downtown French, where chef Jean Joho's "memorable", "one-of-a-kind" meals are the norm and the beauty on the plates is exceeded only by the spectacular, "romantic" evening views of twinkling lights stretching far into the distance; "magnificent service" and an interesting wine list round out an admittedly pricey but "truly satisfying" experience.

Franco's Ristorante | 24 | 15 | 18 | $19 |

300 W. 31st St. (Princeton St.), 312-225-9566
U – "Simple pleasures" – "chargrilled seafood", "home-made pasta" and "friendly waiters" – make this affordable Italian in an "improbable" South Side location an "undiscovered", if "noisy", "gem"; convenience to Comiskey Park makes it "perfect" for a pre-game warm-up.

CHICAGO

| F | D | S | C |

Frontera Grill | 26 | 21 | 20 | $25 |
445 N. Clark St. (bet. Hubbard & Illinois Sts.),
312-661-1434
U – "Yessss, this is what Mexican is all about" say the myriad fans of this "lively" Near North "hot spot"; its "wonderful", "fresh and original" food is a "revelation" compared with standard south-of-the-border fare, and attracts a "cosmopolitan" crowd; the no-reservations policy means you can "grow a beard waiting for a table" and "the staff is sometimes overwhelmed", but satisfied surveyors still think "Chicago needs more places like this one."

Gene & Georgetti | 24 | 13 | 17 | $32 |
500 N. Franklin St. (Illinois St.), 312-527-3718
U – This "classic", "very-male" River North steakhouse offers "huge portions" of "out-of-this-world" steak and "old-fashioned" Italian food complete with "obnoxious" waiters; beloved by many, it's also blasted by some: "if you're not Sinatra you're in Siberia", "women alone are ignored", "The Palm without deodorant."

Gordon/S | 25 | 25 | 24 | $41 |
500 N. Clark St. (Illinois St.), 312-467-9780
U – "Always-steady", "always-special" and "always a pleasure" is Gordon Sinclair's "urbane" River North Contemporary American; despite frequent changes in the kitchen that lead some to christen this "the chef-of-the-week club", the "classy" surroundings, "smooth" service" and "superb style" make this "clearly one of the city's best" for "new and exciting food", with such welcome extras as half-portion entrees, a pre-theater menu, and "civilized" live music and dancing on weekends.

Greenery/S | 25 | 22 | 24 | $31 |
117 North Ave. (Northwest Hwy. & Main St.), Barrington,
708-381-9000
U – Located in an atmospheric "old home", this Northwest Suburban Cajun-Creole manages to exude a sense of "elegance" despite its "cramped quarters" and wins high marks for its "innovative", "light" variations on a New Orleans theme; though some diners are "disappointed", most think this one is "a hidden treasure."

Hatsuhana | 23 | 17 | 20 | $28 |
160 E. Ontario St. (Michigan Ave.), 312-280-8287
M – Chicago's "top" sushi bar (part of a successful international chain) continues to win raves from our reviewers for pristine "fresh" sushi and great theater from the sushi chefs, but the "clean" looking, casual decor may be getting "somewhat tired", and a few raters are tiring of the "nose-up, wallet-out" attitude.

CHICAGO

| F | D | S | C |

Jackie's
| 27 | 22 | 24 | $45 |

2478 N. Lincoln Ave.(bet. Fullerton Pkwy. & Altgeld St.), 312-880-0003
U – The food is "almost too pretty to eat" at this Lincoln Park/De Paul–area French Nouvelle, but once you start, you'll find that Jackie Shen's "innovative" cooking is as good as it looks, especially the "outstanding" desserts (don't miss the "outrageous chocolate bag"); some diners suggest that service can be "erratic" and that the decor suffered a bit in a recent expansion, but solid ratings across the board indicate why it's a favorite place to "impress your friends."

Jimmy's Place
| 27 | 23 | 26 | $47 |

3420 N. Elston Ave. (2½ blocks south of Addison St.), 312-539-2999
M – No perfume, hairspray or smoking are allowed at this Northwest French favorite – owner Jimmy Rohr is allergic to all – but that doesn't deter his many fans, who love the place's "personalized" service, operatic music and chef Kevin Shikami's "innovative", "Asian-influenced" food; predictably, a few of our surveyors label the food "overwrought" and exclaim "talk about taking yourself too seriously!", but the numbers don't lie about this "important restaurant."

La Tour/S
| 25 | 26 | 24 | $48 |

Park Hyatt Hotel, 800 N. Michigan Ave. (Chicago Ave.), 312-280-2230
U – With its "stunning" decor and "beautiful" view of the old Water Tower and Michigan Avenue, this "wonderful but expensive" French is the perfect setting for "power breakfasts", Sunday brunch or an evening of "romance in the heart of the city"; while a scant few detect some "slippage recently", the vast majority of our reviewers agree that the "superb" food and "heavenly" service live up to the "elegant" room, justifying the "lofty" prices.

Le Francais
| 29 | 27 | 27 | $66 |

269 S. Milwaukee Ave. (2 blocks south of Dundee Rd.), Wheeling, 708-541-7470
U – Ranked No. 1 for food in our Chicago Survey, this famed French Classic is still "top of the line" – some say "even better" – under new owners Roland and Mary Beth Liccioni; the "elegant" food, which has been lightened under the Liccionis, and "superb" service approach "perfection", and the country French atmosphere remains homey and comfortable; not surprisingly, there are those who "miss (former owner) Jean Banchet" or complain of pretension and high prices, but to nearly all of our surveyors this is the "ultimate dining experience."

CHICAGO

| F | D | S | C |

Le Mikado/S | 24 | 22 | 21 | $33 |
21 W. Goethe Pl. (Dearborn Ave.), 312-280-8611
U – Since our last Survey, a remarkable thing happened at this North Side Eurasian: the ratings nudged up and the prices came down; as a result, crowds are converging on this "very comfortable", "casual" spot for "exciting" and "innovative" food; the "scrumptious", "intriguing" combinations please the palate, while the $16 prix fixe soothes the pocketbook.

Le Titi de Paris | 26 | 24 | 25 | $44 |
1015 W. Dundee Rd. (Kennicott St.), Arlington Heights, 708-506-0222
U – Fans of the original location may find the new Northwest Suburban version of this French standby a bit "sterile", but "superb" food and the "creative" energy of chef Pierre Pollin keep them coming back to what is a "good runner-up" to Le Francais; relatively modest prices (compared to L.F., at least) and "amiable staff" add to the appeal of this "elegant yet homey" spot; try the six-course degustation menu at $28.

Le Vichyssois/S | 25 | 22 | 23 | $40 |
220 W. Ill. Hwy. 120 (2 miles west of Rte. 12), Lakemoor, 815-385-8221
U – "Far Northwest" doesn't adequately describe the location of this "country French inn" that's a "long drive even from the suburbs", but for many it's "worth the hike": "wonderful seafood" prepared by "talented chef" Bernard Cretier and "huge" portions make this a "real hidden treasure."

Meson Sabika/S | 26 | 24 | 23 | $25 |
1025 Aurora Ave. (Washington Ave.), Naperville, 708-983-3000
U – Emilio's younger sibling in the Western Suburbs is situated in a "quaint" old renovated mansion, winning praise for its "nice setting" as well as for its "interesting variety" of creative tapas and Spanish food; though the "quality is good", "the bill can add up" as you sample.

Montparnasse | 26 | 23 | 23 | $44 |
200 E. Fifth Ave. (1½ blocks east of Washington Blvd.), Naperville, 708-961-8203
U – "An oasis in the 'burbs", this French "hidden treasure" offers "Chicago's greatest wine values", "excellent food" and a "unique" renovated "factory setting" with lofty ceilings; chef Suzy Crofton's "delicate flavors" and "outstanding presentations" (she trained under Jean Banchet) win raves that drown out scattered snipes about high prices and pretension.

CHICAGO | F | D | S | C |

Morton's of Chicago/S | 26 | 20 | 22 | $39 |

1876 First St. (Central Ave.) Highland Park, 708-432-3484
1 Westbrook Corporate Ctr. (intersection of 22nd St. & Wolf Rd.), Westchester, 708-562-7000
Columbia Centre III, 9525 W. Bryn Mawr Ave. (River Rd.), Rosemont, 708-678-5155
Newberry Plaza, 1050 N. State St., lower level (Bellevue Pl.), 312-266-4820

U – Carnivores may be endangered, but they're far from extinct, and for them "there's no better place" than this homegrown chain, overwhelmingly voted "Chicago's best steakhouse" by our surveyors; people may beef about the tourists and the "expensive" à la carte pricing, but if it's steak they want (or a "great veal chop" or lobster), they almost inevitably head to this "clubby", some say "manly", Windy City institution.

95th, The/S | 21 | 26 | 21 | $41 |

John Hancock Bldg., 875 N. Michigan Ave., 95th fl. (bet. Chestnut St. & Delaware Pl.), 312-787-9596

U – The view is so "electrifyingly" "spectacular" at this top-of-the-Hancock restaurant that many surveyors seem to forget the interesting seasonal American food that has "improved greatly" in recent years; a "worthy" Sunday brunch and wine list add to the experience, but the prices are as "lofty" as one might expect.

Pizzeria Uno & Due | 22 | 14 | 16 | $14 |

29 E. Ohio St. (Wabash Ave.), 312-321-1000/L
619 N. Wabash Ave. (Ontario St.), 312-943-2400/LS

M – Ike Sewell invented the now-famous Chicago-style deep-dish pizza at Uno, and these Near North sisters still get the highest ratings in town for their pies – they also seem to generate the most controversy, from "eck" to "excellent", with folks who call this the "best pizza known to mankind" in the clear majority, despite "rude" service, "uncomfortable" quarters and all the tourists.

Printer's Row | 25 | 22 | 23 | $37 |

550 S. Dearborn St. (Congress Pkwy.), 312-461-0780

U – It's "not like Mama cooked American", but this attractive Printer's Row "pioneer" wins admiration for its "innovative menu", interesting domestic wine list and chef-owner Michael Foley's "serious", almost intellectual, approach to food; service is "wonderful", and the "charming", comfortable setting has an "old clubby feel" that's perfect for a "romantic" occasion.

CHICAGO

| F | D | S | C |

Pump Room, The/S | 21 | 25 | 23 | $38 |
Omni Ambassador East Hotel, 1301 N. State Pkwy.
(Goethe St.), 312-266-0360
U – Nostalgia buffs and incurable "romantics" go for this "elegant" Gold Coast "grande dame" with celebrity photos lining the walls, live music and dancing, and "well-executed" Contemporary American cuisine; while it may not be as good as you remember, it's still "a lot better than you think" – and really "should be seen"; P.S. Sunday brunch is particularly popular.

Seasons/S | 26 | 27 | 25 | $43 |
Four Seasons Hotel, 120 E. Delaware St., 7th fl.
(bet. Michigan Ave. & Rush St.), 312-280-8800
U – This strangely unheralded Gold Coast American offers "exceptional" food with a seasonally-changing menu; the "wonderful" Sunday brunch, "impeccable service" and "elegant" dining room win raves; overall, expensive, but a "great value" for a "quality" experience.

Shaw's Crab House and Blue Crab Lounge/S | 23 | 20 | 20 | $27 |
21 E. Hubbard St. (State St.), 312-527-2722
U – This ain't the Grand Central Oyster Bar but it "comes close"; the noise just "seems right" with the "'40s-diner decor" (lots of tile and "stuffed fish on the walls") and the menu has all the "good fresh basics": "the best crab cakes", stone crab and a "wide variety of fish and shellfish"; while a few say "too hustle-bustle" and "too expensive", most agree "everything is done right."

Spiaggia/S | 24 | 26 | 23 | $43 |
One Magnificent Mile Bldg., 980 N. Michigan Ave.,
2nd fl. (Oak St.), 312-280-2750
M – Our surveyors call this "gorgeous" Gold Coast classic overlooking Oak Street Beach "one of the prettiest", "most romantic" rooms in Chicago, but praise is somewhat fainter for the "high-ticket" Italian food; while most applaud the "imaginative" menu and "great little pizzas", critics say that the "revolving door in the kitchen" has led to an occasional "disappointment", but surveyors are certain that the arrival of chef Paul Bartolotta spelled an end to that era.

Tallgrass/S | 27 | 25 | 26 | $48 |
1006 S. State St. (10th St.), Lockport, 815-838-5566
U – "Superb" French Nouvelle cuisine (including a tempting prix fixe), "excellent" service and an "extensive", well-priced wine list are enough to bring foodies from 60 miles away to this Southwest Suburban "find", located in a charming former home in the historic I & M Canal town of Lockport; the "beautiful rooms" are chock-full of antiques and "elegant" tables set with crystal and fine china, and the "inventive menu" changes frequently; the only complaint: "why isn't it in the city?"

CHICAGO

| F | D | S | C |

302 West
| 25 | 23 | 24 | $37 |

302 W. State St. (Third Ave.), Geneva, 708-232-9302
U – "Excellent" Californian cuisine comes to the Western 'burbs and wins plenty of praise (no mean feat) at this "romantic", "innovative" trendsetter housed in an old bank building with soaring ceilings; customers are pleased with the "superb" daily-changing menu that's "artfully prepared" and served by a "superior" staff.

Topolobampo
| 25 | 22 | 23 | $35 |

445 N. Clark (bet. Hubbard & Illinois Sts.), 312-661-1434
U – Customers place this "unusual" Near North Mexican among the top restaurants in Chicago, thanks to its "elegant" setting and "tremendous" blends of "unique flavors" from Mexico's many culinary regions, served by a gracious and "knowledgeable" staff; N.B. some prefer its next-door sister, Frontera Grill.

Trattoria No. 10
| 24 | 22 | 21 | $30 |

10 N. Dearborn St. (bet. Washington & Madison Sts.), 312-984-1718
U – Overcoming its basement boiler-room setting, this popular Loop Italian offers sunny decorations and "romantic" lighting; our reviewers praise the "outstanding" Italian menu and say this "hot" spot has the "best happy-hour" buffet anywhere.

Un Grand Cafe
| 24 | 22 | 23 | $31 |

2300 N. Lincoln Park West (Belden Ave.), 312-348-8886
U – "Paris meets Chicago" at this Lincoln Park French bistro that has a "classy", "European feel", yet many say it's also just like a "neighborhood club", with "terrific food" and fine service; the outdoor cafe is "delightful" in the summer, adding up to an "all-around satisfying experience."

Va Pensiero
| 25 | 21 | 23 | $31 |

1566 Oak Ave. (bet. Davis & Grove Aves.), Evanston, 708-475-7779
U – "The secret is out" about this "hideaway", even if Peggy Ryan (ex Cafe Provencal) is an unlikely moniker for an Italian chef; the "regional specialties" are "splendid", especially since "you get what you pay for", and the staff is "wonderfully helpful."

Vivere
| 21 | 24 | 21 | $33 |

Italian Village, 71 W. Monroe St. (bet. Clark & Dearborn Sts.), 312-332-4040
M – The Capitanini family "went for baroque" when they transformed the old Florentine Room into this "breathtaking" spot that people either love or hate (e.g. "Architectural Digest four-star decor" vs. "the design team must have been on drugs"); the well-rated regional Italian food gets fewer comments, but it can be just as "dramatic" as the room.

CHICAGO

| F | D | S | C |

Walker Bros./SX | 24 | 20 | 20 | $11 |

153 Green Bay Rd. (bet. Central & Lake Aves.),
Wilmette, 708-251-6000
1615 Waukegan Rd. (2 blocks north of Lake Ave.),
Glenview, 708-724-0220
825 W. Dundee Rd. (bet. Rte. 53 & Arlington Heights
Rd.), Arlington Heights, 708-392-6600
U – The lines form early at these area "institutions" for thick apple pancakes and "big portions" of other "yummy" breakfasts, all at rock-bottom prices and served amid "spectacular stained glass" by efficient servers who actually seem to enjoy what they're doing – but oh, those lines.

Yoshi's Cafe/S | 27 | 22 | 25 | $47 |

3247 N. Halsted St. (1 block north of Belmont Ave.),
312-248-6160
U – "Delicate" and "exquisite" dishes that are "beautifully presented" are the hallmarks of chef Yoshi Katsumura's Asian-accented French food, which is consistently among the highest-rated in Chicago; the "lovely", "intimate" atmosphere and "friendly", "attentive" staff also win general applause; true, a handful of detractors say that after 10 years, Yoshi is "resting on his laurels", but they are overwhelmingly outvoted.

DALLAS

TOP 30 RESTAURANTS
(In order of food rating)

Restaurant	Cuisine Type
28 – Riviera	French
French Room	French Classic
Routh Street Cafe	Southwestern
Gaspar's	Amer. Contemp.
27 – Mansion	Southwestern
Laurels	Amer. Contemp.
Actuelle	Amer. Contemp.
26 – L'Entrecote	French Classic
Del Frisco's	Steakhouse
Cafe Pacific	Seafood
Chaplin's	Amer. Contemp.
25 – Lawry's The Prime Rib	Amer. Tradition.
Chez Gerard	French Bistro
Morton's of Chicago	Steakhouse
Pyramid Room	American/Continental
Conservatory	Amer. Contemp.
Old Warsaw	Continental
Ruth's Chris	Steakhouse
York Street	Amer. Contemp.
24 – Adelmo's	Mediterranean
Mr. Sushi	Japanese
Nana Grill	Southwestern
Baby Routh	Southwestern
Clark's Outpost	BBQ
Ruggeri's Ristorante	Northern Italian
Uncle Tai's Hunan Yuan	Chinese
Addison Cafe	French Bistro
Sonny Bryan's	BBQ
Alessio's	Northern Italian
City Cafe	Amer. Contemp.

OTHER TOP PLACES
(In alphabetical order)

Acapella	Pizza
Avner's	Amer. Contemp.
Chimney	Austrian
Gennie's Bishop Grill	Soul Food
India Palace	Indian
Jasmine Restaurant	Chinese
Javier's	Mexican
La Calle Doce	Mexican/Seafood
Ristorante Savino	N/S Italian
Thai Soon	Thai

DALLAS

| F | D | S | C |

Acapella Cafe/S | 21 | 20 | 19 | $15 |
2508 Maple Ave. (bet. McKinney Ave. & Cedar Springs Rd.), 214-871-2262
U – "Sophisticated but casually simple", this "small, charming old house" serves "great yuppie pizzas" in the shadow of the Crescent complex; though some surveyors caution against "offbeat combos" like "pineapple pizza", and many menu items are "routinely out", most say this is a "great value" "for a relaxed, health-conscious dinner."

Actuelle | 27 | 25 | 25 | $42 |
500 Crescent Ct., Ste. 165 (at McKinney Ave. & Cedar Springs Rd.), 214-855-0440
U – One of Dallas's best overall, this "spiffy luxe" New American pleases "top-drawer types" with its "stunning" performance; it recently moved from The Quadrangle to lovely, romantic quarters in The Crescent; the new surroundings complement chef-owner Victor Gielisse's "rarefied, excellent food" and host-owner Clive O'Donoghue's gracious hospitality.

Addison Cafe/S | 24 | 20 | 22 | $29 |
5290 Belt Line Rd. (Montfort Rd.), Addison, 214-991-8824
M – "A-plus overall" say fans of this "undiscovered" North Dallas strip-center French bistro, although what's "cozy and romantic" to some seems "too crowded" to others; a few complain of "stuffy" service, but most think it's a "great neighborhood cafe" and "a real bargain for such quality."

Adelmo's | 24 | 18 | 22 | $27 |
4537 Cole Ave. (near Knox St.), 214-559-0325
U – This tiny, two-story bistro offers a first-class cruise through the Mediterranean – a little Italian food, a little French, even a little Middle Eastern; "loud and lively", this place may be "cramped" and "like dining in a fishbowl", but to some surveyors it's a "European inn" with a Park Cities crowd; the owner, Adelmo Banschetti, is a "perfect host."

Alessio's/S | 24 | 19 | 22 | $29 |
4117 Lomo Alto Dr. (near Lemmon Ave.), 214-521-3585
U – "Reminscent of an intimate NYC Italian restaurant", Alessio Fransechetti's "pricey", "dark and romantic" spot can also be "noisy and crowded, but the food is worth it"; "they have to know you", say folks who consider it "clubby", but once they do, it's "very comfortable and friendly."

DALLAS

| F | D | S | C |

Avner's/L

| – | – | – | M |

2515 McKinney Ave. (bet. Fairmount & Routh Sts.), 214-953-0426

Bringing upscale New American cuisine to a casual, bang-for-the-buck bistro level, chef-owner Avner Samuel crafts a creative menu in a sleek, comfortable urban setting; unusual dishes include Singapore tea soup and "lava-seared" calf's liver; facing the McKinney Avenue trolley line through floor-to-ceiling glass, this restaurant provides a good view of the city.

Baby Routh/S

| 24 | 24 | 22 | $30 |

2708 Routh St. (bet. McKinney Ave. & Cedar Springs Rd.), 214-871-2345

U – "Not as consistent as Big Bro" – chef Stephan Pyles's Routh Street Cafe – but a "very slick and chic" spot in two creatively renovated and connected Victorian houses; while most say the Southwestern cuisine is "interesting and innovative" and decor is "creative down to the napkins (diapers!)", some fault "baby-sized portions", "bad acoustics" and "aloof" waiters.

Cafe Pacific/S

| 26 | 24 | 23 | $27 |

24 Highland Park Village (Mockingbird Lane & Preston Rd.), 214-526-1170

U – Sophisticates flock to this redecorated seafood restaurant, a Highland Park favorite that's "ritzy and high class, with food and service to match", and "always good, always crisp, always consistent"; some say this "dinner with the old guard" comes with "snob appeal" and "a snooty attitude that's not necessary nor appreciated by regular rich clientele."

Chaplin's/S

| 26 | 21 | 22 | $25 |

1928 Greenville Ave. (Oram St.), 214-823-3300

U – Brilliantly crossing Continental with American grill food, this reasonably priced and "laid-back" restaurant (owner Jack Chaplin works the room in Bermuda shorts topped by chef's whites) is "great", "fun" and "innovative"; it's a "nice alternative to typical upscale dining", with a staff that's "sensitive to customers' requests"; sweet-toothed Anglophiles recommend going "just for Port and cheesecake" – made with Stilton cheese.

Chez Gerard

| 25 | 21 | 24 | $29 |

4444 McKinney Ave. (south of Knox St.), 214-522-6865

U – "Small, wonderful oasis" serving "the best Country French" in an informal, "crowded" bistro setting; "friendly" service, "reasonable prices" for "simple but serious" food and a good selection of wine earn fans, although some raters find the service "somewhat impersonal" and the tables "too close."

DALLAS

| F | D | S | C |

Chimney, The
| 23 | 21 | 21 | $26 |

9739 N. Central Expwy. (Walnut Hill Lane exit, west), 214-369-6466

U – An "older crowd", fond of Austrian food and of attentive waitresses dressed up "like milkmaids", finds this a "dependable" and "pleasant" spot, especially for "old-world charm" and "great veal" and venison; they say the "pianist is worth the trip" (especially for the personalized birthday song), and the "snowball" dessert is a special treat, if you get our drift.

City Cafe/S
| 24 | 20 | 21 | $25 |

5757 W. Lovers Lane (west of Tollway), 214-351-2233

M – The weekly-changing, "unique" New American menu gets general praise, but some bristle at the Park Cities prices; a "Highland Park housewife hangout" at lunch, but it's "very popular" at night too; for those who want to avoid the "status-conscious diners" and "smoky open kitchen", a sister carry-out restaurant has opened next door.

Clark's Outpost Bar-B-Q/S
| 24 | 18 | 21 | $16 |

Hwy. 377 (I-35 north to Hwy. 380 E. to Hwy. 377 N.), Tioga, 817-437-2414

U – "Yum yum" Texas BBQ served in a rustic roadhouse 60 miles north of Dallas is "worth the drive" – though some fans "go by limo or helicopter" to this horse-country oasis; the lean, tender stuff is smoked for hours and even days, ranking "right up there with The Mansion and Routh Street"; owner Warren Clark learned barbecuing from late master Sonny Bryan.

Conservatory, The/S
| 25 | 25 | 24 | $44 |

Hotel Crescent Court, 400 Crescent Ct. (Cedar Springs Rd. & Maple Ave.), 214-871-3242

M – Seafood stars on the Contemporary American menu in this newish, richly European, "sumptuous" 52-seat dining room carved out of the hotel's now-downsized Beau Nash; many participants say it falls short of expectations and is long on expense, but agree it's a "beautiful setting", overlooking a landscaped patio through 20-foot-high glass walls; "take the clients here" or save it "for a special occasion."

Del Frisco's Double Eagle
| 26 | 22 | 23 | $32 |

4300 Lemmon Ave. (Wycliff Ave.), 214-526-9811

U – "Best steak in Dallas" is our diners' verdict on this "pricey" but "excellent" restaurant; they give it more blue ribbons for red meat than even Ruth's Chris and Lawry's, and laud its "wonderful clubby atmosphere"; not cheap, but you do get what you pay for.

DALLAS | F | D | S | C |

French Room, The | 28 | 29 | 27 | $48 |
Adolphus Hotel, 1321 Commerce St. (Field St.), 214-742-8200
U – Since last we surveyed, this "plush, plush and more plush" French Nouvelle bastion has captured the No. 2 spot for food; meanwhile, the go-for-baroque dining room maintains its "best decor in Dallas" status; diners pay a pretty price for all of this but have learned to love the gilt: the cherubic ceiling, marble floor and rich appointments make this such "a special place for that special occasion."

Gaspar's | 28 | 20 | 24 | $24 |
150 S. Denton Tap Rd. (bet. Belt Line & Sandy Lake Rds.), Coppell, 214-393-5152
U – This "great neighborhood bistro" in a Coppell shopping area ranks No. 4 for food in our Dallas Survey and is "worth the trip"; chef-owner Gaspar Stantic's frequently-changing menu is "creative and upscale"; diners fond of a "best-kept secret" liken it to "dining at the home of a good friend", with "superb warm service" to match; BYO.

Gennie's Bishop Grill/X | 22 | 13 | 15 | $7 |
321 N. Bishop Ave. (8th St.), Oak Cliff, 214-946-1752
U – "Just what it says it is": "good Soul Food" in a friendly setting that welcomes "everyone from bankers to construction workers"; favorite "homestyle vittles" include chicken-fried steak and a precious peanut butter pie; the new location just up Bishop maintains the same cafeteria style and "good value" as before.

India Palace/S | 22 | 18 | 19 | $16 |
12817 Preston Rd., Ste. 105 (south of I-635), 214-392-0190
U – The "greatest Indian restaurant in town" inspires high marks and higher praise: "better than Bangkok, London or Hong Kong"; the "chicken madras is not to be missed" at this slightly dressy spot – Sunday brunch is a pleaser, too.

Jasmine Restaurant/S | 23 | 23 | 20 | $18 |
4002 Belt Line Rd. (Surveyor Blvd.), Addison, 214-991-6867
M – As Chinese go, the "ritzy" atmosphere soars above the rest; the food also gets high marks as the "best Chinese in Addison", and the live entertainment (piano or harp) is soothing.

Javier's/S | 23 | 21 | 21 | $21 |
4912 Cole Ave. (west of N. Central Expwy.), 214-521-4211
M – When you take the Tex away from Mex, this is the elegant result; "very good upscale Mexican seafood and steaks" are complemented by service with "style and grace" in a "dark, comfortable, candlelit" atmosphere; while most appreciate the menu's Mexico City authenticity, several diners say they would like to see it updated.

DALLAS

| F | D | S | C |

La Calle Doce/S | 23 | 17 | 22 | $12 |
415 W. 12th St. (bet. Bishop and Adams Aves.), Oak Cliff, 214-941-4304
U – A warren of rooms in a one-time home, this is a "fantastic sleeper" for cheap but excellent Mexican seafood, including "first-class frog legs", and service that's solid and reliable; the name, which means "12th Street", has become synonymous with authentic south-of-the-border style.

Laurels | 27 | 28 | 25 | $40 |
Sheraton Park Central Hotel, 12720 Merit Dr., 20th fl. (I-635, Coit Rd. exit), 214-851-2021
U – With "first-rate" regional American fare and a "magnificent view of Dallas" from the hotel's 20th floor, this "elegant restaurant" offers "the best meal in North Dallas"; our raters say its polished service helps "make the evening memorable"; best tip – "ask for a window table" and bring an expense account.

Lawry's The Prime Rib/S | 25 | 23 | 24 | $27 |
3008 Maple Ave. (Carlisle St.), 214-521-7777
U – With a name like this, the top choice has got to be the "mouth-watering" prime rib, served up in "an ornate setting" that's like "the '50s all the time"; waitresses in upstairs-maid uniforms spin your salads for you, and the beef is sliced tableside from rolling deco carts to yield a "cholesterol-lover's dream"; N.B. on the Survey questionnaire, Lawry's was incorrectly typeset as Larry's, and we deservedly took a lot of prime ribbing for it.

L'Entrecote | 26 | 25 | 26 | $43 |
Loews Anatole Hotel, 2201 Stemmons Frwy. (I-35, exit west on Industrial Blvd.), 214-748-1200
U – Excellent haute French food and attentive service bring distinction to this polished hotel dining room, a tiered glass-and-brass oasis; a harpist strikes the right chord for "intimate dining", and the expertly chosen wine list adds luster to this finely faceted "jewel."

Mansion on Turtle Creek, The/S | 27 | 29 | 27 | $45 |
The Mansion on Turtle Creek, 2821 Turtle Creek Blvd. (Gillespie St.), 214-559-2100
U – "Glamorous" and "expensive", this one-time cotton magnate's mansion turned world-renowned hotel weaves a "Xanadu atmosphere" and SW cuisine into one of Dallas's most talked-about dining experiences; star-chef Dean Fearing's menu reads like a patent directory of modern Texas cooking – "lobster taco", "tortilla soup", "SW chicken salad"; once again, for most reviewers it's "simply the best – day in, day out"; only an occasional "haughty" waiter intrudes on what is otherwise "an impeccable dining experience."

DALLAS | F | D | S | C |

Morton's of Chicago/S | 25 | 23 | 24 | $35 |
501 Elm St. (Houston St.), 214-741-2277
U – A handsome "speakeasy setting" with a "masculine business feeling" and professional service are the backdrop for "great steaks", which can be "as big as your head" at this local outpost of one of Chicago's most famous restaurants; portions are so large that some say "there is such a thing as too much food", especially since you have to pay for what you get.

Mr. Sushi/S | 24 | 17 | 21 | $22 |
4860 Belt Line Rd. (Inwood Rd.), Addison, 214-385-0168
U – All agree that experienced chefs and the "freshest fish" at this casual Addison spot make it "the best place for sushi in town"; some say "it helps to know the help", but they still consider it the "Cadillac of sushi."

Nana Grill/S | 24 | 26 | 22 | $32 |
Loews Anatole Hotel, 2201 Stemmons Frwy., 27th fl. (Industrial Blvd. exit west, off I-35), 214-761-7470
U – While the excellent Southwestern-inspired menu draws many ardent admirers, our surveyors are also smitten with the zaftig nude "Nana" painting in the bar and the undeniably "spectacular views of the Downtown skyline"; the family-oriented Sunday buffet wins additional points – all in all, a clear winner.

Old Warsaw, The/S | 25 | 24 | 24 | $41 |
2610 Maple Ave. (bet. McKinney Ave. & Cedar Springs Rd.), 214-528-0032
M – Dark-lacquered wood and "very attentive" European service make this "an enduring classic" in Continental dining; "harps, chandeliers and incredible cuisine" add up to what some say is "the most romantic atmosphere in town"; though a few surveyors think it's "past its prime", high numbers bolster the majority, who deem it "an old favorite."

Pyramid Room, The | 25 | 27 | 25 | $44 |
Fairmount Hotel, 1717 N. Akard St. (Ross Ave.), 214-720-5249
M – A soothing California-on-the-Nile setting and an inspired American-Continental menu combine to make this a "lovely" place "for quiet conversation" – of either the business or romantic kind; service is "polished", if antiquated – waiters dart about with carts for tableside preparation; even though a few reviewers have had "disappointing experiences", a reputation for "gracious dining" makes this "a good place to take clients."

DALLAS

	F	D	S	C

Ristorante Savino/S | 23 | 19 | 22 | $24 |

2929 N. Henderson Ave. (E. of N. Central Expwy.), 214-826-7804

U – "Top-notch Italian" food and "comfortable", neo-Italian decor make this east-of-Central "sleeper" "an experience to look forward to"; modest prices and the "small but reasonable wine list" get applause, too.

Riviera, The/S | 28 | 25 | 27 | $45 |

7709 Inwood Rd. (south of Lovers Lane), 214-351-0094

U – "It just doesn't get much better than this" say fans of the top-rated Provençal-inspired French charmer, whose "sophisticated" and "novel" menu is "innovative without being overwhelming"; Franco Bertolasi, the demonstrative host-owner, gives a kiss of welcome to guests and presides over a staff that's both "gracious" and professional; though some complain of "elbow-to-elbow seating" and wish it were less expensive, for most it's "the best in town."

Routh Street Cafe | 28 | 27 | 27 | $48 |

3005 Routh St. (Cedar Springs Rd.), 214-871-7161

U – This was ground zero in the explosion of Southwestern cuisine in the mid-'80s, and chef-owner Stephan Pyles brings it into the '90s with a "fantastic", "creative" menu emphasizing "excellent game" and a finely tuned atmosphere that ranks No. 3 in Dallas for food; service is "unobtrusive" and "knowledgeable" in a dramatic modern space that, while "austere" to some, is "elegant" to most; yes, it's "expensive", but you're paying for what many argue is "the most exciting dining experience in Dallas."

Ruggeri's Ristorante/S | 24 | 22 | 23 | $25 |

2911 Routh St. (Cedar Springs Rd.), 214-871-7377

U – "Very consistent" and "excellent" Northern Italian fare in a "pretty setting" make this a great place for romancing business or making a business of romance; expect "good people-watching" and "consistently good" preparations of lasagna, osso buco and lamb chops in the bricked interior, though the noise level "can be deafening."

Ruth's Chris Steak House/S | 25 | 19 | 21 | $31 |

5922 Cedar Springs Rd. (bet. Inwood Rd. & Mockingbird Lane), 214-902-8080

M – "High-stakes steaks" get high marks at this local offshoot of a nationwide New Orleans–based chain; for some, this is the ultimate "cholesterol orgy" and "a steak-lover's dream come true", though stiff prices for dry-aged beef are prime gripes; the creekside location near Love Field has die-hard fans; a few dissenters simply say "no cow should die for this."

DALLAS | F | D | S | C |

Sonny Bryan's/SX | 24 | 8 | 11 | $10 |
2202 Inwood Rd. (bet Harry Hines Blvd. & Forest Park), 214-357-7120
302 N. Market St. (West End), 214-744-1610
U – "God's BBQ gift to Dallas", the original location is "the best BBQ in the worst dump", which accounts for the fact that most people order takeout; smoke-house beef, ribs, onion rings and baked beans created a cult that makes a pilgrimage to the parking-lot seating of Sonny's first "shabby" shack; for the same good food, in "excruciatingly clean, more touristy" digs, try the West End location; our raters say "Sonny may be gone (he sold out several years ago), but the quality remains."

Thai Soon/S | 23 | 11 | 16 | $13 |
2018 Greenville Ave. (3 blocks north of Ross Ave.), 214-821-7666
M – Chili peppers fuel a vegetarian fervor at this narrow, citified Lower Greenville Thai; a recent expansion may have taxed the kitchen and tempered some raters' superlatives, but most say the "Austin crowd" enjoys "good and hot" stuff at "reasonable prices."

Uncle Tai's Hunan Yuan/S | 24 | 21 | 20 | $25 |
Galleria, 13350 Dallas Pkwy., 3rd fl. (I-635 at Tollway), 214-934-9998
U – "High-dollar Chinese", "but worth every penny", because this stylish, sophisticated spot offers "great, innovative dishes" to enjoy with a skating-rink view; some surveyors say it's "expensive for what you get", but it's still the top-rated Chinese in town – a "wonderful, upscale" Oriental dining experience.

York Street | 25 | 16 | 21 | $31 |
6047 Lewis St. (Skillman & Live Oak Sts.), 214-826-0968
U – Like the thumbnail-sized restaurants of San Francisco, this "tiny husband-and-wife operation" is a "treat", with a "European feel" and "innovative yet classic" New American food; even though many find it expensive, it's "worth trying", and since they take no reservations, be prepared to wait; wine and beer only.

FORT LAUDERDALE

TOP 20 RESTAURANTS
(In order of food rating)

Restaurant	Cuisine Type
27 – Cafe Max	Amer. Contemp.
25 – Primavera	Nuova Cucina Italian
Plum Room	Continental
By Word of Mouth	Amer. Contemp.
Cafe Arugula	Amer. Contemp.
24 – Cafe Seville	Spanish
Ruth's Chris	Steakhouse
La Ferme	French Bistro
23 – Left Bank	French
Casa Vecchia	No. Italian/Meditteranean
Newman's	French Bistro/No. Italian
Cypress Room	Amer. Contemp.
Armadillo Cafe	Southwestern
La Coquille	French
Never on Sunday	French Nouv./No. Italian
Su Shin	Japanese
22 – Le Dome	Continental
Paesano	Northern Italian
Down Under	Seafood/Steakhouse
La Tavernetta	Northern Italian

OTHER TOP PLACES
(In alphabetical order)

Brasserie Max	Amer. Contemp.
Burt & Jack's	Seafood/Steakhouse
French Quarter	French Creole
Il Tartuffo	Northern Italian
La Bonne Crepe	French
La Reserve	French Classic
Le Mesquite	Amer. Contemp./French
Raindancer	Amer. Trad./Steakhouse
Silverado Cafe	Amer. Contemp.
Studio One Cafe	Continental

FORT LAUDERDALE

| F | D | S | C |

Armadillo Cafe/S | 23 | 16 | 20 | $28 |
4630 S.W. 64th Ave. (Griffin Rd. & Davie Blvd.), Davie, 305-791-4866
U – "Innovative" and "creative" best describe the Southwestern food served at this unpretentious place in the heart of Broward's horse country, which sports a "casual atmosphere" and "crayons on the table to scribble with"; reserve well in advance to beat the crowds driving up from Miami for "great black and white soup" (black beans on one side, jalapeno cheese on the other) and other "change-of-pace" dishes.

Brasserie Max/S | 20 | 20 | 20 | $21 |
Fashion Mall, 321 N. University Dr. (bet. Sunrise & Broward Blvds.), Plantation, 305-424-8000
M – After you've shopped till you've dropped at the Fashion Mall, you could do far worse than this trendy American "oasis" for a "lite bite"; the "affordable" "mall food with flair" – trendy pastas, pizza and the like – is enjoyed by a majority of our surveyors, but even they acknowledge that this place is "not worth a special trip."

Burt & Jack's/S | 22 | 24 | 20 | $35 |
Berth 23 (South Terminal), Port Everglades, 305-522-5225
M – Fans say this "hard-to-find" dockside steak-and-lobster spot is "worth the search" for the "beautiful view of the cruise ships", piano music and five crackling fireplaces that set a romantic mood, but the old-fashioned American menu, though very good, "isn't as special as the setting" and service can be "forgetful"; still, it's "impressive to tourists" – especially when co-owner Burt Reynolds stops by.

By Word of Mouth | 25 | 15 | 21 | $28 |
3200 N.E. 12th Ave. (½ block north of Oakland Pk. Blvd.), Ft. Lauderdale, 305-564-3663
M – Despite its unpromising location next to the railroad tracks, this "reverse chic" caterer-cum-eatery's "yuppie but yummy" Contemporary American fare is tremendously popular with our surveyors; with a daily-changing menu and food "almost too good to be true", the only problems are the mild case of "attitude" and "trains whizzing by."

FORT LAUDERDALE | F | D | S | C |

Cafe Arugula/S | 25 | 21 | 22 | $35 |
3150 N. Federal Hwy. (½ mile south of Sample Rd.),
Lighthouse Point, 305-785-7732
U – This "top-notch" Contemporary American "on the cutting edge" (lots of Mediterranean, Floridian and Southwestern influences) "gets better all the time" according to respondents; "great service" and a "cozy, elegant", "cosmopolitan" setting, with "outstanding presentation" to match, are proof that chef-owner Dick Cingolani "goes the extra distance to please"; though expensive, it's "worth every penny" and "a must for the serious diner."

Cafe Max/S | 27 | 21 | 25 | $36 |
2601 E. Atlantic Blvd. (W. Atlantic Blvd. & E. 26th Ave.),
Pompano Beach, 305-782-0606
U – Capturing the top food rating in the Fort Lauderdale area, this "endlessly inventive" Contemporary American is genuinely "sublime", with an "always exciting" and daily-changing menu based on fresh local ingredients, as well as a "knowledgeable" staff and a "great wine list"; chef Oliver Saucy's open kitchen is the focal point of a room that's cozy and comfortable, and while a few complain of an air of "self-importance", such a quibble is tiny compared with raves for an "exciting dining experience."

Cafe Seville | 24 | 17 | 21 | $26 |
2768 E. Oakland Park Blvd. (Bayview Dr.),
Ft. Lauderdale, 305-565-1148
U – "A true find", this "delightful little storefront cafe" in Oakland Park "would still be filled if it were twice the size", thanks to its "high-quality" Spanish food, professional service and "affordable prices"; the guitarist adds to the "European atmosphere" of this sleeper.

Casa Vecchia/S | 23 | 27 | 23 | $38 |
209 N. Birch Rd. (Alhambra St., off A1A),
Ft. Lauderdale, 305-463-7575
M – This "lovely old house on the Intracoastal" is "the place to go for ambiance" in the area, but reviewers can't agree on the rest; some consider it "one of the greats" for romantic, Italian-Mediterranean dining, with "excellent food, attractively presented", "lovely", "antique-filled surroundings" and a "helpful and knowledgeable" staff, but others scorn the "uneven" kitchen and "stuffy" waiters and complain that wines are often out of stock; everyone agrees, too, that prices are high, but not whether they're merited.

FORT LAUDERDALE | F | D | S | C |

Cypress Room | 23 | 26 | 25 | $37 |
Westin Cypress Creek Hotel, 400 Corporate Dr. (I-95 & Cypress Creek Rd. E.), Ft. Lauderdale, 305-772-1331
M – "One of the most attractive restaurants in South Florida" is this "real sleeper" that offers "solid", "updated" Contemporary American food, "leisurely service" and a "classy", "understated" setting of "old-fashioned elegance"; though some surveyors find it "too stuffy" and "pretentious", the new owners "are really trying" and mostly succeeding; the "lovely wine room for private parties" is a bonus.

Down Under/S | 22 | 24 | 21 | $35 |
3000 E. Oakland Park Blvd. (Intracoastal), Ft. Lauderdale, 305-563-4123
M – "A little tired, but still better than most", this "comfortable" waterside steak-and-seafood spot was the first of Leonce Picot's award-winning establishments in the area; while it remains "a tourist spot that locals also enjoy", with "a beautiful view and honest food", some diners suspect "they read too many good reviews and stopped trying"; an impressive wine list doesn't compensate for food these critics regard as "nothing special" and service that "could be friendlier."

French Quarter | 22 | 24 | 21 | $31 |
215 S.E. 8th Ave. (bet. Broward & Las Olas Blvds.), Ft. Lauderdale, 305-463-8000
M – Billed as "French-Creole", it's "not really either", but this nonetheless "elegant", well-hidden bistro has "tasty" food and "beautiful" decor that "work in harmony"; many feel it's "best for lunch" or the prix fixe pre-theater dinner, when you can spot the "who's who crowd"; neither its laxness in honoring reservations nor the "somewhat abrupt" service interfere with the enjoyment of the "very well-prepared" cuisine.

Il Tartuffo/S | 21 | 19 | 19 | $32 |
2980 N. Federal Hwy. (1 block south of Oakland Pk. Blvd.), Ft. Lauderdale, 305-564-0607
M – "The perfect quaint little Northern Italian" delights many of our reviewers; this Lauderdale "hideaway" features "food prepared with loving care", an "intimate setting", high-flown service and a chef who sings "romantic serenades" for customers; the raves aren't universal – critics find the service "pretentious" and the cooking "not very great"; still, solid numbers suggest why it's popular enough that reservations are a must.

FORT LAUDERDALE | F | D | S | C |

La Bonne Crepe | 21 | 15 | 19 | $17 |
815 E. Las Olas Blvd. (2 blocks south of Broward Blvd.),
Ft. Lauderdale, 305-761-1515
U – A "real find" on Las Olas, this "cute" creperie strikes most as "comfortable, cheerful and original", with "one-of-a-kind for Florida" fare made on a large Brittany crepe-maker; "lovely for lunch", it has a "very-French feel" and "solicitous service" that make the "good prices" seem even better.

La Coquille/S | 23 | 18 | 22 | $28 |
1619 E. Sunrise Blvd. (N.E. 16th Terrace),
Ft. Lauderdale, 305-467-3030
U – A Suburban shopping center might not seem the most promising location for an "excellent, true French" restaurant, but this "quaint little spot" delivers with an "old-fashioned but delightful" menu of "home cooking"; "family-run", "cordial" and "reasonably priced", it's hailed for its early-bird dinners and proximity to Parker Playhouse.

La Ferme/S | 24 | 20 | 23 | $33 |
1601 E. Sunrise Blvd. (16th Ave.), Ft. Lauderdale,
305-764-0987
U – The Survey's top-rated French for Broward County has attracted a loyal coterie with its consistently "excellent", "authentic Country French cooking", deftly prepared by chef-owner Henri Terrier; the "warm" "storefront atmosphere", "friendly service", "attention to detail" and "always dependable" kitchen make it "one of the area's best" of any kind; P.S. it's also "convenient to Parker Playhouse."

La Reserve | 21 | 23 | 21 | $37 |
3115 N.E. 32nd Ave. (northeast side of Oakland Pk. Bridge), Ft. Lauderdale, 305-563-6644
M – "Elegant" if somewhat "pompous", this three-tiered "Traditonal French" dining room with a "lovely view" of the Intracoastal Waterway has many admirers for its "gorgeous setting", "very reserved" air and often "excellent" food; naysayers are equally insistent, deeming it "haughty" and "no big deal"; the summer prix fixe menu is a good value.

La Tavernetta/S | 22 | 17 | 20 | $26 |
Colony Ctr., 8455 W. Macnab Rd. (bet. University Dr. & Pine Island Rd.), Tamarac, 305-722-1831 ·
M – The "old favorites" on the menu make this "casual", "family-owned" storefront Northern Italian an "all-around treat" for most of its customers, especially in light of the "tableside music" and "complimentary port after dinner"; a few dissenters complain that it's "cramped" and "noisy", with "rushed" service and "too-close" tables.

FORT LAUDERDALE

| F | D | S | C |

Le Dome/S
| 22 | 25 | 22 | $35 |

333 Sunset Dr., 12th fl. (½ block south of E. Las Olas Blvd.), Ft. Lauderdale, 305-463-3303

M – Soft piano music, crystal chandeliers and a "beautiful view" of Ft. Lauderdale from the 12th-floor penthouse of the Four Seasons condominium rekindle "romantic memories" at this Continental, which most diners consider "first-rate in all aspects"; critics blast food that tastes "mass-produced" and a "menu that hasn't changed in 20 years."

Left Bank/S
| 23 | 19 | 22 | $31 |

214 S.E. 6th Ave. (bet. Las Olas & Broward Blvds.), Ft. Lauderdale, 305-462-5376

U – Tableside cooking and a "romantic atmosphere" distinguish this recently expanded French, which features "excellent" food with Floridian overtones and "attentive service"; "if you can find it, you'll love it."

Le Mesquite
| 22 | 19 | 19 | $28 |

1015 S.E. 17th St. (bet. U.S. 1 & Cordova Rd.), Ft. Lauderdale, 305-522-6795

M – "European" ambiance highlights this "very relaxing", "very small" French with New American touches (hinted at in the name); it's "a rare find", considering the cooking, "charming" atmosphere and "good wine list"; foes may say it's "too expensive" for "small portions" of "nothing-special" fare and warn of "slow service", but the prevailing view is that it's "a true treat."

Never on Sunday/S
| 23 | 21 | 22 | $29 |

(aka Darcy's)
129 N. Federal Hwy. (bet. Griffin & Stirling Rds.), Dania, 305-923-1000

M – "Quaint and intimate", this "charming" old house in Dania is "one of the most romantic" around, according to our surveyors, who also laud the "always good" Northern Italian–French Nouvelle food; although some say the "hearty" fare exhibits "no imagination" and feel it's "too expensive for what you get", the majority say it's "perfect for a quiet evening."

Newman's La Bonne Auberge
| 23 | 20 | 22 | $30 |

4300 N. Federal Hwy. (43rd St.), Ft. Lauderdale, 305-491-5522

U – "A favorite of many", this Country French with Northern Italian touches manages to be "warm and cozy" despite its location on busy Federal Highway; even though they concede it's "out of touch" with current culinary trends, many surveyors say they've "never had a bad meal" here, and the "comfortable" "bistro atmosphere" and "friendly" service make it "always dependable"; the bargain "early-bird dining" menu is an added attraction.

FORT LAUDERDALE | F | D | S | C |

Paesano | 22 | 20 | 21 | $27 |
1301 E. Las Olas Blvd. (S.E. 13th Ave.),
Ft. Lauderdale, 305-467-3266
M – The "hearty" Northern Italian fare at this "comfortable", "solid trattoria" located in the old Las Olas section may be "heavy" and the atmosphere reminiscent of an "elitist" "men's club", but that's just fine with its regular clientele of local "movers and shakers", who come for "well-prepared" food and "Frank Sinatra"; service can be "aloof" at times, and while critics charge that the menu hasn't changed "for 10 years", it's still a "favorite."

Plum Room, The/LS | 25 | 25 | 25 | $42 |
Upstairs at Yesterday's, 3001 E. Oakland Park Blvd. (west side of Intracoastal), Ft. Lauderdale, 305-561-4400
U – "Make reservations in advance" for this "very New York City" Continental on the Intracoastal, with an "adventuresome menu", "luxurious" art deco setting, "top-notch view" and top honors for service in Broward County; fans say it's the "ultimate" for a "romantic special occasion" – though a few critics quibble that it's "so dark and romantic, the waiters can't find your table."

Primavera/S | 25 | 22 | 24 | $34 |
840 Plaza, 830 E. Oakland Park Blvd. (bet. 6th Ave. & Dixie Hwy.), Ft. Lauderdale, 305-564-6363
U – Near the top of everyone's list is this "real treat" of a "classy Contemporary Italian", where "you'll feel like you're in Italy" – even though you're actually in a shopping plaza; "always creative" food, "elegant surroundings" and "dynamite waiters", plus a "display table" laden with interesting antipasti, add up to a "wonderful experience"; the only drawbacks are minor: "they can't always accommodate the big crowds" they attract and it's possible "you'll leave broke."

Raindancer/S | 21 | 18 | 22 | $26 |
3031 E. Commercial Blvd. (just west of Intracoastal Bridge), Ft. Lauderdale, 305-772-0337
M – "Superb beef" is the draw at this "noisy, very crowded" "sharp operation" of a steakhouse, offering "solid American food" in a web of dining rooms upstairs and down; though admirers (in the majority) laud the "excellent service" and "one of the best salad bars around", a few dissenters counter that it's "nothing special" and the steaks are "hit-and-miss."

FORT LAUDERDALE | F | D | S | C |

Ruth's Chris Steak House/S | 24 | 19 | 21 | $36 |
2525 N. Federal Hwy. (bet. Oakland Pk. & Sunrise Blvds.), Ft. Lauderdale, 305-565-2338
M – Even "meat-and-potatoes guys" are divided about the Lauderdale branch of a New Orleans–originated steakhouse chain; while aficionados insist it's "the only place if you're into red meat", others say the "quality seems inconsistent" and don't like their steaks "drenched in butter"; there's agreement about everything else, however, from plaudits on the "extensive wine list" to complaints about the "stuffy" decor and "unrealistic" prices.

Silverado Cafe/S | 21 | 18 | 19 | $28 |
3528 S. University Dr. (bet. Rte. 595 & Griffin Rd.), Davie, 305-474-9992
M – "Yuppies" flock to this Contemporary American, despite its "weird location in the middle of nowhere"; not everyone is enchanted by the "creative" menu, but many say the return of chef-owner Larry Berford has brought improvement already; expect a "very good wine list" and "friendly" if relaxed service.

Studio One Cafe | 21 | 16 | 18 | $21 |
2447 E. Las Olas Blvd.(Bayview Dr.), Ft. Lauderdale, 305-565-2052
U – For "real value with personality", many of our surveyors tout this "surprisingly good" and remarkably tiny Continental across from the Galleria Shopping Center; its "creative food" in a somewhat cramped setting represents a "best buy", especially if you go with the bargain prix fixe menu, and service is "generally good"; dinner only.

Su Shin/S | 23 | 16 | 18 | $19 |
4595 N. University Dr. (bet. Commercial & Oakland Pk. Blvds.), Lauderhill, 305-741-2569
U – "Sushi superiority" distinguishes this "frenetic" but "consistently great" Japanese that's been around since before "Japanese became trendy"; though the staff is "friendly" and the atmosphere "authentic", neither has as much to do with the place's popularity as the "fantastic" food; "reserve the room in the back."

FORT WORTH

TOP 10 RESTAURANTS
(In order of food rating)

Restaurant
26 – Saint-Emilion
　　 Reflections
25 – Cafe Matthew
　　 Enjolie
　　 Cacharel
24 – Piccolo Mondo
23 – Le Chardonnay
　　 Angelo's Barbeque
　　 Balcony
　　 Charles Kinkaid Grocery

Cuisine Type
French Bistro
Amer. Contemp.
Continental
French Nouvelle
French Classic
Italian
French Bistro
BBQ
Continental
Hamburgers

OTHER TOP PLACES
(In alphabetical order)

Byblos — Middle Eastern
Cafe Aspen — Amer. Contemp.
Carriage House — Continental
Celebration — Amer. Tradition.
Joe T. Garcia's — Mexican
La Playa Maya — Tex-Mex
Michael's — Amer. Contemp.
Old Swiss House — Continental
Tours — Continental
Via Real — Mexican

F	D	S	C

Angelo's Barbeque/X | 23 | 13 | 14 | $10 |
2533 White Settlement Rd. (bet. University Dr. & Bailey Ave.), Fort Worth, 817-332-0357
U – "Old-west flavor" in both food and atmosphere has some raters calling this "the best BBQ in Fort Worth" – "maybe as good as Sonny Bryan's" in Dallas; the fact that the joint is "a dump" and so noisy that customers should "wear earplugs" seems to come with the territory.

Balcony, The | 23 | 22 | 22 | $24 |
6100 Camp Bowie Blvd. (bet. Bryant Irvin Rd. & Westridge Ave.), Fort Worth, 817-731-3719
M – "A standby of the old guard", this highly rated old-line Continental is "one of the best in Fort Worth", and its hidden-away second-floor location overlooking Camp Bowie can make for a very "special occasion"; dissenters say it's "overpriced" and "unexciting", but they're easily outvoted.

FORT WORTH

| F | D | S | C |

Byblos/S | – | – | – | M |
1406 N. Main St. (Central Ave.), Fort Worth,
817-625-9667
Joseph Hedary, a son of Fort Worth's famed Lebanese restaurant family, has refurbished a 1904 building to continue the tradition of fine Middle Eastern food at favorable prices; 14-foot ceilings and an open kitchen give this newcomer a helping of history to go with its casual, contemporary feel; the restaurant, which bears the name of an ancient Lebanese city, is between Downtown and the Stockyards, and draws an eclectic crowd for its outstanding baked chicken and falafel.

Cacharel | 25 | 24 | 24 | $31 |
2221 E. Lamar Blvd. (Watson Rd. exit, north of I-30), Arlington, 817-640-9981 (metro)
U – "This is the best in Arlington", especially for customers who are "putting on the dog"; the French food by chef Hans Bergman is classic yet imaginative; most consider the "pinks-and-pastels" atmosphere "romantic" and enjoy the view of the twinkling lights at Six Flags Over Texas; though pricey, it's a "good special-occasion place" that compares favorably with top spots in Fort Worth and Dallas.

Cafe Aspen | – | – | – | M |
3416 W. 7th St. (2 blocks west of Camp Bowie Blvd.), Fort Worth, 817-877-0838
An unassuming regional American menu, a dozen tables and a simple, warm atmosphere make this casual local hangout a popular Survey write-in; customers from young to old mix in plain surroundings that are dressed up with art loaned by a nearby gallery; dinner is served Thursday through Saturday only, featuring fish specials and a limited but savory selection of desserts.

Cafe Matthew | 25 | 23 | 23 | $29 |
8251 Bedford-Euless Rd., Ste. 231 (Old Town Sq.), North Richland Hills, 817-577-3463 (metro)
M – Admirers say the "strip-center location hides a pretty interior" and "an elegant surprise" at this SW-influenced Contemporary Continental between Fort Worth and the DFW airport; its "well-presented food" tends toward salsas and grilling plus a variety of pasta dishes; there's a good wine list, and the sleek, citified setting is "plush 'n' superb."

FORT WORTH | F | D | S | C |

Carriage House | 22 | 20 | 22 | $27 |
5136 Camp Bowie Blvd. (4 blocks north of I-30), Fort Worth, 817-732-2873
M – "The standard with old-line Fort Worth", this garishly elegant Continental has been a "good, reliable choice" for decades; though trendies might consider it stuck in the '60s, many of our critics say "it can't be beat" for "excellent service and an interesting menu variety"; one self-styled art critic finds the numerous oil paintings of Rubenesque ladies "dressed in a bit too little" "a bit too much."

Celebration/S | 21 | 16 | 19 | $14 |
4600 Dexter Ave. (Camp Bowie Blvd.), Fort Worth, 817-731-6272
U – This is home cooking you can feel at home with; "very generous portions" of "good, solid" food and "seconds on entrees", as well as side dishes served family-style, make this one-time hippie leather joint a real favorite; its popularity means patrons should "arrive early or wait hours."

Charles Kincaid Grocery/X | 23 | 10 | 14 | $7 |
4901 Camp Bowie Blvd. (2 blocks north of I-30), Fort Worth, 817-732-2881
U – In the Fort Worth dictionary, Kincaid means hamburger; this "one-of-a-kind joint" is boldly back-to-basics, offering "great burgers that you eat standing up in a grocery" or at one of the tables; N.B. the junior burgers are great for kids and those with smaller appetites.

Enjolie | 25 | 25 | 23 | $32 |
Marriott Mandalay Hotel, 221 E. Las Colinas Blvd. (Urban Center), Las Colinas, 214-556-0800
U – Showing improvement since this "beautiful" hotel French Nouvelle was first taken over by Marriott, this "excellent restaurant" is considered by many to be "the crème de la crème of hotel dining in the SW"; while it's "good for hotel guests", this "lovely but dark" place also draws a business-oriented Las Colinas power crowd.

Joe T. Garcia's/XS | 18 | 17 | 17 | $13 |
2201 N. Commerce St. (1 block east of N. Main St.), Fort Worth, 817-429-5166 (metro) or 817-626-4356
M – A Fort Worth "institution", this "family-style Mexican" may have been "surpassed by new places" and taken over by tourists, but raters uniformly love the mariachis and the "nice patio during summer"; this "local legend" is the "best place for a family with children"; one naysayer claims that it's "overrated – their P.R. department is better than their food."

FORT WORTH

| F | D | S | C |

La Playa Maya
| - | - | - | M |

3200 Hemphill (Barry St.), Fort Worth, 817-924-0698
Mexican seafood makes a splash in a city known more for its Tex-Mex; this small (74 seats plus a becoming patio) spot was crafted from a charming bungalow in the distressed Fort Worth neighborhood, and is home to such delicacies as shrimp soup and fried whole catfish; the mixed clientele is entertained by mariachis and treated to a mid-priced taste of Mexico's coastline.

Le Chardonnay/S
| 23 | 23 | 21 | $24 |

2443 Forest Park Blvd. (bet. Park Hill Dr. & Park Pl.), Fort Worth, 817-926-5622
M – "Good, reliable" French food at a "fair price", in a "quaint" bistro; this "simple yet beautiful" woodland setting invites guests to "sit out on the patio and watch the cardinals fly by", preferably while sampling one of more than 30 wines offered by the glass; a few say that service, normally good, can be "Parisian" (read: "rude").

Michael's
| - | - | - | E |

3413 W. Seventh St. (bet. Montgomery & University), Fort Worth, 817-877-3413
The cuisine evolving at this pricey but popular new spot is described as "Contemporary Ranch" by chef Michael Thomson of the now-defunct Epicure on the Park; stark white walls and concrete floors provide a soothing backdrop for such off-the-range fare as pan-seared beef tenderloin with goat cheese tart, or sage-brushed pork rack with chipotle-chili sauce; an upscale clientele has made this the talk of the town.

Old Swiss House
| 22 | 21 | 23 | $25 |

1541 Merrimac Circle (University exit, south of I-30), Fort Worth, 817-877-1531
U – "Classic Continental" makes this "old-reliable" establishment a "wonderful place to go", especially for special occasions, and surveyors say the country-club "setting is extra nice"; a new wine–bar room serves a revolving selection of wines by the glass.

Piccolo Mondo/S
| 24 | 18 | 21 | $21 |

829 E. Lamar Blvd. (north of I-30, west of Hwy. 157), Arlington, 817-265-9174 (metro)
U – This classy, "always-consistent" Northern and Southern Italian in Arlington gets many votes as the "best Italian in the Mid-Cities", boasting a light, elegant atmosphere, "good attitude" and "thoughtful presentation", all at nonexorbitant prices; service can be slow, but "the food is worth waiting for."

FORT WORTH

| F | D | S | C |

Reflections | 26 | 24 | 23 | $32 |
Worthington Hotel, 200 Main St. (2nd St.), Fort Worth, 817-870-1000

U – One of the top restaurants in Fort Worth, this is *"elegance in Cowtown"*; it's loved for its Nouvelle American menu and the *"best service in town"*, plus a lovely art deco setting that many surveyors consider *"first class all the way"*; though it's not cheap, soaring scores in all categories indicate that you certainly get what you pay for here.

Saint-Emilion | 26 | 21 | 23 | $29 |
3617 W. 7th St. (Montgomery St.), Fort Worth, 817-737-2781

U – This *"charmingly authentic Country French restaurant"* with *"excellent food"*, professional service and a good wine list attracts some of *"Fort Worth's most interesting people"*; *"intimate and friendly"*, this *"cozy place"* is a *"delightful hidden-away treat."*

Tours | 23 | 23 | 21 | $23 |
3500 W. 7th St. (east of Montgomery St.), Fort Worth, 817-870-1672

U – This spot is *"simple"* and *"Continental all the way"*, with *"superb food"* and *"lots of ambiance"*, including an upstairs area with a fantastic view of Downtown Fort Worth at night; a more casual menu and service were added last year, including afternoon selections and pre- and post-theater dining.

Via Real | 23 | 21 | 20 | $16 |
4020 N. MacArthur Blvd., Ste. 100 (south of Northgate Dr.), Irving, 214-255-0064

U – Easily affordable *"yuppie Mexican food"* in fresh surroundings makes this a Las Colinas favorite; *"delicious squash enchiladas"* are among the *"imaginative"*, *"upscale"* Mexican-Southwestern offerings served in this *"refined"*, *"pleasant setting."*

HONOLULU

TOP 20 RESTAURANTS
(In order of food rating)

Restaurant	Cuisine Type
27 – Roy's Restaurant	Pacific Rim
26 – Maile Restaurant	Continental
25 – La Mer	French
Hy's Steak House	Steakhouse
Kua Aina Sandwich	Hamburgers/Sandwiches
Swiss Inn	Swiss
24 – Secret	Continental
Ono Hawaiian Foods	Hawaiian
Bali-By-The-Sea	Continental
Prince Court Restaurant	Pacific Rim
Bon Appetit	Continental/French
Keo's Thai Cuisine	Thai
Michel's Restaurant	Continental/French
23 – La Salle	Japanese
Orchids	Amer. Contemp.
Cafe Haleiwa	Diner
Yanagi Sushi	Japanese
Mekong Thai Restaurant	Thai
Keo's at Ward Centre	Thai
Restaurant Suntory	Japanese

OTHER TOP PLACES
(In alphabetical order)

Cafe Sistina	Northern Italian
Golden Dragon	Chinese
Hajjibaba's	Moroccan
John Dominis	Seafood
Nick's Fishmarket	Continental/Seafood
Phillip Paolo's	Northern Italian
Quintero's	Mexican
Ruth's Chris Steak House	Steakhouse
Shogun	Japanese
Willows	Continental

F	D	S	C

Bali-By-The-Sea/S | 24 | 26 | 23 | $43 |
Hilton Hawaiian Village, 2005 Kalia Rd., Waikiki,
Honolulu, 808-949-4321, x43
M – For "oceanside ambiance", there are few to top this "incredible", "serenely romantic", "delightful" Continental, and the food, though very pricey, also wins high marks; dissenters call the service "extremely slow" and think the food is "just ok"; still, with these top scores, it's obvious that fans outnumber foes.

HONOLULU

| F | D | S | C |

Bon Appetit French Restaurant & Cafe/L
| 24 | 20 | 22 | $33 |

Waikiki-Discovery Bay, 1778 Ala Moana Blvd., Waikiki, Honolulu, 808-942-3837

U – This "consistently good" bistro offers what may be "the best French-Continental cuisine in Honolulu" in a "small", "intimate", "very romantic" setting; although some say the "tables are too close together", the "creative specials", "excellent service" and prix fixe lunch menu prepared by "friendly chef-owner" Guy Banal more than compensate.

Cafe Haleiwa/X
| 23 | 17 | 17 | $13 |

66-460 Kamehameha Hwy., Haleiwa, 808-637-5516

U – The "best breakfast in the countryside" is yours at this informal North Shore diner, bustling with ravenous surfers and denizens of the country who read the morning paper over hefty "el rollos" (vegetarian burritos) and breakfast quesadillas; the early-morning crowd (this is strictly a breakfast-and-lunch joint) "has got to be seen to be believed – it's a surf-out."

Cafe Sistina
| 23 | 20 | 19 | $22 |

1314 S. King St. (First Interstate Bank Bldg.), Honolulu, 808-526-0071

M – The "hottest place in town", this Northern Italian "up-and-comer" has "good jazz" on Friday and Saturday; located a few blocks from Ala Moana Center, it serves "fabulous food" in a room accented with "wonderful graphics" by the chef-owner; on the downside, it's hard to get a table on weekends, it's often "loud and crowded", and critics say it still has some kinks to work out, but with these high ratings, the kinks must be few and far between.

Golden Dragon/S
| 23 | 22 | 21 | $29 |

Hilton Hawaiian Village, 2005 Kalia Rd., Waikiki, Honolulu, 808-941-2254

U – Chinese "fine dining" can be a "once-in-a-lifetime treat", especially with the "fabulous service and surroundings" at this "elegant" lagoonside restaurant in Waikiki's Hilton Hawaiian Village; "always-outstanding Beggar's Chicken" – a trademark – is a major attraction; although "expensive", our respondents report that it's "innovative, daring and fulfilling."

Hajjibaba's
| 22 | 22 | 21 | $26 |

4614 Kilauea Ave., Ste. 102, Honolulu, 808-735-5522

U – "Novel for Hawaii", this "trendy" Moroccan restaurant in Kahala features belly dancers and caftan-clad waiters, and is a "fun ethnic experience" where you "just use your fingers" to eat the "interesting food"; the authentic atmosphere, however, has its downside – the floor-seating is "uncomfortable" – "not for the infirm or aged" and "way too cramped"; still, says one fan, "the food was better than in Morocco."

HONOLULU

| F | D | S | C |

Hy's Steak House/S | 25 | 23 | 24 | $34 |
2440 Kuhio Ave. (Uluniu St.), Waikiki, Honolulu, 808-922-5555
U – "Impeccable food", "luxury attention", and "very good" steaks in a "masculine", "pleasantly clubby atmosphere" mark this old-time favorite steakhouse adjacent to the Waikiki Park Heights Hotel, pricey as always, but "consistent" and ever-popular; the "greatest steaks in town" are here, but "seafood is equally good", and the pasta and desserts aren't bad either.

John Dominis Restaurant/S | 20 | 25 | 20 | $41 |
43 Ahui St. (off Ala Moana Blvd.), Honolulu, 808-523-0955
M – Though the seafood is "fresh" and "quite good" and the room "elegant" at this oceanview restaurant in industrial Kewalo, both pale in comparison to the "enchanting" view of surfers out the window; at these prices, though, little wonder that so many call it "overpriced seafood with a million-dollar view" – one fan says he "never left hungry...or wealthy"; Sunday brunch is "the best bet" and "worth the price."

Keo's at Ward Centre/S | 23 | 21 | 19 | $24 |
Ward Centre, 1200 Ala Moana Blvd. (bet. Ward & Auahi Sts.), Honolulu, 808-533-0533
U – Thai ranks high at this Ward Centre shopper's stop, which a "profusion of orchids" turns into a "charming" destination for spicy dishes with "excellent" flavoring; Keo's trademark – "Evil Jungle Prince" (a currylike dish seasoned with basil and coconut milk) and the green papaya salad are must-tries; complaints include: service can be "slow" at peak hours, "small portions" make the food seem "overpriced" and outdoor seats are exposed to "auto exhaust and noise."

Keo's Thai Cuisine | 24 | 22 | 20 | $26 |
625 Kapahulu Ave. (Date St.), Honolulu, 808-737-8240
U – For "glamour seekers", this orchid-drenched, casually chic Thai-food mecca in Honolulu is where "the best spicy food in town" can be found; it's tropical and "exotic", with an "exquisite menu" and service that is usually – but not always – "gracious"; the "consistently good", "world-class Thai cuisine" and celebrity-watching make this the pick for out-of-towners.

Kua Aina Sandwich/SX | 25 | 11 | 14 | $10 |
66-214 Kamehameha Hwy., Haleiwa, 808-637-6067
U – "Hamburger heaven" and the "No. 1 sandwich spot on Oahu" are the consensus on this inexpensive, "neat lunch stop enroute to the North Shore surf spots" in rural Haleiwa; order at the counter and then move to the roadside tables to enjoy their famous fries and "the best burgers on the island"; "worth the drive", it has a huge following – some fans "never do a circle-island tour without the mahi-mahi sandwich"; BYO.

HONOLULU

| F | D | S | C |

La Mer Restaurant/S | 25 | 27 | 26 | $54 |
Halekulani Hotel, 2199 Kalia Rd. (bet. Lewers St. & the beach), Waikiki, Honolulu, 808-923-2311
M – The epitome of "Hawaiian elegance", this "gorgeous" French spot in the Halekulani is "first-class all the way", with its "romantic" view of Diamond Head and the ocean; though a few find the menu "over-ambitious", the prevailing view is that it's "heaven on earth"; a small number aren't sure about a "slightly silly" atmosphere in which jackets and ties for men are required and "socks are optional", but most swoon over the "pure luxury"; N.B. it's perfect on OPM (other people's money).

La Salle/S | 23 | 20 | 23 | $27 |
Pagoda Hotel, 1525 Rycroft St., Honolulu, 808-941-6611
U – "Elegant dining that's easy on the pocketbook" is the strong suit at this internationally minded Japanese seafood spot; perhaps the menu "could be more creative", but when you're presented with a plate of "very good sushi" by a staff that treats you like royalty", it's hard to quibble; nightly karaoke sing-alongs are offered in the cocktail lounge for fledgling pop stars.

Maile Restaurant/S | 26 | 24 | 26 | $49 |
Kahala Hilton Hotel, 5000 Kahala Ave., Honolulu, 808-734-2211
M – "Flawless dining that becomes an investment in memories", say devotees of this "conservative but dependable" Continental at the luxurious Kahala Hilton; the "superb", albeit "old-fashioned" cooking and "excellent service" by a tuxedoed- and kimono-clad staff both win ratings among Honolulu's best; nonetheless, fault-finders wish it were a little less stuffy and had an ocean view; still, this is definitely "tops for a cost-is-no-object dinner."

Mekong Thai Restaurant/S | 23 | 13 | 18 | $18 |
(fka Mekong Restaurant)
1295 S. Beretania St., Honolulu, 808-521-2025
U – "The pleasant family-style setting and prices", plus "modest but tasty" food, win kudos for this Thai eatery, owned by the folks who run Keo's; the simple dining room is nothing like its glamorous sister restaurant's, but it's "less frantic" and "cheaper"; BYO.

HONOLULU | F | D | S | C |

Michel's Restaurant/S | 24 | 26 | 23 | $43 |
Colony Surf Hotel, 2895 Kalakaua Ave. (bet. Bobby McGee & Outrigger Canoe Club), Waikiki, Honolulu, 808-923-5751
M – If you "love being on the beach" while eating at a "fine-dining" restaurant, try this Classic French–Continental at Diamond Head, a "romantic" and "classy" (albeit "expensive") place "for those special occasions"; some complain that the setting is superior to the "overpriced" food and that the service can be "snobby", but fans call it "the best restaurant on the island"; the budget-conscious go for breakfast or lunch, when prices are more reasonable.

Nick's Fishmarket Restaurant/LS | 22 | 19 | 22 | $38 |
Waikiki Gateway Hotel, 2070 Kalakaua Ave. (Kuhio Ave.), Waikiki, Honolulu, 808-955-6333
M – "You'll feel like Cinderella" at this high-ticket, high-profile Continental-seafood restaurant in Waikiki, with "excellent" food and a happenin' atmosphere; they "make you feel important", especially if you're "out-of-town folks"; however, the "dark", "very New York/Chicago atmosphere", especially at the active bar, and high prices turn some off; insiders recommend the "great Caesar salad" and say the fish is always fresh.

Ono Hawaiian Foods/X | 24 | 7 | 16 | $12 |
726 Kapahulu Ave. (bet. Date & Kamuela), Kapahulu, Honolulu, 808-737-2275
U – "Ono" (delicious) Hawaiian food is "no ka oi (the best) on Oahu" here at this "very local", matchbox-size and always crowded "favorite" in Kapahulu; there's "no decor", and you have to "come early to get a seat" or face the long lines outside the door, but it's "cheap", tasty and buzzing with local color – "a good place to take Mainland guests"; "yippee!" says one enthusiastic fan.

Orchids/S | 23 | 27 | 24 | $35 |
The Halekulani Hotel, 2199 Kalia Rd. (bet. Lewers St. & the beach), Waikiki, Honolulu, 808-923-2311
U – The "moon over Diamond Head", the ocean and the "bikinis walking by on the beach" make this Waikiki landmark "the standard for an open-air restaurant in Hawaii", with American food "as delightful as the atmosphere is romantic"; "fabulous service" and sparkling Swiss linens complete the "elegant" experience at this "real slice of paradise"; N.B. the "best brunch in town" draws crowds every Sunday for "unbeatable oceanfront dining."

HONOLULU

| F | D | S | C |

Phillip Paolo's Italian Restaurant/S
| 22 | 18 | 19 | $27 |

2312 S. Beretania St. (bet. McCully & Isenberg), Honolulu, 808-946-1163

M – It "feels like home" at this "charming" Italian tucked away in a "beautiful" old house on a semiresidential McCully street, serving "awesome food" in such "mammoth portions" that "five truck drivers could eat off your plate and you'd still be satisfied"; however, some say that the "quantity doesn't make up for the quality", and that it's "too high-priced" and too "overreaching for a neighborhood cafe."

Prince Court Restaurant/S
| 24 | 23 | 24 | $36 |

Hawaii Prince Hotel Waikiki, 100 Holomoana St. (bet. Hobron Ln. & Ala Moana Blvd.), Waikiki, Honolulu, 808-956-1111, x61

U – There's "fine dining par excellence" at this harborside Waikiki restaurant, which serves "very creative" Pacific Rim specialties; "nice views" of the harbor and "good service" make this a "luxurious treat"; though several respondents call the decor "sterile" and "cold", the "extensive" wine list and "fantastic" Sunday brunch help warm things up.

Quintero's/SX
| 22 | 14 | 15 | $16 |

2334 S. King St. (Isenberg St.), Honolulu, 808-944-3882

U – Authentic, homestyle Mexican food is served in this quirky, "hole-in-the-wall" of a McCully neighborhood family-run restaurant; it's "short-staffed", and the room's no bigger than a cubicle, but it's always crowded with cognoscenti who clamor for ceviche, tortilla soup and other "surprisingly good" things not often found in Mexican restaurants.

Restaurant Suntory/S
| 23 | 22 | 22 | $32 |

Royal Hawaiian Shopping Ctr., 2233 Kalakaua Ave., 3rd fl., Bldg. B (Orchid St.), Waikiki, Honolulu, 808-922-5511

U – "Chefs perform great feats" at this "real McCoy", "authentic Japanese gourmet" restaurant that's recommended for "the best teppanyaki and sushi in Honolulu"; it's "pricey" but "worth it", "tops all around", with a "Zen-like formal atmosphere" and "service in English"; it's a Japanese power scene.

HONOLULU

| F | D | S | C |

Roy's Restaurant/S | 27 | 21 | 24 | $33 |
Hawaii Kai Corporate Plaza, 6600 Kalanianaole Hwy., Hawaii Kai, Honolulu, 808-396-7697
U – "Innovative" is the word for Roy Yamaguchi's "Nouvelle Pacific" cuisine, emerging from the open kitchen into a "beautiful" "LA-chic", Spago-style room overlooking Hawaii Kai's Maunalua Bay; this "winner" has "excellent everything", but specializes in "first-class" fresh local ingredients and a creative commingling of tastes and flavors; you can't go wrong if you ask the advice of the "knowledgeable" waiters, though the acoustics are "terrible" and there's little privacy at the crowded tables; still, it's "a great place to entertain guests."

Ruth's Chris Steak House/S | 23 | 16 | 20 | $31 |
Restaurant Row, 500 Ala Moana Blvd. (bet. Punchbowl & South Sts.), Honolulu, 808-599-3860
U – The "food quality is primo" at this pricey Restaurant Row steakhouse, "the best in town for hungry steak lovers"; while the decor is scarcely more than "glorified coffee shop", the "melt-in-your-mouth" beef and attentive staff consistently please our surveyors.

Secret, The/S | 24 | 24 | 24 | $42 |
Hawaiian Regent Hotel, 2552 Kalakaua Ave. (Ohua St.), Waikiki, Honolulu, 808-922-6611
U – "Consistently tops" for food, decor and service, this "warm" and "wonderful" Continental in Waikiki's Hawaiian Regent Hotel is "ideal for that very special occasion"; it boasts "excellent" classical food, "friendly, helpful staff" and "lots of privacy" in a "quiet", "romantic atmosphere."

Shogun/S | 23 | 20 | 21 | $22 |
Pacific Beach Hotel, 2490 Kalakaua Ave., Waikiki, Honolulu, 808-922-1233
U – "You'll be surprised" by the "excellent Japanese lunch buffet" and generally "good Japanese food" at this huge Waikiki dining room, which shares Oceanarium's view of a spectacular three-story aquarium through walls of glass; although there's a complete à la carte menu, the "bountiful" buffets are a particularly "good" value, with "nice presentation" and professional, attentive service.

Swiss Inn/S | 25 | 17 | 24 | $25 |
Niu Valley Shopping Ctr., 5730 Kalanianaole Hwy., Niu Valley, Honolulu, 808-377-5447
U – "Dependable, friendly and relaxed", this Suburban Niu Valley Swiss is "the perfect neighborhood restaurant" – "like coming home" to "an Alpine Village but larger and more charming"; it offers "consistently good Swiss food" and a "warm, hospitable" staff; "gemutlich for all."

HONOLULU

| F | D | S | C |

Willows, The/S | 19 | 24 | 20 | $25 |
901 Hausten St. (bet. Kapiolani & Date Sts.), Honolulu, 808-946-4808
U – Thatched roofs, carp ponds and a "charming", "lush" setting grace this Honolulu Continental with "the best Hawaiian decor in Oahu", but the food is clearly secondary to the "wonderful" "tropical" setting and open-air entertainment; it's a "must for tourists", especially on "poi supper days", but locals see it for what it is: "a beautiful setting with adequate food"; N.B. the Kama'aina Suite, with its separate chef and menu, is preferred by the cognoscenti.

Yanagi Sushi/LS | 23 | 17 | 17 | $23 |
762 Kapiolani Blvd. (Cooke St.), Honolulu, 808-537-1525
U – "Artfully served Japanese favorites" and fair prices are the stock in trade of this popular sushi spot in Kakaako near Downtown Honolulu, which also boasts a comfortable, modern atmosphere and "nice private rooms" for groups; this one has "charisma."

HOUSTON

TOP 30 RESTAURANTS
(In order of food rating)

Restaurant	Cuisine Type
28 – DeVille	Southwestern
27 – Tony's	Continental
26 – La Reserve	French Classic
Chez Nous	French Bistro
Empress of China	Chinese/French
Rotisserie for Beef/Bird	Amer. Contemp.
Damian's Cucina	Northern Italian
Brenner's Steak House	Steakhouse
Anthony's	Northern Italian
Cafe Annie	Southwestern
Brennan's of Houston	Creole
Kelly's Del Frisco	Steakhouse
25 – Frenchie's Italian	N/S Italian
Chez Georges	French Bistro
24 – Ruggles Grill	Amer. Contemp./SW
Carrabba's	Nuova Cucina Italian
Ritz-Carlton Hotel	Continental
Rivoli Restaurant	Continental
Lynn's Steakhouse	Steakhouse
La Colombe d'Or	French Classic
Grotto	Southern Italian
Patisserie Descours	Dessert/Sandwiches
Hunan	Chinese
Quail Hollow Inn	Swiss
Dolce & Freddo	Coffee House/Dessert
Enzo's Pasta e Vino	Northern Italian
Charley's 517	Continental
Ginza Japanese	Japanese
Nino's	N/S Italian
23 – Churrascos	So. Amer./Steakhouse

OTHER TOP PLACES
(In alphabetical order)

Green's Barbecue	BBQ
Nit Noi Thai	Thai
Pappadeaux Seafood Kit.	Cajun/Seafood
Pappasito's Cantina	Tex-Mex
Quilted Toque	American/International
River Oaks Grill	Amer. Contemp.
Sasaki Restaurant	Japanese
Star Pizza	Pizza
Taj Mahal	Indian
Taste of Texas	American/Steakhouse

HOUSTON | F | D | S | C |

Anthony's/S | 26 | 25 | 24 | $28 |
4611 Montrose (Chelsea Market), 713-524-1922
M – A rose-colored glow not only emanates from the pretty Italian dining room of this highly touted Museum-area Northern Italian but tends to color diners' impressions; typical comments include "a winner", "excellent", "makes me feel good"; sure, there are complaints – "crowded and noisy", "they don't honor reservations" and "service is so attentive it drove me crazy" – but the bottom line is that 655 surveyors give it rave ratings.

Brennan's of Houston/S | 26 | 26 | 25 | $29 |
3300 Smith (Stuart St.), 713-522-9711
U – This sibling to New Orleans's famed Commander's Palace is a "safe bet" for romancing or "entertaining those you want to impress"; its secret – "they make you feel special"; "warm greetings" and "great ambiance" set the stage for "consistently good" Creole cuisine that includes oyster specialties, seafood, turtle soup (which "cures the flu"), bread pudding and delicious pralines to put in your pocket for later; "first class" all the way; there's also a patio that's "delightful in the right weather."

Brenner's Steak House/S | 26 | 16 | 22 | $31 |
10911 Katy Frwy./I-10 W. (near Wilcrest), 713-465-2901
U – There is no printed menu (the waitress tells you what's available) – just one of the idiosyncracies at this untrendy 1950s-style ranch house that serves "the best steak in the city"; it's a longtime favorite among locals, many of whom drive 15 miles to get here from the inner Loop – they come for the "unbelievable" Roquefort dressing, apple strudel and German fried potatoes, as well as for "the wonderful salty pan juices that make the melt-in-your-mouth steak perfect."

Cafe Annie | 26 | 25 | 24 | $35 |
1728 Post Oak Blvd. (San Felipe), 713-840-1111
M – "Exquisite food" and "polished" service on a "par with either coast's best" is our surveyors' consensus on chef-owner Robert Del Grande's award-winning restaurant; though it comes in "arty, tiny, expensive portions", his SW cuisine is said to be "worth every dollar", "the optimal in town and in Texas"; despite complaints, e.g. "snooty" and "way too noisy", there's no denying that this "coolly sophisticated" venue is among the city's "very finest."

HOUSTON | F | D | S | C |

Carrabba's/S | 24 | 19 | 20 | $19 |
3115 Kirby (Branard), 713-522-3131
1399 S. Voss (Woodway), 713-468-0868
U – The only thing wrong with this pair of "great trattorias" is that they're "too popular"; as a result, you may face a long wait at peak hours and you should "bring earplugs"; once seated, you can expect to eat "the best tomato-basil pizza in town", "fresh pastas" and sausage and peppers that reflect the "modest objectives but excellent execution" of the two first-rate kitchens; both restaurants are attractively decorated.

Charley's 517 | 24 | 23 | 23 | $33 |
517 Louisiana (bet. Texas & Prairie), 713-224-4438
M – Set smack in the heart of the Downtown Theater District and featuring a nationally respected wine list, this "classy" Continental ("you can wear your flirty little dinner dress") offers "consistently fine food with excellent service" to make a memorable evening; though most consider it "a little jewel", a few say it's "riding on its reputation."

Chez Georges | 25 | 21 | 22 | $30 |
11920-G Westheimer (Kirkwood), 713-497-1122
U – "A true diamond in the rough", this "quaint" and "beautiful" West Side Classic French bistro is "very romantic" and a "best value" for the "excellent" food and atmosphere and "consistent, friendly" service, all at moderate prices; even though it's "halfway to LA from Downtown, it's worth the trip."

Chez Nous | 26 | 22 | 25 | $27 |
217 S. Ave. G (Granberry), Humble, 713-446-6717
U – This "good little French" may be "hard to find" up in Humble, but it's an "out-of-the-way oasis" for moderately priced and classically prepared Country French fare (escargot, onion soup, etc.), plus "terrific atmosphere in an old church" and owners who give it a "personal touch"; the "crowds haven't found it yet", but it's "worth the drive" to make Chez Nous, chez vous.

Churrascos/S | 23 | 20 | 20 | $22 |
9788 Bissonnet (Beltway 8), 713-541-2100
2055 Westheimer (S. Shepherd), 713-527-8300
M – At this "beefeater's paradise", the namesake churrascos (beef tenderloin basted with chimichurri sauce) served with fried plantains and perhaps a side of empanadas are the things to order; though some say this Latin steakhouse is "congested, noisy" and "not as good as its reviews", many more hail the "unusual" pan–South American food and "excellent" wine list; even vegetarians say "I'll eat meat here."

HOUSTON

| F | D | S | C |

Damian's Cucina Italiana | 26 | 22 | 23 | $26 |
3011 Smith (near Elgin), 713-522-0439
U – The "best of the Mandola brothers' restaurants", this "classy" and "romantic" Italian trattoria on the south side of Downtown exudes elegance and serves "wonderful old-world food" – including the "best carbonara", gnocchi, eggplant dishes and a "delightful antipasto selection" – in a comfortable, pleasantly lived-in atmosphere; "personable" service and "confident", consistent food at a "good value" ensure popularity at both lunch and dinner, however, so you may "risk waiting", even for reserved tables.

Deville/S | 28 | 26 | 25 | $36 |
Four Seasons Hotel, 1300 Lamar (bet. Austin & Caroline), 713-650-1300
U – "Sublime", say the cognoscenti of this Southwestern "classic", backed by Survey ratings that bestow top honors for food; typical comments include: "undiscovered gem", "such a great restaurant", "superb cuisine in a lovely atmosphere"; food is pricey but "wonderfully creative" and beautifully presented, and the service is first-class; perhaps it's "a bit stuffy", but most call it "excellent formal dining", wonderful for "a serious meal or business" and "awesome" at Sunday brunch.

Dolce & Freddo/L | 24 | 17 | 17 | $8 |
5515 Kirby (near Sunset Blvd.), 713-521-3260
7595 San Felipe (near S. Voss), 713-789-0219
U – Sleek as Milano espresso bars, these "superhip" Italian-style dessert-and-coffee specialists offer the "trendiest ice cream in town", including "gelato you can't pronounce" and "the best" cappuccino and espresso; "long waits" mar the experience for some ("it's just an ice cream parlor, after all"), but most say they're "worth standing up for – and you often have to"; the decadent liqueur-spiked ice creams are a "divine" splurge.

Empress of China/S | 26 | 19 | 24 | $17 |
5419-A FM 1960 W. (Champions Village), 713-583-8021
U – An impressive wine list and "outstanding and inventive" "Franco-Chinese food" are unexpected finds in this attractive Far North Champions-area restaurant; "take a group to sample everything" on the "unusual" menu that features "superb Nouvelle cuisine, prepared in an interesting way"; "nice folks" and "fair prices" are just an added bonus.

Enzo's Pasta e Vino | 24 | 15 | 20 | $18 |
720 W. NASA Rd. 1 (Texas Ave.), Webster, 713-332-6955
U – "Priced to use nightly", this unprepossessing Italian that "no one but natives knows is here" offers the "best Italian food in the area" and a surprisingly good wine list; service is "great", and the "top-quality" food always satisfies.

HOUSTON

| F | D | S | C |

Frenchie's Italian Restaurant | 25 | 13 | 20 | $17 |
1041 NASA Rd. 1 (El Camino), 713-486-7144
M – The "homestyle Italian" served up here is "great food", but "there's a long wait" most evenings; locals are fiercely proud of the "good plain grub" and "tacky decor" at this friendly, family-run eatery; "this place is an institution, in a category by itself."

Ginza Japanese | 24 | 19 | 19 | $21 |
5868 San Felipe (near Fountain View), 713-785-0332
U – Small, intimate, tidy-looking Tanglewood-area sushi bar boasting good tempura and some of the "best sushi in town" – the fish is "always fresh" – plus lunch that's "a bargain"; this "authentic" spot is "favored by local Japanese", which most respondents think is a point in its favor.

Green's Barbecue/LX | 23 | 12 | 17 | $12 |
5404 Almeda (near Southmore), 713-528-5501
U – "Taste with soul" at this offbeat stand on the Med Center that fans say serves up the "best BBQ in town"; it's been a barbecue-lover's mainstay for more than 25 years, but wimps beware: the peppery sauce is lip-singeing, and the dicey location makes it a destination "for the adventuresome" only.

Grotto/S | 24 | 22 | 22 | $20 |
Highland Village, 3920 Westheimer (bet. Weslayan & Drexel), 713-622-3663
M – A bawdy mural sets the "mischievous tone" at this lively Highland Village Neapolitan trattoria, which draws a "who's-who", "see-and-be-seen" crowd – "wear your best dressy casual"; it's "trendy", yes, "too popular" even, but fans say it "keeps improving"; look for "excellent" pizza, pastas, gnocchi and osso buco, but don't be surprised by a "long wait" due to the no-reservations policy (for parties fewer than 6); also, it can be "too noisy unless you eat outside."

Hunan | 24 | 24 | 22 | $19 |
The Pavilion, 1800 Post Oak Blvd. (near San Felipe), 713-965-0808
U – What our surveyors term "the classiest Chinese in Houston" has overtaken Uncle Tai's on our scoreboard, the result not only of serving "consistently excellent" Hunan classics but of James and Gigi Huang's practice of making "all the customers feel like special-dinner guests"; it's well-known as George Bush's favorite, and given the fact that he served a tour of duty in Peking, his taste in Chinese restaurants deserves respect.

HOUSTON

| F | D | S | C |

Kelly's Del Frisco
| 26 | 17 | 21 | $26 |

14641 Gladebrook (Stuebner-Airline), 713-893-3339
U – Fans of "steaks at their best" praise the Kellys for carrying "the homey concept to the nth degree"; a "somewhat out-of-the-way" location matters not at all, because "for steak and seafood, it's first class"; caveat: the portion sizes are "almost too much" – split them and you've got a bargain.

La Colombe d'Or/S
| 24 | 24 | 22 | $34 |

La Colombe d'Or Hotel, 3410 Montrose (Harold), 713-524-7999
U – Highly rated (some say "superb"), this Classic French has lovely quarters in a tiny luxury hotel, once the manse of a local oil baron; our surveyors say the food is "pricey" but "excellent" and the "comfortable elegance" is "perfect for a romantic evening" – or a leisurely power lunch; the vast majority call it "special"; and where else can you "have a cigar and cognac in the library" after dinner?

La Reserve
| 26 | 26 | 25 | $35 |

Omni Houston Hotel, 4 Riverway (Woodway & S. Post Oak Lane), 713-871-8177
U – "Chefs change, but the food stays outstanding" at this lavish (and pricey) Classic French; "caviar pie appetizer to die for, excellent soufflés") and service that's a "dream" explain why this charming dining room "deserves top ratings in all categories"; even those few who call it a little "stuffy" admit that it's still "dining par excellence."

Lynn's Steakhouse
| 24 | 19 | 21 | $31 |

9551½ Dairy Ashford (bet. I-10 W. & Memorial), 713-870-0807
U – An "intimate setting" and careful hands-on management by owner Lynn Taylor provide a "family touch" at this West Side steak-and-chop house; "huge servings" of "excellent steaks" and side dishes (especially the famous bread) will fill you up, and you can "feed the family and guests on leftovers"; considering the prices, though, it's not surprising that some consider this "strictly an expense-account affair."

Nino's
| 24 | 16 | 20 | $20 |

2817 W. Dallas (bet. Waugh & Montrose), 713-522-5120
U – Recent interior renovations are not reflected in the unimpressive decor score above, but there's no missing the outstanding Italian food served in this cozy Moonstruck setting; one fan says he'd pick it "for my last meal" (fried calamari, perhaps, or the "best veal chop in the world").

HOUSTON | F | D | S | C |

Nit Noi Thai | 23 | 12 | 18 | $15 |
Rice Village, 2462 Bolsover, 713-524-8114
U – The name means "little bit", but whether it refers to the noshing or the floor space is not clear, since this "tiny" (some say "intimate"), redolent Thai has only a handful of tables and is often overcrowded; "seafood dishes are excellent", but "service can be slow" – even so, it's "loved by those who know about it."

Pappadeaux Seafood Kitchen/S | 23 | 18 | 19 | $18 |
2525 S. Loop W. (Kirby), 713-665-3155
13080 Northwest Frwy./290 (Hollister), 713-460-1203
6015 Westheimer (near Fountain View), 713-782-6310
12711 Southwest Frwy./59 S. (Corporate Dr.), Stafford, 713-240-5533
2226 FM 1960 (Kuyendahl), 713-893-0206
U – These "consistently outstanding" Cajun seafooders are just one more chapter in the Pappas family success story; like most of the others, they are "impossibly crowded on weekends" and always "too noisy" – "couldn't even hear the waitress"; large portions of "fine food, served pleasantly" and at "fair prices" more than compensate.

Pappasito's Cantina/S | 23 | 19 | 19 | $15 |
20099 Gulf Frwy./I-45 S. (NASA Rd. 1 exit), Webster, 713-338-2885
6445 Richmond (Hillcroft), 713-784-5253
15280 North Frwy./I-45 N. (Airtex), 713-821-4500
12000 Southwest Frwy./59 S. (Wilcrest & Murphy exit), Sugarland, 713-240-0099
10005 FM 1960 Bypass (U.S. Hwy. 59 N.), Humble, 713-540-8664
13070 Northwest Frwy. (Hollister), 713-462-0245
2515 S. Loop W. (Astrodome), 713-668-5756
2536 Richmond (Kirby), 713-520-5066
10409 Katy Frwy. (Westbelt), 713-468-1913
M – The "circus atmosphere" in these enormous Tex-Mex cantinas, complete with roving mariachis, is "great for parties" and as a "fun date place"; try the carne asada, fajitas or "huge shrimp on a sizzling platter"; ironically, a few say "portions are too large"; more common is the observation that "there's such a long wait."

Patisserie Descours | 24 | 12 | 19 | $14 |
1330-B Wirt St., Ste. B (Westview), 713-681-8894
U – You're in "dessert heaven" at this tiny bakery-cum-sandwich storefront in Spring Branch, where many of the city's status wedding cakes are ordered; the surroundings are nothing special, but stop by anyway for a slice of what could be the "best carrot cake on earth" or "great goodies to take home."

HOUSTON

| F | D | S | C |

Quail Hollow Inn/S | 24 | 20 | 23 | $20 |
214 Morton St. (3rd St.), Richmond, 713-341-6733
U – Set in Downtown Richmond inside a lovely old building, this "superlative and very Swiss" inn features a "diversified menu with a great Sunday spread" and excellent service; a few complain that it's becoming "too touristy", but they probably just want to keep this "excellent small-town classic" for themselves.

Quilted Toque, The/S | – | – | – | M |
(fka Evan's)
3939 Montrose Blvd. (bet. Richmond & W. Alabama), 713-942-9233
This talk of the town in the Museum District is proving a winner with American food of global influence served at breakfast, brunch, lunch and dinner; moderate prices, an in-house bakery that turns out innovative breads, and private dining in the loft all make Monica Pope's new Toque tops!

Ritz-Carlton Hotel/S | 24 | 27 | 24 | $34 |
1919 Briar Oaks Lane (San Felipe), 713-840-7600
M – Despite changes in menu and personnel, "polished" and "wonderful" Continental dining endures at this "gorgeous" hotel that fans (the majority) call "the most beautiful in Texas" and "ne plus ultra", with the "best food around", enhanced by "excellent" service; the Grill, "always a favorite", is now the place to go on weekends with dancing", while the rosy Garden Room is the spot for "magnificent lunches"; however, nostalgic critics think it was "better as the Remington."

River Oaks Grill | 23 | 22 | 21 | $29 |
2630 Westheimer (Kirby), 713-520-1738
U – An "elegant hunt-club atmosphere" and prime River Oaks location make this American-Continental the place where many of Houston's social types come to see and be seen; "excellent grilled salmon in town" as well as a slew of richly indulgent meat dishes make up the "risk-free" menu, and the service is "10-star"; the takeover by the Parlante family is good news.

Rivoli Restaurant | 24 | 23 | 24 | $32 |
5636 Richmond (near Chimney Rock), 713-789-1900
U – "Soooo romantic, always good" say lovers of this "contemporary yet classic" Continental; while it may indeed be a "socialite's restaurant", the "excellent service" and painstaking attention to detail mean you need "never hesitate to entertain someone here"; the death of longtime owner Ed Zeilinsky prompts many to say "we'll miss Ed", but fans say quality remains.

HOUSTON

| F | D | S | C |

Rotisserie for Beef and Bird | 26 | 23 | 24 | $30 |
2200 Wilcrest (north of Westheimer), 713-977-9524
U – "Wonderful American-Continental food and excellent wines" make this gently sophisticated country inn the West Side's most highly regarded restaurant; duck, venison and wild boar dishes are particularly renowned; insiders say "take a wine aficionado", because The Wine Spectator–*praised list gets as much attention as the food.*

Ruggles Grill/S | 24 | 18 | 21 | $21 |
903 Westheimer (east of Montrose), 713-524-3839
M – "The wave of the future is here now" at the "best revamped restaurant in Houston", a trendy bistro serving an innovative menu of Southwestern and other fresh, Contemporary American food; some complain that this "good casual spot" is in a "lousy part of town", but the food and value are worth the inconvenience; insiders advise "don't go without reservations – the bar is too small for a pleasant wait."

Sasaki Restaurant* | 24 | 18 | 18 | $24 |
8979 Westheimer (Fondren), 713-266-5768
U – The "best sushi in town" is served in this oddball setting with plump club chairs and a tangle of video wiring on the small stage; it's not as well-known as some other Japanese spots around Houston, so the clientele is less yuppified; too bad "service is slow."

Star Pizza/S | 22 | 11 | 14 | $11 |
2111 Norfolk (bet. S. Shepherd & Greenbriar), 713-523-0800
140 S. Heights Blvd. (Washington), 713-869-1241
U – This highly rated pizza joint's reputation is built (partly, at least) on its famous spinach and garlic pie – "try a Joe's and say it ain't a real satisfaction"; it's "not much on service or atmosphere", but you'll find the city's "yummiest pizza plus free movies" upstairs.

Taj Mahal/S | 22 | 13 | 18 | $14 |
8328 Gulf Frwy./I-45 S. (Bellfort), 713-649-2818
U – "Unsurpassed" Indian south of the Loop" has been a Gulf Freeway fixture for more than a decade; the nondescript decor is no match at all for the food, which continues to thrill: "I'll drive 50 miles for their nan bread" says one fan and there's a "great lunch buffet."

HOUSTON | F | D | S | C |

Taste of Texas/S | 23 | 20 | 20 | $22 |
10505 Katy Frwy./I-10 W. (bet. Beltway 8 & Gessner), 713-932-6901
M – A recent move has made the crowds at this popular steakhouse even larger than before – there's an "unbelievable wait on Friday or Saturday night"; everyone comes for their "favorite American food" at a value price that even covers an appetizer and cinnamon coffee; foes warn that it's "overblown, overpriced, and overcrowded", but most diners are "surprised how good it is."

Tony's | 27 | 27 | 26 | $40 |
1801 Post Oak Blvd. (south of San Felipe), 713-622-6778
M – In Houston, this dining-out "phenomenon" is a sleek and pricey, power-brokering Italian-Continental that many surveyors say is "the best place to celebrate anything"; critics, however, say "it's too tony for me", and that inconsistency and stuffiness are big drawbacks – "if you're a nobody, they seat you and forget you"; fans counter that it's in a class by itself, citing "elegant" food, "first-class service", "beautiful" decor and an "outstanding" wine list.

KANSAS CITY

TOP 30 RESTAURANTS
(In order of food rating)

Restaurant	Cuisine Type
26 – Tatsu's	French
Cafe Allegro	Eclectic
Peppercorn Duck Club	Amer. Tradition./Eclectic
25 – La Mediterranee	French
Venue	Eclectic
Plaza III	Steakhouse
24 – Woks	Chinese
Stroud's	American/Southern
Classic Cup	Eclectic
Hunan Empire	Chinese
Andre's Confiserie Suisse	Swiss
Red Dragon House	Chinese
Ruby's Soul Food	Soul Food
Rozzelle Court	Eclectic
American Restaurant	American
23 – Le Picnique	Amer. Tradition.
California Taqueria	Mexican
Parkway Market Cafe	Eclectic
Bristol Bar & Grill	Seafood/Steakhouse
New Peking	Chinese
Stephenson's Farm	Amer. Tradition.
Smoke Stack Bar-B-Q	BBQ
Bellucci's	Continental/Eclectic
Paradise Diner	Southwestern
Jasper's	Northern Italian
Royal China	Chinese
Savoy Grill	Seafood/Steakhouse
Mrs. Peter's	Amer. Tradition.
Princess Garden	Chinese
Nikko Steak House	Steakhouse

OTHER TOP PLACES
(In alphabetical order)

Athena on Broadway	Greek
Boulevard Cafe	Middle Eastern
Fedora Cafe & Bar	International
Grand Street Cafe	Eclectic
Metropolis	Eclectic
Murray's Ice Cream	Desserts
Nabil's Mediterranean	Middle Eastern
Veco's Italian Restaurant	N/S Italian
West Side Cafe	Middle Eastern

KANSAS CITY | F | D | S | C |

American Restaurant | 24 | 26 | 23 | $33 |
Halls Crown Center, 200 E. 25th St. (Grand Ave.),
816-426-1133
M – No one disputes the prominent role played by Crown Center's crown jewel restaurant in putting Heartland cooking on the map, and its high ratings confirm the public's approval; but some find "uneven food and service" at odds with its lofty reputation and high prices: "when it's good, it's good, when it's not, it's expensive"; the "stunning decor" wins unanimous praise; dinner only.

Andre's Confiserie Suisse/X | 24 | 20 | 20 | $10 |
5018 Main St. (50th St.), 816-561-3440
M – Great Gstaad, there's "always something to yodel about" at this Swiss "ladies' lunch place" just south of the Plaza, thanks to its "always delicious" food, "cute Alpine decor", low prices and pastries so tasty that "dessert is the main course"; but it's "no place for a starving man", and critics deplore its line-inducing "no reservations" policy; lunch only.

Athena on Broadway | 22 | 17 | 19 | $15 |
3535 Broadway (Armour Blvd.), 816-756-3227
U – Modest prices and a menu that ranges well beyond predictable Greek cooking attract an urbane crowd to this "intimate and romantic" Midtown standby; its "fresh food is presented beautifully" and waiters are "always attentive."

Bellucci's | 23 | 18 | 18 | $11 |
303 W. 10th St. (bet. Broadway & Central Ave.),
816-471-4667
U – A "quaint European feel" attracts the lunch and pre-theater crowd to this cramped Downtown Eclectic-Continental cafe; despite a "classy, cosmopolitan menu", prices are mostly moderate; pasta salads and "yummy desserts" top the recommended list.

Boulevard Cafe | – | – | – | M |
703 Southwest Blvd. (Broadway & Summit),
816-842-6984
Here's a cafe that brings something different to the table: Middle Eastern tapas; it is probably the only place in the area where "grazing" – sampling a lot of dishes (especially someone else's) – can be undertaken without embarrassment; an ideal spot for late-night dining and for those who enjoy an urban flavor.

KANSAS CITY | F | D | S | C |

Bristol Bar & Grill/S | 23 | 23 | 22 | $21 |
4740 Jefferson St. (bet. W. 47th & W. 48th Sts.),
816-756-0606
U – High energy and noise go hand in hand at this pricey, dark, clubby Country Club Plaza fish house; land-locked patrons are so grateful for "consistently good seafood" that they may ignore an impressive selection of steaks, "heavenly" biscuits and great Sunday brunch; choicest seats are in the curtained booths or under the back room's stained-glass dome.

Cafe Allegro | 26 | 22 | 24 | $29 |
1815 W. 39th St. (State Line Rd.), 816-561-3663
U – Inventive, seasonal Eclectic food, fantastic bread, a fine wine list and "warm atmosphere" add up to "one of the best dining experiences in KC"; the arty, bistrolike look of this Midtown favorite near the Kansas state line belies a semi-formal service style; regulars commend owner Steve Cole for his personal attention.

California Taqueria/X | 23 | 9 | 16 | $7 |
2316 Summit St. (bet. Southwest Blvd. & 23rd St.),
816-474-5571
U – This near-Downtown "hole-in-the-wall" features "huge portions" of "great, homemade Mexican food"; fans like the "honest tamales and chicken enchiladas"; there's "no table service" or decor, but "talk about cheap!" – muy bueno!; closes at 5:30 PM except on Friday when it's open "late", i.e. 8 PM.

Classic Cup, The/S | 24 | 17 | 20 | $15 |
4130 Pennsylvania Ave. (1 block west of Broadway),
816-756-0771
301 W. 47th St. (Central Ave.), 816-753-1009
U – "Unique and refreshingly different", the original Pennsylvania Avenue site is a "charming cafe" set in a Westport coffee, specialty grocery and classical music store; the new Plaza location is equally attractive, with sidewalk and back deck seating; both outlets are praised for their limited, mid-scale menus that range from a vegetarian club sandwich to brunchtime strawberry brie pancakes and "great, unusual desserts."

Fedora Cafe & Bar/S | 22 | 24 | 21 | $22 |
210 W. 47th St. (bet. Main St. & Wornall Rd.),
816-561-6565
M – This flashy, "everybody-who's-somebody" restaurant on the Country Club Plaza draws a "young, attractive crowd" who laud the French-accented Italian menu for its "designer pastas and pizzas" and favorites ranging from carpaccio to tartufo; not everyone likes it, but as Yogi Berra says, "nobody goes there anymore – it's too crowded."

KANSAS CITY

| F | D | S | C |

Garrozzo's Ristorante | 23 | 15 | 21 | $14 |
526 Harrison (north of Independence Ave.), 816-221-2455
12801 E. 40 Hwy. (east of Blueridge Mall), 816-737-2400
U – These St. Louis–style Ethnics have found a KC audience for their first-rate, moderately priced food – "great pastas and eggplant parmesan take Southern Italian to its highest level"; decor and "close quarters" come with the Sinatra music.

Grand Street Cafe/X | – | – | – | M |
4740 Grand (Main St. & Brush Creek), 816-561-8000
Paul Koury and Bill Crooks have the knack for creating popular, visually exciting restaurants; their latest venture sparkles with color, spice, people and an Eclectic menu of salads, sandwiches and more substantial main courses that caters to most tastes and budgets; P.S. the pork chop with homemade apple sauce is divine.

Hunan Empire/S | 24 | 19 | 19 | $12 |
Glenwood Manor Shopping Ctr., 9058 Metcalf Ave. (91st St.), 913-341-9888
U – This comparatively new, stylish Japanese-looking entry has made a favorable impression in Overland Park; devotees call its competitively priced Chinese menu "the standout in a field of heavy hitters", praising dishes as diverse as shrimp toast, hot-and-sour soup and "great whole fish in spicy sauce"; service can be "disorganized."

Jasper's | 23 | 21 | 23 | $30 |
405 W. 75th St. (Wornall Rd.), 816-363-3003
M – Some surveyors liken this extravagantly decorated, uncompromisingly formal Midtowner to Antarctica ("too many penguin waiters walking around"), while others say it makes them feel on top of the world ("first class all the way" with "service fit for kings and queens"); few dispute the Mirabile family's grasp of French-influenced Northern Italian cooking; dinner only.

La Mediterranee | 25 | 22 | 23 | $29 |
4742 Pennsylvania Ave. (48th St.), 816-561-2916
M – Chef Gilbert Jahier's expensive, straightforward French restaurant is a longtime fixture on the Country Club Plaza; regulars tout his lobster in vanilla sauce and confide that "lunch is a bargain"; "dated decor" and "pompous service" garner the most complaints.

Le Picnique | 23 | 24 | 20 | $11 |
Seebree Gallery, 301 E. 55th St. (Brookside), 816-333-3387
U – Here's a "great luncheon spot" that serves "ladies' portions" in the midst of a tony Midtown antiques shop; the soup/salad/sandwich/dessert menu is moderately priced despite the restaurant's reputation as "headquarters for the Junior League"; lunch only.

KANSAS CITY | F | D | S | C |

Metropolis | 22 | 23 | 21 | $22 |
303 Westport Rd. (bet. Broadway & Main St.), 816-753-1550
M – "Nuevo" Eclectic cuisine and "Euro-tech-to-the-max" decor are the stuff of controversy at this recent Westport entry; "trendy, lovely and innovative", say its fans, while critics who feel "overcharged and underfed" say "their chef must take drugs – so did the designer"; all agree it's "unique" but "noisy."

Mrs. Peter's/S | 23 | 19 | 22 | $11 |
4960 State Ave. (3 blocks west of Indian Springs Shopping Ctr.), 913-287-7711
U – Motherly cooking in a "charming, squeaky-clean setting" draws fried chicken fanciers to KC, Kansas; inexpensive down-home dishes plus "all the trimmings" are served family-style with doting servers in "Martha Washington getup" as the finishing touch.

Murray's Ice Cream and Cookies/X | – | – | – | I |
4120 Pennsylvania (Westport Rd.), 816-931-5646
Nobody does ice cream better than Murray's; the shop probably has the highest sugar per square foot ratio in the KC area, and the truly addicted frequent the place up to four times a week; the changing selection of ices and ice creams are made on the spot; N.B. the cookies should not be overlooked.

Nabil's Mediterranean/X | 22 | 17 | 20 | $18 |
3605 Broadway (bet. 36th & 37th Sts.), 816-531-0700
U – This "teeny, tiny" Aegean on Broadway north of Westport "does a delicious take on Middle Eastern food" that's "sophisticated enough to have sweetbreads on the menu"; our surveyors celebrate "classy presentation" and "good value."

New Peking/S | 23 | 22 | 21 | $14 |
540 Westport Rd. (Broadway), 816-531-6969
U – The art deco decor may come as a shock, but many see this Westport Chinese as "a step above the rest"; if specialties like the "excellent lemon chicken and orange beef" command prices slightly higher than the Chinese norm, they're more than fair for what you get; service stresses "individual attention."

Nikko Steak House | 23 | 23 | 23 | $17 |
Overland Park Marriott, 10800 Metcalf Ave. (I-435), 913-451-8000
M – Another of the city's Japanese teppan specialists, this one located in the Overland Park Marriott, gets generally high marks and has show-off chefs who are "invariably entertaining"; still, dissenters knock the "small portions at expense-account prices"; dinner only.

KANSAS CITY | F | D | S | C |

Paradise Diner/S | 23 | 20 | 21 | $13 |
Oak Park Mall, 11327 W. 95th St. (Quivira Rd.),
913-894-2222
U – "They should call it 'Paradox Diner' " for bringing
"first-rate Southwestern specialties" to a shopping mall
setting; some complain that "service is not consistent"
and "the trendy decor is out of sync", but no one faults
the "original dishes" or the fair tab.

Parkway Market Cafe | 23 | 20 | 20 | $14 |
2820 W. 53rd St. (Shawnee Mission Pkwy.), 913-432-3030
M – Admirers like the "creative International cuisine",
"attractive, pink-and-turquoise color scheme" and open
kitchen at this mezzanine restaurant; critics say the
"takeout food is far superior to the restaurant's
expensive output" and that "service tends to be uneven."

Pepper Corn Duck Club/S | 26 | 26 | 25 | $28 |
Hyatt Regency Crown Ctr., 2345 McGee St. (Pershing
Rd.), 816-421-1234
U – The Hyatt Regency's entry in the special-occasion
sweepstakes specializes in excellent rotisserie-cooked
duckling and a dessert bar so chocolate-drenched "they
should serve insulin as a chaser"; our reviewers find no
faults at this top-of-the-line Crown Center American –
as one fond admirer says, "when you want to be
pampered, this is it."

Plaza III – The Steakhouse/S | 25 | 23 | 23 | $25 |
4749 Pennsylvania Ave. (Ward Pkwy.), 816-753-0000
U – This Country Club Plaza cornerstone's redo as a
steakery has been warmly received despite some
carping about "ridiculous à la carte prices" and the
"ritual display of raw meat"; the handsome, "leather-
lined men's-den feeling" is also highly praised, as is
the signature steak soup, a perennial favorite.

Princess Garden/S | 23 | 17 | 21 | $14 |
8906 Wornall Rd. (89th St.), 816-444-3709
8505 College Blvd. (1 block east of Antioch Rd.),
913-339-9898
U – Seen by many as "the first good Chinese restaurant
in town", this 18-year-old Szechuan-Mandarin (now with
a second location in Johnson County) continually
strengthens its preeminence with new menu additions;
Chang family members are always in charge and "they
treat you like a guest in their home"; "order the Peking
duck", its admirers advise.

KANSAS CITY

| F | D | S | C |

Red Dragon House | 24 | 20 | 20 | $11 |
312 W. 8th St. (bet. Central Ave. & Broadway), 816-221-1388
U – Surveyors call this "Oriental surprise" in Downtown's Garment District "an urbane place" to eat excellent Chinese food at "very fair prices"; "high ceilings and lots of plants" give it "a different look" that most respondents clearly like.

Royal China/S | 23 | 21 | 22 | $11 |
7800 W. 63rd St. (bet. Antioch Rd. & Metcalf Ave.), 913-384-1688
U – This unassuming, but quite attractive, Chinese in Overland Park comes highly recommended for specialties like "beggar's chicken baked in clay" and "excellent sesame beef" at "surprisingly painless prices"; our participants praise management that "genuinely seems to care."

Rozzelle Court/S | 24 | 27 | 17 | $12 |
Nelson-Atkins Museum of Art, 4525 Oak St. (45th St.), 816-751-1279
U – Many see the Nelson Gallery's "gorgeous" enclosed courtyard as "the classiest place in town for lunch"; the buffet line offers two entrees plus soups, sandwiches, "lovely scones" and luscious desserts at prices that are low considering the surroundings; "if you found this in Florence, you'd write home about it."

Ruby's Soul Food/X | 24 | 11 | 18 | $9 |
1506 Brooklyn St. (15th St.), 816-421-8514
U – "Super Soul Food served buffet-style" at super low prices brings a cross section of famished Kansas Citians daily to Ruby's Center City doorstep; count fried chicken, "butter-doused cornbread" and homemade ice cream among its perennial favorites; a principal feature of the funky decor is a series of sometimes-bawdy signs that reflect the spirited owner's outlook.

Savoy Grill/LS | 23 | 23 | 22 | $23 |
Hotel Savoy, 219 W. 9th St. (Central Ave.), 816-842-3890
M – You can "step back into history" at this turn-of-the-century Downtown steak-and-seafood house that's "so old and so delicious" – only the bill is up-to-date; surveyors find the choicest seats in the historic Grill Room and dismiss other rooms as "dumpy"; veteran waiters in starched white jackets are seen by some as "slow and stuffy", by others as reflecting "old-fashioned elegance."

Smoke Stack Bar-B-Q | 23 | 17 | 19 | $12 |
13441 Holmes Rd. (I-150), Martin City, MO, 816-942-9141
8920 Wornall Rd. (89th St.), 816-444-5542
8129 S. 71 Hwy. (north of 85th St.), 816-333-2011

KANSAS CITY | F | D | S | C |

Smoke Stack Bar-B-Q (Cont.)
U – This Suburban BBQ chain is noted for its "unique, hickory-smoked fresh fish" as well as top-rated, typically inexpensive barbecue specialties like ribs and brisket; such side dishes as onion rings (stacked on a pole) and "gloriously smoky pit-baked beans" also win raves, and the quaintly countrified decor is a cut above the BBQ norm.

Stephenson's Old Apple Farm/S | 23 | 22 | 22 | $16 |
16401 E. 40 Hwy. (just east of Nolan Rd.), 816-373-5400
U – Real country charm may be only a memory at this sprawling, city-surrounded Eastsider, but steady customers still call the homey decor "heart-warming"; moreover, hickory-smoked meats, grandmotherly entrees such as smothered chicken, and side dishes such as corn relish and frozen fruit salad continue to please at a modest, all-inclusive price; Stephenson's "famous apple fritters" are the "coup de grace."

Stroud's/S | 24 | 16 | 20 | $12 |
1015 E. 85th St. (Troost), 816-333-2132
5410 N.E. Oak Ridge Dr. (at I-35 & Vivion Rd.), 816-454-9600
U – The pan-fried chicken at these twins may be "the best cholesterol ever made"; the same goes for the pork chops and chicken-fried steak, and if that's not enough, there are homemade cinnamon rolls and cracklin' gravy so good they should bottle it, all included at a rock-bottom tab; folksy service, checkerboard curtains and a warped wooden floor help preserve the "early roadhouse" authenticity; Stroud's "we choke our own chickens" T-shirts are a don't-miss.

Tatsu's/S | 26 | 13 | 21 | $21 |
4603 W. 90th St. (Roe Ave.), 913-383-9801
U – Finding a first-class French restaurant out in suburban Prairie Village, Kansas, is a delightful surprise; Japanese chef-owner Tatsuya Arai honors his classic French training with excellent proven favorites such as scallops in lemon butter; although some respondents think a new menu and upgrading of the "horrible" decor are sorely needed, most agree that this is as good as French gets in Kansas.

Veco's Italian Restaurant | – | – | – | M |
1803 W. 39th St. (Bell), 816-931-2101
Not as dressy or pricey as Vic Fontana's previous Italian eateries, this one serves good, garlicky fare at moderate prices; one wonders whether Vic is competing against himself with Charlie Charlie virtually across the street, but in the meantime, he continues to expand in the hottest restaurant district in town.

KANSAS CITY | F | D | S | C |

Venue | 25 | 18 | 23 | $35 |
4532 Main St. (just north of 47th St.), 816-561-3311
M – Dennis and Gabrielle Kaniger, both veterans of LA's International-Eclectic City Restaurant, have brought some of the same outlook to the New American menu and ambiance at their own restaurant near the Country Club Plaza; most surveyors praise the "California-chic food" and "wonderful presentations"; what hasn't traveled well, however, are the "microscopic portions" at top-end prices, and the "stark, chilly atmosphere" causes some to say "you'll either love it or leave it, with no in-between."

West Side Cafe/X | 23 | 13 | 18 | $12 |
723 Southwest Blvd. (Summit St.), 816-472-0010
U – The retired Downtown gas station redone in pink and lime sherbet serves inexpensive "ethereal Middle Eastern cuisine" and "cosmic curries"; to partake of "a unique experience", sit inside or out on old-fashioned metal folding chairs; either way, enjoy "careful, considerate service"; open Thursday and Friday for lunch and dinner, Saturday dinner only.

Woks, The/S | 24 | 24 | 23 | $10 |
Westchester Sq., 8615 Hauser Dr. (87th St.), 913-541-1777
U – This popular newcomer in the Kansas suburbs "does sensational things with Szechuan and Mandarin food"; a "special favorite" is "seven stars and moon" (tempura shrimp over assorted meats and seafoods); regulars praise its "friendly proprietor" and "suave, subdued decor"; it's hard to even imagine getting better for less.

LOS ANGELES

TOP 30 RESTAURANTS
(In order of food rating)

Restaurant	Cuisine Type
28 – Patina	Californian/French
Matsuhisa	Pacific New Wave
27 – Shiro	Pacific New Wave
Chinois on Main	Pacific New Wave
Diaghilev	French Classic/Russian
C'est Fan Fan	Pacific New Wave
26 – Citrus	Californian/French
Valentino	Italian
Locanda Veneta	Italian
La Toque	French Nouvelle
Sushi Nozawa	Japanese
Le Chardonnay	Californian/French Bistro
25 – Dynasty Room	French Classic
L'Orangerie	French Classic
Water Grill	Seafood
Bel-Air Hotel	Californian/French
Checkers	Amer. Contemp./French
Spago	Californian
Katsu	Japanese
Yujean Kang's	Chinese
Campanile	Cal./Mediterranean
Rockenwagner	Californian/Eclectic
Rex II Ristorante	Italian
Granita	Californian
Parkway Grill	Californian
Cafe Katsu	French/Oriental
24 – Lawry's Prime Rib	Amer. Traditon.
Joe's	Californian
Michael's	Californian
Ivy	Amer. Contemp.

OTHER TOP PLACES
(In alphabetical order)

Bombay Cafe	Indian
Ca'Brea	Italian
Chaya Brasserie	Pacific New Wave
Drago	Italian
Grill	Seafood/Steakhouse
Jody Maroni's	Frankfurters
Pinot	French Bistro
Regent Beverly Wilshire	Continental
Saddle Peak Lodge	Amer. Contemp.
72 Market Street	Amer. Contemp.

LOS ANGELES

| F | D | S | C |

Bel-Air Hotel/SM | 25 | 28 | 26 | $46 |
Bel-Air Hotel, 701 Stone Canyon Rd. (¼ mile north of Sunset Blvd.), Bel Air, 310-472-1211

U – One of the top hotel restaurants in LA is appropriately found in one of the top hotels in America; there's hardly a spot in town more "romantic" or "exquisite"; the "swans gliding across the lake" are worth the price at this "dreamlike" Nouvelle Californian–French where the food and service are almost as "heavenly" as the setting; it's "an elegant escape from LA in LA."

Bombay Cafe/S | 23 | 11 | 18 | $18 |
12113 Santa Monica Blvd. (Bundy Dr.), W. LA, 310-820-2070

U – The "best Indian in town" is a "funky storefront" in a West Side mini-mall serving "authentic street food" from the subcontinent; though decor is nonexistent, the food is "better than anything we've had in India"; "freshly made chutneys" and regional specialties like "fiery Bombay frankies" and crunchy "chips and dips, Indian-style", are served by "the nicest people around."

Ca'Brea/M | 24 | 20 | 20 | $31 |
346 S. La Brea Ave. (3 blocks north of Wilshire Blvd.), LA, 213-938-2863

U – "The best Italian food outside of Italy" is found at this large economy-sized sibling of top-rated trattoria Locanda Veneta; built inside a former French relic, it offers "super food" served by "legitimate Italian waiters" in a "noisy, crowded" setting; in exchange for the "reasonable prices", expect "long waits even with reservations" – "you'll be well-rewarded for patience."

Cafe Katsu/SM | 25 | 15 | 20 | $29 |
2117 Sawtelle Ave. (north of Olympic Blvd.), West LA, 310-477-3359

U – Praised as "the best thing to happen to a strip mall", this "sterile" "minimalist" French-Japanese "bento box" of a restaurant offers what's been described as "Michael's food at McDonald's" prices; the "stark" setting only makes the "wonderful" "creative" cooking stand out better at this tribute to "subtle seasonings"; the consensus: "we've never had better seafood anywhere."

Campanile/M | 25 | 23 | 21 | $40 |
624 S. La Brea Ave. (½ block north of Wilshire Blvd.), LA, 213-938-1447

M – This "pleasantly trendy" Mediterranean-Californian was once an office complex built by Charlie Chaplin; with great care, chef Mark Peel and his baker-wife Nancy Silverton (don't forget to stop by her La Brea Bakery next door) have made it a temple to the fine flavors of Southern France and Italy; already a "landmark in LA eating", with the addition of casual breakfast, it has become one of the top power spots in town, with many a celeb nursing espresso as the sun rises over the La Brea Tar Pits.

LOS ANGELES

| F | D | S | C |

C'est Fan Fan/S | 27 | 12 | 23 | $33 |
3360 W. First St. (Virgil Ave.), LA, 213-487-7330
U – At this "truly great" Pacific New Waver, you sit at what used to be a sushi bar (there are no tables) and watch a "fantastic" chef create dishes that are "worth a long drive" to the problematic edge of Silver Lake; enjoy the "wonderful dishes custom-made for you" at this "Chinois for those who do not need to be hip"; "when you eat in the kitchen, the chef can't hide anything"; but, then again, you don't expect fancy decor in a kitchen.

Chaya Brasserie/SM | 24 | 23 | 21 | $35 |
8741 Alden Dr. (east of Robertson Blvd., bet. 3rd St. & Beverly Blvd.), LA, 310-859-8833
U – West Hollywood hideaway near Cedars-Sinai ("you can stop for a last meal before a tummy tuck"); popular with the "Spago and Morton's crowd" and those who "can't handle the hassle at The Ivy", it serves some of the "best and most creative food in town" in a barnlike room looking like "a koala bear's habitat"; after a tumultuous decade, it's still one of the "trendiest spots" in a very trendy town.

Checkers/SM | 25 | 26 | 24 | $44 |
Checkers Hotel Kempinski, 535 S. Grand Ave. (bet. 5th & 6th Sts.), Downtown, 213-624-0000
U – The far-flung Kempinski chain seems committed to keeping Checkers Downtown's best hotel dining room, where morning meetings are served "the best breads in town" and the Contemporary French–American lunch and dinner menus are "daring" and "dazzling"; its fans call it a "gem" in an "elegant", "sophisticated", "thoroughly civilized" "oasis."

Chinois on Main/SM | 27 | 22 | 22 | $44 |
2709 Main St. (bet. Rose Ave. & Ocean Park Blvd.), Santa Monica, 310-392-9025
U – Many consider this Californian-Japanese-Chinese–Pacific New Waver "one of the best restaurants in America", and for good reason – this is the "most creative and unusual" of Wolfgang Puck's constantly expanding dynasty (Spago in LA, Las Vegas and Tokyo; Granita in Malibu, Postrio in SF); a "David Lynchian fantasy" with "an awesome noise level" and "absolutely brilliant cuisine", "it's good as gold", and nearly as expensive.

Citrus/M | 26 | 22 | 22 | $43 |
6703 Melrose Ave. (1 block west of Highland Ave.), LA, 213-857-0034
U – Cheerful, avuncular chef Michel Richard's best creation is this French-Californian restaurant where the ladies who lunch and the power brokers overlap over salads and grilled fish; this is "haute cuisine that's worth the price of admission", with "heavenly food" served in an "airy atmosphere"; don't miss the "legendary lemon raspberry tart" at this "apogee of LA cuisine."

LOS ANGELES | F | D | S | C |

Diaghilev | 27 | 28 | 28 | $54 |
Bel Age Hotel, 1001 N. San Vicente Blvd. (south of Sunset Blvd.), West Hollywood, 310-854-1111
U – "You'll feel like a czar" at this Franco-Russian hotel "beauty" offering some of the "most romantic", "most elegant" dining in town; it's a "special occasion" place where you wear your Chanel and Armani while nibbling on caviar and drinking flavored vodka, cared for by "the best maitre d' in LA"; plan to be "pampered"...but "bring along your savings book"; dinner only.

Drago | 24 | 20 | 20 | $37 |
2628 Wilshire Blvd. (26th St.), Santa Monica, 310-828-1585
U – Chef Celestino Drago's Wilshire eatery is simply "the best Sicilian", a "highly polished" Modern Italian specializing in the fish-and herb-intensive flavors of his homeland, found in dishes like the pasta flavored with bottarga, a pressed, dried salted fish roe called bottarga – "these are not subtle tastes", but they do make for "great Italian"; "Celestino does it again."

Dynasty Room/SM | 25 | 27 | 26 | $46 |
Westwood Marquis Hotel, 930 Hilgard Ave. (bet. Weyburn & Le Conte Aves.), Westwood, 310-208-8765
U – "Quiet", "dressy", "elegant" Classic French in the middle of chaotic Westwood near UCLA; the "beautiful living room–like atmosphere" is "great for business breakfasts" and "special occasions"; it's "surprisingly great for a hotel", a "hidden gem" that some say "equals the best of SF and NY."

Granita/SM | 25 | 25 | 22 | $41 |
23725 W. Malibu Rd. (Webb Way & P.C.H.), Malibu, 310-456-0488
U – Though Chinois ranks higher, this may be "Wolfgang Puck's best restaurant" – an "incredibly casual" celebrity-filled, excitingly decorated, underwater fantasy where the food is basically "Spago-by-the-Sea", which means pizza and pastas, and lots of grilled seafood dishes; that it's the "best restaurant in Malibu" goes without saying (there's no competition); the only real grumbles involve the "impossible reservation policy" and, to a few, "overly cute" decor – the "Little Mermaid meets Frank Gehry."

Grill, The/M | 24 | 20 | 23 | $37 |
9560 Dayton Way (bet. Camden & Rodeo Drs.), Beverly Hills, 310-276-0615
U – "American food at its very best" is what you'll find at this steak and seafood "classic" that has "the feel of San Francisco in Beverly Hills" and serves "the best steaks, chops" and "incredible spuds"; the decor is macho traditional with lots of wood, brass and leather, where "a man's got to be a man to be a man."

LOS ANGELES

| F | D | S | C |

Ivy, The/SM | 24 | 23 | 19 | $41 |
113 N. Robertson Blvd. (bet. 3rd St. & Beverly Blvd.), LA, 310-274-8303
M – Next to Spago, this is one of the surest spots in town to see celebrities, who show up in droves at this "attitude uber alles" Modern American, where your ability to get a reservation has long been a reflection of the success of your last mini-series; the famous and the famous wannabes crowd into this ersatz cottage where they serve the "best crabcakes anywhere", but service can be "supercilious"; don't be fooled by the tatty picket fence in front – "when you're insulted here, you're insulted by the best."

Jody Maroni's | 24 | 6 | 14 | $8 |
Sausage Kingdom/SMX
2011 Ocean Front Walk (The Boardwalk, north of Venice Blvd.), Venice, 310-306-1995
U – Effusive, ebullient Jody has made the Venice Boardwalk "the sausage capital of LA" by setting a "new sausage quality standard"; he operates out of nothing more than a simple stand, but it has a great floor show that features Jody himself cajoling roller bladers, muscleheads and floss bikini-wearers to sample "the best sausages anywhere"; go for the exotic flavors (sausage flavored with bacon and maple syrup!) at this "pig – and other creatures – heaven"; N.B. Jody's dogs are now at LAX and Dodger Stadium.

Joe's/S | 24 | 15 | 22 | $30 |
1023 Abbot Kinney Blvd. (bet. B'way & Westminster Ave.), Venice, 310-399-5811
U – Chef Joe Miller (ex Brentwood Bar & Grill) "hits his stride" in the storefront that propelled Hans Rockenwagner to fame and fortune; this "favorite discovery" is the place to go for outstanding food on a limited Californian menu that includes "the best vegetable soup in LA" and "great roast pork" at "very good prices"; the consensus: "Joe is doing everything right."

Katsu/M | 25 | 20 | 21 | $33 |
1972 Hillhurst Ave. (2 blocks east of Vermont Ave.), Los Feliz, 213-665-1891
U – This "minimalist masterpiece" ranks as "one of the best sushi houses in town" (only Matsuhisa and Sushi Nozawa rate higher), serving food that's "art at its peak of realization" – "beautiful", "elegant" and "delicate"; "expensive and worth every penny", orders of raw fish are created by "magicians with knives" who are "true artisans working with fish as their medium."

LOS ANGELES | F | D | S | C |

La Toque/M | 26 | 21 | 23 | $43 |
8171 Sunset Blvd. (bet. La Cienega & Crescent Hts. Blvds.), West Hollywood, 213-656-7515
U – Chef-owner Ken Frank's "intimate and interesting" Nouvelle French is a "high-quality classic" respected by most local foodies, who find Frank a "better chef than a restaurateur" serving "some of the best food in LA"; the fare is "always a taste treat" at this "imaginative", "never pretentious", "fab" experience.

Lawry's Prime Rib/SM | 24 | 20 | 23 | $31 |
55 N. La Cienega Blvd. (½ block north of Wilshire Blvd.), Beverly Hills, 310-652-2827
M – This "must for visiting Japanese friends" is what you might expect "if Disney opened Meatland" – a beef-intensive Southern California tradition, where generations of locals have taken Mom for her birthday and Dad for Father's Day; it's generally considered the place to go for the "best prime rib anywhere, ever", carved to order at your table, and served by waitresses who "sound like audio-automatons"; it's not just "classic", it's downright "mythic"; dinner only.

Le Chardonnay/M | 26 | 26 | 24 | $42 |
8284 Melrose Ave. (Sweetzer Ave.), LA, 213-655-8880
U – "Very romantic" Melrose Avenue replica of a Parisian bistro serving "bistro food, California-style", i.e. no cassoulet and no choucroute garnie, but lots of "lip-smacking roast chicken" and "well-prepared fish" in a "luxurious" "art nouveau" setting; some call this the "most romantic bistro east of the Left Bank" and a "trip to Paris for the evening"; "the best seat in the house is in front of the fire with the one you love."

Locanda Veneta/M | 26 | 16 | 21 | $34 |
8638 W. Third St. (bet. San Vicente & Robertson Blvds.), LA, 310-274-1893
U – LA's top-rated trattoria is "better than anything we found in Venezia"; it's an "always-crowded" "Venetian beach shack" across from Cedars-Sinai, where reservations are the "toughest in town", and for good reason: this is "authentic Italian", perhaps the "best pasta in the whole city", with "gnocchi so light they need to be tied to the plate."

L'Orangerie/SM | 25 | 28 | 24 | $55 |
903 N. La Cienega Blvd. (bet. Melrose Ave. & Santa Monica Blvd.), West Hollywood, 310-652-9770
M – "Gorgeous", "elegant", "chic" and "lovely" are just a few of the raves directed at this last bastion of "incredibly expensive" Classic French dining; this "mini-Versailles" is home to the "best French food this side of the Rockies"; "if you can afford it, there's nothing better" than this "Lutece West"; it's the "best place in town" to be "romanced by food, wine and a wealthy lover"; dinner only.

LOS ANGELES

| F | D | S | C |

Matsuhisa/SM | 28 | 15 | 22 | $43 |

129 N. La Cienega Blvd. (½ block north of Wilshire Blvd.), Beverly Hills, 310-659-9639

U – Only Joachim Splichal's Patina ranks higher than Nobu Matsuhisa's "awesome" Japanese seafooder, with just a fraction of a point separating the two; the man who may be the "best Japanese chef in the world" works in a "simple", "casual" storefront, creating dishes that "have no equal" in a cooking style that's part Peruvian and part Nobu's alone; this remains one of the most popular spots in LA, offering the "best sushi outside of Japan" and "seafood dishes like we've never tasted anywhere else"; "hauntingly good", this food is "absolutely world-class."

Michael's/SM | 24 | 25 | 22 | $46 |

1147 3rd St. (n. of Wilshire Blvd.), Santa Monica, 310-451-0843

U – Although Michael McCarty, one of the fathers of Californian cuisine, spends half the year dealing with his New York branch, this New American remains one of the "quintessential" LA dining experiences; a "truly special place", it's "worth every penny" to sit in Michael's art-filled dining room, or on his celebrity-filled patio, eating the "best Californian cuisine in California"; you "can't beat the garden on a warm summer's night" for going "first-class in everything."

Parkway Grill/SM | 25 | 23 | 22 | $33 |

510 S. Arroyo Pkwy. (north of California Blvd.), Pasadena, 818-795-1001

U – Reviewers regularly compare it to Spago (e.g. "Spago for the rest of us") but "Parkway has a life of its own"; this "trendy", reasonably priced Californian offers the same open kitchen, the same designer pizzas and the same innovative food, but "at a fraction of the cost"; fans say "it's worth the trip" to eat some of "the best food in Southern California", and if "Spago has the PR...Parkway has everything else."

Patina/SM | 28 | 23 | 25 | $49 |

5955 Melrose Ave. (1 block west of Cahuenga Blvd.), LA, 213-467-1108

U – For a second year, master chef Joachim Splichal's "superb", "incredibly innovative", "understated" flagship restaurant (with sibling Pinot, recently opened in Sherman Oaks) is No. 1 for food in LA; reviewers rave that this stylish modern French-Californian is "unquestionably the best in town, and maybe in America"; equally praised is "lack of attitude" (it's incredible how friendly the staff is); in short, "it's pretty damn good."

LOS ANGELES

| | F | D | S | C |

Pinot/M
| | - | - | - | E |

12969 Ventura Blvd. (bet. Coldwater Canyon & Fulton Aves.), Studio City, 818-990-0500
Joachim Splichal goes Val, gutting La Serre to create a bistro, Splichal-style, which means a Magrittan interior and dishes that are bistro north-by-northwest; the early word is "fantastic", though the curse of the Valley has yet to be broken – suburban crowds don't like to spend major money on curious food.

Regent Beverly Wilshire/SM
| 24 | 27 | 25 | $43 |

Regent Beverly Wilshire Hotel, 9500 Wilshire Blvd. (1½ blocks west of Beverly Dr.), Beverly Hills, 310-274-8179
U – Replacing the legendary, mawkish El Padrino Room, this "elegant" Continental has become a center for "serious" dining "as good as any hotel restaurant in the world"; it's one of three "very civilized" places to eat at the Regent, including the "lovely" Lobby Lounge and the "perfect" coffee shop; all in all, this is the "most European site to dine in LA."

Rex II Ristorante/M
| 25 | 28 | 24 | $54 |

617 S. Olive St. (bet. 6th & 7th Sts.), Downtn., 213-627-2300
M – Next to L'Orangerie the most expensive restaurant in LA, and easily one of the top Italians, Mauro Vincenti's flagship art deco "masterpiece" "will impress the true gourmet"; it's a "best-of-the-best" "very special-occasion" restaurant where you get elegant, "small portions of remarkable food for lots of dough"; it's just a pity "you can't eat the Lalique."

Rockenwagner/SM
| 25 | 20 | 22 | $39 |

2435 Main St. (bet. Pico & Ocean Park Blvds.), Santa Monica, 310-399-6504
U – This "architecturally incredible", "bright and shiny" Californian-Eclectic, not far from Chinois, presents the "awesome cooking" of chef-owner Hans Rockenwagner, who serves "dishes touched by genius"; the cooking at this big brother to Fama is "as good as it gets", thanks to the signature "perfect crab soufflé", "wonderful lamb" and "great sea scallops"; be sure to try Hans's very European breakfasts, his "unique breads" and cheeses, which you can eat on the patio while smelling the fresh breezes off the ocean a few blocks away.

Saddle Peak Lodge/S
| 23 | 27 | 23 | $40 |

419 Cold Canyon Rd. (east of Malibu Canyon Rd., bet. Mulholland Hwy. & Puma Rd.), Calabasas, 818-222-3888
M – "Great game in a breathtaking, romantic setting", where you "can almost hear the theme from Wild Kingdom"; this "rustic", "very nonvegetarian" Contemporary American, situated high in the "mountains of Malibu", is one of LA's most "exotic" destination restaurants and always "worth the trip" for the "roaring fireplaces"; with "heads and horns" on the walls, it's an eatery that "makes men feel manly."

LOS ANGELES

| F | D | S | C |

72 Market Street/SM | 24 | 21 | 21 | $39 |
72 Market St. (bet. Pacific Ave. & Venice Boardwalk), Venice, 310-392-8720
U – This "totally cool" American Comfort Food specialist is the place to go for "great meat loaf", "fabulous kick-ass chili" and "wonderful mashed potatoes" served in an artfully minimalist room, where co-owner Dudley Moore shows up to play piano and partner Tony Bill holds court at the front table; this "Venice oasis" is big brother to Beverly Hills's Maple Drive.

Shiro/S | 27 | 14 | 22 | $34 |
1505 Mission St. (½ block west of Fair Oaks Ave.), South Pasadena, 818-799-4774
U – "Zen minimalist" French–Japanese "Pacific Rim seafood house", where afishionados purr over the "best catfish in the world"; equally praised are the "outstanding Mexican shrimp", "peppered tuna", "salmon mousse ravioli", and "blueberry and pear wontons"; some find this "real surprise" in restaurant poor South Pasadena a semi-religious experience – "if God cooked fish, this is how it would taste"; dinner only.

Spago/LSM | 25 | 20 | 20 | $41 |
1114 Horn Ave. (Sunset Blvd.), West Hollywood, 310-652-4025
U – The restaurant that "every visitor to LA wants to go to" remains the toughest ticket in town if you're a civilian, though celebs get in with ease – it's the "ultimate proof there's no such thing as democracy"; Wolfgang Puck's little pizza shop–cum–Californian trend-setter is the one place where everyone who's anyone wants to see, be seen and eat; it "meets the test of time" and the test of the palate as well, still serving "the best" pizza grills and desserts in a "stunning" setting overlooking all of L.A.

Sushi Nozawa/M | 26 | 11 | 17 | $31 |
11288 Ventura Blvd. (2 blocks west of Vineland Ave.), Studio City, 818-508-7017
U – "All bow to Nozawa, King of Fishes" at this understated Valley "sushi bar for purists" that's simply "the best" – "in town"; fans give high praise to "absolutely excellent", "superb" sushi prepared by a "master" chef who "really knows what he's doing"; says one worshiper, "a businessman from Japan told me this is the best sushi he's ever had."

LOS ANGELES | F | D | S | C |

Valentino/M | 26 | 23 | 24 | $47 |
3115 Pico Blvd. (2 blocks west of Bundy Dr.), Santa Monica, 310-829-4313
U – LA's Top Italian for the fourth year in a row transcends its jewellike status; "charming" Piero Selvaggio's many regular diners call this "cozy yet modern" space "one of the great restaurants of the world", the "equal of Gualtiero Marchesi and San Domenico" and even "better than anything we had in Italy"; expect "stratospheric prices", but also expect a "class act" that "coddles you with classic cuisine in a classic restaurant"; dinner only, except lunch on Friday.

Water Grill/SM | 25 | 24 | 23 | $37 |
544 S. Grand Ave. (bet. 5th & 6th Sts.), Downtown, 213-891-0900
U – Praised as "LA's best" seafood house since the day it opened, this "very San Francisco" fish and shellfish eatery became an "instant classic", with a "remarkable" oyster bar and a "luxurious, clubby" feeling; the cooking tends to be regional – the menu divided into dishes from Hawaii, the Pacific Northwest, etc. – and though it "can be expensive", it does offer bargains: the smoked seafood sandwiches are "the best deals in town."

Yujean Kang's/SM | 25 | 18 | 22 | $34 |
67 N. Raymond Ave. (bet. Walnut St. & Colorado Blvd.), Pasadena, 818-585-0855
M – "Some of the best Chinese food in the world" is found at this "wildly innovative" Nouvelle Chinese, an understated room on a Pasadena side street where "each bite is a new experience"; reviewers often use the term "gourmet Chinese" to describe the "small portions" of outstanding tea duck, cloud soup, lamb and eggplant, Chinese polenta and "stupendous" when it comes to the closing cheesecake.

MIAMI

TOP 30 RESTAURANTS
(In order of food rating)

Restaurant	Cuisine Type
29 – Mark's Place	Amer. Contemp.
26 – Chef Allen's	Amer. Contemp.
Grand Cafe	Continental
Fish Market	Seafood
25 – Casa Larios	Cuban
Le Festival	French Classic
"a Mano"	Amer. Contemp.
Joe's Stone Crab	Seafood
Aragon Cafe	Amer. Contemp./Seafood
Le Pavillon	Continental
Palm	Steakhouse
24 – Brickell Club	Amer. Contemp.
Casa Rolandi	Northern Italian
Bistro	French Bistro
Forge	Amer. Tradition.
Il Tulipano	N/S Italian
La Bussola	Northern Italian
Christy's	Steakhouse
Caffe Abbracci	Northern Italian
Dominique's	Continental
Ramiro's	Spanish
Hy-Vong	Vietnamese
23 – Caffe Baci	Nuova Cucina Italian
Osteria del Teatro	N/S Italian
Didier's	French
Su Shin	Chinese
Dining Galleries	Amer. Tradition.
B.C. Chong	Chinese
Ruth's Chris	Steakhouse
Yuca	Cuban

OTHER TOP PLACES
(In alphabetical order)

Cafe Chauveron	French Classic
Casa Juancho	Spanish
Charade	Continental
Fleming	Continental/Seafood
Mezzanotte	Nuova Cucina Itaian
Monty's Stone Crab	Seafood
Rascal House	Jewish
Thai Orchid	Thai
Unicorn Village	Health Food
Veranda	Amer. Contemp.

MIAMI | F | D | S | C |

"a Mano"/S | 25 | 23 | 23 | $45 |
Betsy Ross Hotel, 1440 Ocean Dr. (bet. 14th & 15th Sts.), Miami Beach, 305-531-6266
M – Star-chef Norman Van Aken "dares to be original" at this Contemporary American that has taken South Beach by storm with its "four-star-quality food" and "warm and inviting" atmosphere; while a few find the food "too eclectic" and "contrived", the great majority adore the "incredibly creative" "New World Cuisine" and like to watch the "beautiful people" who come to be seen, be spoiled and eat at what some are already calling "the best in Miami."

Aragon Cafe | 25 | 26 | 25 | $40 |
Colonnade Hotel, 180 Aragon Ave. (Ponce de Leon Blvd.), Coral Gables, 305-448-9966
M – "One of Coral Gables's classiest joints" offers "marvelous" Contemporary Florida seafood and "almost too attentive service" in a "most elegant" setting; a few feel it's inconsistent for the price, and that it's "detached and a bit stuffy", but the majority report that the ever-changing menu is "exciting" and even "superb"; chef Lisa Palermo is adding more pizzazz.

B.C. Chong/S | 23 | 17 | 19 | $23 |
915 Lincoln Rd. (bet. Jefferson & Michigan Aves.), Miami Beach, 305-672-1688
U – "An interesting departure from typical Chinese", this newly relocated "upscale" restaurant's "imaginative seafood" makes it "a welcome addition" to the Lincoln Road area; the sophisticated setting is a major improvement over the old Coconut Grove address, and though a few feel it's "expensive for Chinese", most rate it "the best in South Florida."

Bistro, The/S | 24 | 22 | 23 | $32 |
2611 Ponce de Leon Blvd. (bet. Valencia & Almeria Sts.), Coral Gables, 305-442-9671
U – "An old favorite that keeps up with the times", this "charming, cozy and crowded" French bistro in the Gables offers "consistently high-quality" food (e.g., rack of lamb, veal steak with lemon sauce and grilled shrimp with basil vinaigrette) and solid service; though it produces "few surprises", the excellent preparation and fresh ingredients make innovation unnecessary; business lunches are especially popular.

Brickell Club | 24 | 28 | 25 | $35 |
Capital Bank Bldg., 1221 Brickell Ave., 27th fl. (bet. 12th & 13th Sts.), Miami, 305-536-9000
U – "Beautiful vistas of Downtown Miami and Biscayne Bay" are the most obvious attraction at this elegant rooftop private club that's open to the public only at dinner; "excellent gourmet" Contemporary American food, "posh" ambiance and "very personal" service help lead our surveyors to conclude that this is "what Miami is all about."

MIAMI | F | D | S | C |

Cafe Chauveron/S | 22 | 23 | 22 | $42 |

9561 E. Bay Harbor Dr. (southeast corner of Kane Concourse), Bay Harbor, 305-866-8779
M – Older New Yorkers still recall the days when this was a NYC French standout; now just as many Floridians consider this "very elegant" "oldie-but-goodie" spot to be their own; though it offers "excellent" Traditional French cooking, a few describe it as "haughty", "old" and "tired"; P.S. the inside word is that it has improved of late.

Caffe Baci | 23 | 21 | 22 | $31 |

2526 Ponce de Leon Blvd. (bet. Andalusia & Valencia Aves.), Coral Gables, 305-442-0600
U – Its many devotees find this "cousin of Caffe Abbracci" "superb in all respects"; this "little Italian jewel", with its "upbeat, friendly feeling" and "consistently good food" "makes for an elegant lunch", but some say that during the crowded dinner hour you can't hear yourself think.

Caffe Abbracci/LS | 24 | 22 | 22 | $32 |

318 Aragon Ave. (bet. Le Jeune Rd. & Salzedo St.), Coral Gables, 305-441-0700
U – "If you can stand the noise", you'll enjoy this bustling Northern Italian's "dependable", "excellently prepared" meals and "tiramisu to die for"; plan to wait at "this very 'in' spot", but once you're seated, Nino Pernetti, "the most charming restaurateur in Miami", "makes you feel like a personal friend" with abbracci and baci (hugs and kisses).

Casa Larios/S | 25 | 16 | 20 | $13 |

Palm Plaza Shopping Mall, 7929 N.W. 2nd St. (Flagler St.), Miami, 305-266-5494
M – This expanded, traditional Cuban is loved for its "family atmosphere" (Dad cooks, son and daughter run the front and Aunt Lala makes the "incredible desserts"), as well as what many say is simply "the best Cuban food in town" (though a few critics call it merely ordinary); with food and value this solid, it's no wonder the place is often crowded.

Casa Rolandi/LS | 24 | 22 | 21 | $35 |

1930 Ponce de Leon Blvd. (bet. Navarre & Majorca Aves.), Coral Gables, 305-444-2187
M – This "authentic and warm" Tuscan tops the Survey's list of Dade's best Italian restaurants for good reason: reviewers rave about the kitchen's "flair and imagination" and a "chef who is as much fun as the food"; service ranges from "crisp" to "inattentive", and the "cozy" room and stiff prices also get mixed responses.

MIAMI | F | D | S | C |

Casa Juancho/LS | 20 | 21 | 19 | $29 |
2436 S.W. 8th St. (bet. 24th & 25th Aves.), Miami, 305-642-2452
M – "Spanish food – not Cuban" is the draw at this "boisterous", "smoky and crowded" Little Havana "institution" that's a "nice place to take visiting tourists"; though a few critics think it's "all show and no substance", most consider it "quite good" for what it is and say that "the later it is, the better it is", especially around the tapas bar.

Charade/S | 22 | 25 | 21 | $29 |
2900 Ponce de Leon Blvd. (Palermo Ave.), Coral Gables, 305-448-6077
U – For "traditional Gables dining" Continental-style, this "always dependable" if rarely inspiring "classic" makes for "the perfect Mother's Day restaurant"; the "beautiful", "country-fresh" room is the main attraction, especially for "Sunday brunch"; while ratings remain high across the board, the efficient but "often impersonal" staff and "tasty" but "not memorable" food leave a few diners disappointed.

Chef Allen's/S | 26 | 22 | 24 | $39 |
19088 N.E. 29th Ave. (1 block east of U.S. 1, 191st St.), N. Miami Beach, 305-935-2900
U – "As close to perfection as you can get" say many surveyors about this "innovative" Contemporary American in Aventura, whose talented chef Allen Susser has helped put South Florida on the American culinary map; if his menu "sometimes misses the mark" with its "crazy combinations", Susser's "batting average is very high", producing meals "worth dreaming about"; the "hip", crisp, modern setting, with its dramatic open kitchen, has recently been enlarged; P.S. don't forget to order the "fabulous chocolate souffle."

Christy's/S | 24 | 20 | 23 | $33 |
3101 Ponce de Leon Blvd. (Malaga Ave.), Coral Gables, 305-446-1400
M – Carnivores crowd this "consistently good" steakhouse for "heavy-duty meat eating" in an "English-club" setting; the "1950s-style" American food and slightly "stuffy" decor may strike some as "stodgy", but it's a hit with local "power brokers" and a longtime local favorite – "where June and Ward Cleaver take the family."

Didier's | 23 | 20 | 22 | $34 |
325 Alcazar Ave. (bet. Le Jeune Rd. & Salzedo St.), Coral Gables, 305-448-0312
U – "The "new King of French", this Gables "touch of Provence" combines "lighter sauces" and "authentic" cooking with a "charming" – albeit "cramped" – bistro setting and "obliging" service to create a "culinary treat"; though some surveyors wish the menu selection were broader, chef-owner Didier Collongette has kept it small to focus on quality, offering "gracious dining" at fair prices.

MIAMI | F | D | S | C |

Dining Galleries, The/S | 23 | 26 | 24 | $39 |
Fontainebleau Hilton, 4441 Collins Ave. (44th St.), Miami Beach, 305-538-2000
U – Our surveyors enthusiastically report that this well-rated American restaurant at the Fontainebleau offers "elegance all the way": the "ultimate Sunday brunch", a "beautiful" French setting and "consistently good service"; "you forget you're in a hotel" in this "great place to make an impression."

Dominique's/S | 24 | 25 | 22 | $42 |
Alexander Hotel, 5225 Collins Ave. (Arthur Godfrey Blvd.), Miami Beach, 305-861-5252
M – Walk through the glass-enclosed garden to this "lush" enclave "of the rich and famous", with its French-accented Contemporary Continental "food as entertainment" – alligator and rattlesnake on the menu – "high-class" decor and "pampering" staff; most call it "all-around excellent", though for a few it's "a big disappointment."

Fish Market, The/S | 26 | 24 | 23 | $34 |
Omni International Hotel, 1601 Biscayne Blvd. (1 mile north of Bayside Marketplace), Miami, 305-374-4399
U – In the Downtown Omni is a "secret" "waiting to be discovered" – "one of Miami's great places for seafood", a mirrored, marbled, high-ceilinged dining room that many find "superlative"; the "impeccable service" makes it "a nice place to take out-of-towners", especially if they're paying – but even if you are.

Fleming | 23 | 17 | 21 | $25 |
8511 S.W. 136th St. (U.S. 1), Miami, 305-232-6444
U – "A local favorite, and deservedly so", this Continental specializing in seafood remains one of the area's "best bets" for "reliable" dining at moderate prices; its popularity can be attributed to "large portions" of "solid" – some say "heavy" – food in simple, warm surroundings; it's a good idea to "reserve a week in advance."

Forge, The/S | 24 | 26 | 23 | $39 |
432 Arthur Godfrey Rd. (bet. Pinetree Dr. & Alton Rd.), Miami Beach, 305-538-8533
U – Only two of the rooms in this "landmark" of "elegant American dining" have reopened after the restaurant was partially destroyed by fire; although the "renowned wine cellar" and hodgepodge of "museum-quality" artifacts that created its "bizarrely opulent decor" were spared, it may take years to restore the entire restaurant to its former glory.

MIAMI

| F | D | S | C |

Grand Cafe/S | 26 | 27 | 25 | $42 |
Grand Bay Hotel, 2669 S. Bayshore Dr.,
Coconut Grove, 305-858-9600
U – The Grand Bay Hotel's "simply grand" Contemporary Continental is beloved for its "East-meets-West cuisine" and its "romantic and beautiful" setting; the "luscious food", "outstanding now that Chef Suki is back in the kitchen", makes it "almost a must" even if it weren't for the "nearly perfect service" and the "grand dining room", which rivals "the prettiest in town"; "for a special occasion", it's "a justified blowing of megabucks."

Hy-Vong/SX | 24 | 8 | 12 | $19 |
3458 S.W. 8th St. (bet. 34th & 35th Aves.), Miami,
305-446-3674
U – Proving that "good things come in small packages" is this "always-crowded" Vietnamese storefront bargain hidden in the heart of Little Havana; "this place may be a dump, but the food is extraordinary", and the "sweet people" will explain the menu to you; so what if "you wait forever" for your food?

Il Tulipano | 24 | 18 | 20 | $41 |
11052 Biscayne Blvd. (110th Terrace), N. Miami,
305-893-4811
M – "Some of the best food" in South Florida goes hand in hand with an infamous "attitude problem" at this "congested" but attractive North Miami roadside trattoria; "the pasta dishes make you feel like you're in heaven", but the "uncomfortable" atmosphere and an "aggressive" staff that "caters to steadies" and sometimes has problems totaling the bill may bring you back to earth; still, fans say the hassles "are worth it."

Joe's Stone Crab/S | 25 | 16 | 20 | $34 |
227 Biscayne St. (south of 1st St., bet. Washington & Collins Aves.), Miami Beach, 305-673-0365
U – After more than three-quarters of a century, South Beach's "most famous landmark" still rates "the best for stone crabs" – in fact, most think there's "no comparison" with any other; "go very early" or at lunch to avoid the "intolerable waits" and "madhouse atmosphere"; "the maitre d' must be the richest man in Miami."

La Bussola/S | 24 | 22 | 23 | $33 |
270 Giralda Ave. (west of Ponce de Leon Blvd.), Coral Gables, 305-445-8783
U – This stylish Gables Northern Italian has a very good reputation, and it's largely earned; a kitchen that "can be extraordinary" (the pumpkin ravioli "gives new meaning to the word ecstasy"), the "very European" frescoed room and "delightful service" all add up to a place that's "pricey, but the quality is there."

MIAMI | F | D | S | C |

Le Festival | 25 | 23 | 25 | $34 |
2120 Salzedo St. (Alcazar Ave.), Coral Gables, 305-442-8545
U – For some 15 years, this place has set "the Gables French standard", delivering "old-fashioned", "honest" Gallic fare that "never disappoints"; "conservative and refined", with "superb service" and a "lovely" flower-filled room, it's "superb for entertaining" and for quiet conversation in "one of the smaller rooms"; its only possible flaw is that it's "too formal to be much fun."

Le Pavillon | 25 | 27 | 25 | $44 |
Intercontinental Hotel, 100 Chopin Plaza, Biscayne Blvd. (bet. S.E. 1st & 2nd Sts.), Miami, 305-577-1000
U – Set within a splendorous Downtown hotel, this pricey – but worth it – bastion of "conservative dining" is "professionally perfect", if "a bit stuffy"; it's the sort of place where you can "expect to meet a celebrity" and are safe taking important clients; the "enjoyable" Continental fare helps make this right for "a wonderful special-occasion lunch or dinner."

Mark's Place/S | 29 | 24 | 25 | $41 |
Sans Souci Shops, 2286 N.E. 123rd. St. (west side of Broad Causeway), N. Miami, 305-893-6888
U – "It seems impossible", but what many consider to be the "best restaurant in South Florida" just gets better and better; star-chef Mark Militello prepares "state-of-the-art", regionally derived cooking that's "innovative and consistently rewarding", served in a "trendy", postmodern setting with a "bright" open kitchen and unparalleled people-watching; sure, it's pricey, but "never mind the cost" – "imagination plus execution and quality equals great food."

Mezzanotte/LS | 22 | 17 | 16 | $33 |
1200 Washington Ave. (12th St.), Miami Beach, 305-673-4343
M – "Always crazy and noisy", this "hip" Nuova Cucina Italian in the Art Deco District is a hotbed of "people-watching people" who "bring their own mirrors" (you may want to "bring your own earplugs" too); this "best late-night spot" for the "Miami Vice crowd" serves food that's "better than you'd expect", though maybe "not worth the wait" caused by a no-reservations policy.

Monty's Stone Crab/S | 19 | 18 | 17 | $27 |
2550 S. Bayshore Dr. (Aviation Ave.), Coconut Grove, 305-858-1431
M – The action's outside at this bayside seafood restaurant, where a "typically Floridian beer-drinking clientele" sits at picnic tables, munches on "good conch fritters" and dances to reggae music; inside you'll find a "dark" room redeemed by a "wonderful raw bar"; it's frequently compared to Joe's: detractors dismiss Monty's as an "imitator", while admirers say it's "every bit as good, without the wait."

MIAMI | F | D | S | C |

Osteria del Teatro/S | 23 | 17 | 21 | $35 |
1443 Washington (Espanola Way), Miami Beach, 305-538-7850
M – "See and be seen" at this "trendy", "crowded" Italian located in the old art deco Cameo Theater building; one of the first of a slew of Italian restaurants to open in South Beach, it remains one of the best, thanks to its "wonderful food" and "great service"; although a few say it's "overrated, overpriced" and "lacks finesse", most surveyors find it "congenial and accommodating."

Palm, The/S | 25 | 17 | 20 | $41 |
9650 E. Bay Harbor Dr. (1 block north of Kane Concourse), Bay Harbor, 305-868-7256
U – "Nothing succeeds like excess" should be the motto of this branch of the "top-notch" New York–based steakhouse chain, whose "steaks and lobsters too large to eat" come with "Big Apple prices" to match; a "clubby" setting and "surly" waiters also make transplanted New Yorkers feel at home.

Ramiro's/S | 24 | 23 | 24 | $41 |
2700 Ponce de Leon Blvd. (Almeria), Coral Gables, 305-443-7605
M – "Sensational Nouvelle Spanish cuisine", "beautiful decor" and "great waiters" make this Gables favorite a "wonderful dining experience" for most of our respondents; even those who find the surroundings pretentious and the staff "erratic" and "glib" concede that the dishes are "creative and tantalizing to the eye"; "what food!! what prices!!!"

Rascal House/SX | 23 | 9 | 17 | $16 |
17190 Collins Ave. (172nd St.), N. Miami Beach, 305-947-4581
U – If you don't mind having "first-quality food thrown at you", this "historic palace of overeating" with the "best Jewish food around", "vintage waitresses with starched hankies" and "dinerlike atmosphere" will suit you fine; "a real experience and an old favorite", this place "should be put in the Smithsonian."

Ruth's Chris Steak House/S | 23 | 20 | 20 | $38 |
Intracoastal Mall, Sunny Isles, 3913 N.E. 163rd St. (bet. A1A & Biscayne Blvd.), N. Miami Beach, 305-949-0100
M – North Miami Beach's outlet of the popular coast-to-coast steakhouse chain doesn't always live up to the group's fine reputation due to an "inconsistent kitchen"; nonetheless, most diners still think the pricey steaks and à la carte side orders are "the best in town."

MIAMI

| F | D | S | C |

Su Shin/S | 23 | 15 | 19 | $20 |
14316 Biscayne Blvd. (143rd St.), N. Miami Beach, 305-956-9180
10501 S.W. 88th St. (bet. 107th Ave. & Rte. 874, Kendall Dr. exit), Kendall, 305-271-3235
U – "The very best of Japan in South Florida" can be found at these "excellent, consistent and quick" "standbys" with pleasant, "clean" surroundings; "unequaled sushi", along with "friendly service" and "dependable value", more than make up for "no real decor."

Thai Orchid/S | 22 | 20 | 21 | $20 |
Sunset Shops, 9565 S.W. 72nd St. (95th Ave.), Kendall, 305-279-8583
317 Miracle Mile (bet. Salzedo St. & Le Jeune Rd.), Coral Gables, 305-443-6364
U – "A treat for the senses", these twin Thais have many fans who rate them among the "best of their kind in South Florida"; not only is the cooking "excellent and consistent", but the decor – dominated, of course, by orchids – is unremittingly "pleasing to the eye."

Unicorn Village/S | 21 | 21 | 18 | $19 |
Waterways Shopping Ctr., 3565 N.E. 207th St. (1 mile east of U.S. 1), Aventura, 305-933-8829
M – "You don't have to be a health-food lover to enjoy" this natural food restaurant overlooking a marina; most diners say its "fresh and varied" menu is "so good you don't know it's health food"; it's "perfect for curing junk-food guilt."

Veranda at Turnberry Isle Resort Club/S | 22 | 26 | 23 | $35 |
1999 West Country Club Dr. (behind Aventura Mall), Aventura, 305-932-6200
U – A "first-class, imaginative menu" from the kitchen of chef Robbin Haas and a "beautifully elegant" room make this New American, open to resort guests and club members only, "a treat", even if a few find its "great potential not yet fully realized" (fans are hoping that it soon goes public); the service "needs a little practice", but this is a quibble.

Yuca/S | 23 | 21 | 21 | $35 |
177 Giralda Ave. (east of Ponce de Leon Blvd.), Coral Gables, 305-444-4448
U – "One of the most exciting restaurants in Miami", this "fabulous Nouvelle Cuban" has food writers from all over the country swarming; chances are that "Mama never cooked like" chef Douglas Rodriguez, whose "elegant", "modern" interpretations strike many as "unbelievably delicious"; naysayers, a small minority, say it "tries too hard to be different" and go ballistic over the prices; now in larger quarters, it's got a full bar for mingling with the rich and famous.

MILWAUKEE

TOP 5 RESTAURANTS
(In order of food rating)

Restaurant
26 – Sally's Steak House
25 – Grenadier's
24 – English Room
23 – Karl Ratzsch's
       Immigrant Room

Cuisine Type
Steakhouse
Continental
Amer. Tradition./French
German
Amer. Tradition.

OTHER TOP PLACES
(In alphabetical order)

Mader's German
Mimma's Cafe
Pandl's in Bayside
Sanford Restaurant
Three Brothers

German
Northern Italian
Amer. Tradition.
Amer. Contemp./French
Serbian

| F | D | S | C |

English Room, The/S | 24 | 24 | 23 | $35 |
Pfister Hotel, 424 E. Wisconsin Ave. (Jefferson St.),
Milwaukee, 414-273-8222
U – Kind of like the Cape Cod Room" in Chicago but better, this "fine old" hotel dining room offers "superb" "traditional" French-American cuisine equal to the "elegance" of the environs, plus "unusual seasonal specials" that keep return visits "interesting."

Grenadier's | 25 | 22 | 24 | $36 |
747 N. Broadway (Mason St.), Milwaukee, 414-276-0747
M – Perfect for "business or romance", this "elegant" Continental in an unlikely location "beneath a noisy parking garage" is "among the best Milwaukee has to offer"; critics sniff that visitors "don't need Manhattan in Milwaukee", no matter how good the food or the proper "English" service may be.

Immigrant Room, The/S | 23 | 25 | 24 | $40 |
The American Club, Highland Dr. (bet. Orchard & School Sts.), Kohler, 414-457-8888
M – "Fine", "hearty" regional Midwestern fare prepared with French accents plus an "exceptional wine list" recommend this "très expensive" dinner spot, where the decor is "beautiful" and jackets are required; the food may be "wonderful", but there are scattered complaints of "strange" service by "Stepford people – like robots."

MILWAUKEE

| F | D | S | C |

Karl Ratzsch's/S | 23 | 23 | 22 | $26 |
320 E. Mason St. (Broadway & Milwaukee Sts.), Milwaukee, 414-276-2720
U – Hey it's Milwaukee, and you're going to eat German food, so it might as well be this "big", "traditional" "institution" with its "great old-world" ambiance, "romantic" string trio and the "best" German food in "Milwaukee", "Wisconsin" or "on the planet" – it's "good times" all around.

Mader's German Restaurant/S | 22 | 23 | 21 | $23 |
1037 N. Old World Third St. (Highland Ave.), Milwaukee, 414-271-3377
M – This historic, "old-world Milwaukee institution" is understandably "crowded" due to its "good heavy German eats", a "cozy", "friendly atmosphere" and an entertaining second-floor museum; though detractors call it "touristy" and "too commercial", it's "a must when you're in the area."

Mimma's Cafe*/S | 23 | 17 | 20 | $27 |
1307 E. Brady St. (Arlington St.), Milwaukee, 414-271-7337
M – It was undergoing remodeling at the time of our Survey, so the decor rating for this cafe may be unfairly low, but the "very good" Northern Italian specialties win praise even though they may be "relatively expensive."

Pandl's in Bayside*/LS | 20 | 20 | 21 | $23 |
8825 N. Lake Dr. (Brown Deer Rd.), Milwaukee, 414-352-7300
M – The "excellent" Sunday brunch with the "huge", "yummy" pancakes is one of the "best values" in Milwaukee according to our respondents, who say the rest of the food is "nothing to get excited about", but the "pleasant" setting and "warm" service make this the kind of place people return to.

Sally's Steak House | 26 | 20 | 23 | $25 |
Knickerbocker Hotel, 1028 E. Juneau St. (bet. Prospect & Astor Sts.), Milwaukee, 414-272-5363
U – It's "like a movie set" at this "roaring-'20s" Milwaukee Italian steakhouse decorated with little white lights that make it look like Christmas year round; our reviewers call it "one of the best steakhouses anywhere"; besides the "stupendous" steaks, there are well-liked seafood and pasta dishes, too.

MILWAUKEE

| F | D | S | C |

Sanford Restaurant* | 28 | 25 | 26 | $41 |
1547 N. Jackson St. (Pleasant St.), Milwaukee,
414-276-9608
U – Although located in a prosaic storefront, this "sophisticated" 65-seater wins accolades for its carefully prepared and well-presented French–New American food, "attractive" decor and "superb" service, making it one of "Milwaukee's No. 1" serious restaurants.

Three Brothers, The*/SX | 23 | 15 | 20 | $21 |
2414 S. St. Clair St. (2 blocks north of Russell Ave.), Milwaukee, 414-481-7530
U – The three brothers plus "Mom, Dad, sister, aunt and uncle, too" make this "hard-to-find" Milwaukee Serbian a "friendly spot" where the host's smile is nearly "worth the trip" in itself; the turn-of-the-century tavern setting and tasty food are enough to "save you a trip to the Balkans."

NEW ORLEANS

TOP 30 RESTAURANTS
(In order of food rating)

Restaurant	Cuisine Type
28 – Grill Room	Amer. Tradition.
27 – Commander's Palace	Haute Creole
Bistro at Maison de Ville	Haute New Orleans
La Provence	French Classic
Brigtsen's	Cajun
Galatoire's	Nouvelle Creole
26 – Emeril's	Nouvelle Creole
Versailles	French Classic
Ruth's Chris Steak House	Steakhouse
Sal & Judy's	Italian
25 – Bayona	Haute New Orleans
Young's	Steakhouse
Crozier's	French Bistro
Gautreau's	Nouvelle Creole
Lafitte's Landing	Cajun/Creole
Mr. B's	Haute New Orleans
La Riviera	Italian
Mosca's	Creole/Italian
Christian's	Haute Creole
Andrea's Restaurant	Northern Italian
24 – Trey Yuen	Chinese
Sazerac	Continental
Casamento's	Seafood
Louis XVI	French Classic
23 – China Blossom	Chinese
Little Tokyo	Japanese
Tony Angello's	Italian
Antoine's	Haute Creole
Bon Ton Cafe	Creole
Central Grocery	Sandwiches

OTHER TOP PLACES
(In alphabetical order)

Arnaud's	Haute Creole
Bacco	Creole/Italian
Brennan's Restaurant	Haute Creole
Clancy's	Continental/Creole
Genghis Khan	Chinese
La Cuisine	Creole
L'Economie	French Bistro
Le Jardin	Continental
Little Greek	Greek
Mike's on the Avenue	Eclectic
Palace Cafe	Creole
Uglesich	Seafood
Upperline	Amer. Contemp./Creole

NEW ORLEANS

| F | D | S | C |

Andrea's Restaurant/SM | 25 | 22 | 22 | $29 |
3100 19th St. (bet. Causeway Blvd. & Ridgelake Dr.),
Metairie, 504-834-8583
U – "Bellissima" sums up most of the comments about this Suburban Northern Italian with "wonderful pasta dishes and antipasto"; while the food and attractive decor get high marks, overbooking and long waits, even with reservations, do not.

Antoine's/M | 23 | 23 | 23 | $38 |
713 St. Louis St. (bet. Bourbon & Royal Sts.), 504-581-4422
U – A 150-year-old New Orleans tradition, locals say this grande dame "can be wonderful", but "inconsistent", especially given its top-of-the-line prices; still, many feel it's "New Orleans's most gala experience", especially if you stick to the outstanding appetizers, excellent filet with marchand de vin sauce and soufflé potatoes; locals know the key to dining success here: have your personal waiter call you when something special is on the menu and slip you through the back door to avoid waiting with the tourists.

Arnaud's/SM | 22 | 24 | 23 | $33 |
813 Bienville St. (bet. Bourbon & Dauphine Sts.),
504-522-8767
U – Another New Orleans traditional restaurant, this sprawling, wood-paneled, two-floor classic offers a beautiful setting in a choice of rooms and some of the best food in town (don't miss the shrimp remoulade); though popular with the locals and an excellent place to take out-of-town visitors, some say "it tries hard but sometimes misses"; others brag about the Sunday brunch and point out the especially good luncheon values.

Bacco/SM | – | – | – | VE |
Hotel de la Poste, 310 Chartres St. (bet. Bienville & Conti Sts.), 522-2426
The latest entry from Ralph Brennan and his sister Cindy, of Mr. B's fame, this beautifully appointed Italian is a welcome addition to the French Quarter; the interior decor includes hand-painted, vaulted ceilings and an upscale white-on-white color scheme; the classy, pricey menu offers chef Fernando Saracchi the opportunity to present elegant regional Italian dishes otherwise hard to come by hereabouts, and there's a first-class wine list and good service, too.

Bayona/M | 25 | 24 | 21 | $30 |
430 Dauphine St. (bet. Conti & St. Louis Sts.), 504-525-4455
U – Chef Susan Spicer (ex Bistro at Maison de Ville) has created this French Quarter charmer as one of the "brightest stars" in New Orleans's culinary firmament (try the shrimp and coriander appetizer and the crawfish curry); while some think it's a little noisy, most find the restaurant elegant and Spicer's self-described "New World" cuisine "light and creative."

NEW ORLEANS | F | D | S | C |

Bistro at Maison de Ville/SM | 27 | 23 | 23 | $30 |
Maison de Ville Hotel, 733 Toulouse St. (bet. Royal & Bourbon Sts.), 504-528-9206
U – The exodus of chef John Neal does not seem to have hurt this wonderful, petit French Quarter favorite; his sous-chef, CIA graduate Randy Windham, is carrying on the tradition of creative, original and well-prepared gourmet dishes using New Orleans–area seafoods and spices; if there is a complaint, it's that the space is too cramped.

Bon Ton Cafe/M | 23 | 18 | 21 | $21 |
401 Magazine St. (bet. Poydras & Natchez Sts.), 504-524-3386
U – A variety of crawfish dishes and one of the best bread puddings with whisky sauce keep this CBD old-timer busy; the "quintessential Creole cafe", it's a great business-lunch spot, in part because of its "consistently good" food and in part because of the wonderful, faithful waitresses.

Brennan's Restaurant/SM | 22 | 25 | 22 | $38 |
417 Royal St. (bet. St. Louis & Conti Sts.), 504-525-9711
U – Start with a ramos gin fizz or some champagne and it's still "the best breakfast in town, day or night", even if it's "the most expensive breakfast you'll ever eat"; dinners featuring haute Creole dishes are also good, also cher, but if you start with a cocktail in "the greatest garden patio in the French Quarter", you can expect a meal that's "always delicious."

Brigtsen's/M | 27 | 19 | 23 | $32 |
723 Dante St. (bet. Maple St. & River Rd.), 504-861-7610
U – A small converted house with small but intimate rooms in the Carrollton bend of the river location is home to what many feel is New Orleans's best example of Cajun cuisine; praise is high for chef-owner Frank Brigtsen's "imaginative use of local seafood and fowl"; what some describe as a "happy atmosphere", others complain is "crowded and noisy", but all agree "the man can cook!"

Casamento's/SX | 24 | 18 | 19 | $13 |
4330 Magazine St. (bet. General Pershing & Napoleon Aves.), 504-895-9761
U – "A treasure", "a unique New Orleans experience", "a place where you can eat off the floor", are a few of the glowing words of praise about this spanking clean and easily affordable Uptown seafood old-timer that still has its fabulous tiled walls and floor; the oysters are the stars here, raw or fried, on the half shell or in a crispy po' boy; check the hours – they're a little unorthodox.

NEW ORLEANS

| F | D | S | C |

Central Grocery/SMX | 23 | 15 | 14 | $9 |
923 Decatur St. (bet. St. Philip & Dumaine Sts.),
504-523-1620
U – "The best muffalettas in town...which means the
best in the whole world" is the overwhelming consensus
on this version of the unique New Orleans sandwich
made from meats, cheeses and cracked olive salad in
a special round loaf; the counter help in this fragrant
old-style grocery doesn't get such high marks, though:
"they never smile", "bad attitude"; eat in if you must, but
you might enjoy your sandwich more if you walk over to
the levee and watch the mighty Mississippi River roll by.

China Blossom | 23 | 18 | 21 | $17 |
1801 Stumpf Blvd. (Wright St.), Gretna, 504-361-4598
U – A West Bank Chinese that gets high ratings for its
tasty food and low prices from almost all our reviewers;
"best Chinese in town", "most creative in New Orleans"
and the "whole trout is amazing" are a few of the
reactions; simple but neat furnishings give a slightly
more "dressed-up" feeling than many other Chinese.

Christian's/M | 25 | 24 | 23 | $30 |
3835 Iberville St. (N. Scott St.), 504-482-4924
U – Eating the haute Creole cuisine in this old,
remodeled church can be a "blessing", even though
long tables and pewlike seating arrangement are "too
close" and it's often "more than a little noisy"; local foodies
praise the smoked soft-shell crabs, terrific bouillabaisse
and oysters en brochette and "thank goodness they're
open for lunch again", even if it is only on Thursdays
and Fridays; perhaps more prayers are in order.

Clancy's/M | 22 | 17 | 20 | $27 |
6100 Annunciation St. (Webster St.), 504-895-1111
U – This Creole-Continental serves as a local hangout
for the Uptown chic crowd and politicos who love it
because it's "comfortable" and "very friendly"; while a
minority of our reviewers feels the best that can be said
of the food is that it's "safe", the majority praises the game
and "excellent seafood" and recommends trying the
soft-shell crawfish, sweetbreads and any of the fish dishes.

Commander's Palace/SM | 27 | 27 | 27 | $36 |
1403 Washington Ave. (Coliseum St.), 504-899-8221
U – "One of the country's great restaurants", this elegant
haute Creole is "consistently the top in New Orleans"
according to the overwhelming opinion of our reviewers;
they say that "chef Jaimie Shannon is doing an excellent
job", adding that the turtle soup and bread pudding
soufflé are as outstanding as ever; Ella Brennan (along
with brothers Dick and John and sister Dottie) wields
that special Southern charm that makes everyone feel
like royalty; don't miss the weekend jazz brunch.

NEW ORLEANS

| F | D | S | C |

Crozier's
| 25 | 20 | 23 | $29 |

3216 W. Esplanade Ave. (Causeway Blvd.),
N. Metairie, 504-833-8108

U – The move to suburban Metairie from New Orleans East hasn't altered the excellent French provincial food which many fans feel is "French cooking at its best" in "marvelous country-style"; moderate prices add to the attraction and so do the bistro atmosphere and friendly service.

Emeril's/M
| 26 | 21 | 21 | $30 |

800 Tchoupitoulas St. (Warehouse Dist., Julia St.),
504-528-9393

U – This swanky, high-tech Warehouse District restaurant, owned and operated by Emeril Lagasse (ex Commander's Palace) is "the hit of the town"; raves for Nouvelle Creole cuisine that is "creative and delicious" and for the stylish, modern decor overwhelm the few complaints about the high noise level which comes with great popularity; all agree, Emeril's has a "brilliant future" and is definitely "one of the places to see and be seen in New Orleans."

Galatoire's/SX
| 27 | 23 | 25 | $29 |

209 Bourbon St. (bet. Iberville & Bienville Sts.),
504-525-2021

U – It's hard to explain to out-of-towners why a restaurant that makes you wait in a line outside (no-reservations policy), looks a bit like a barber shop on the inside and won't take credit cards is so beloved; but loyal New Orleanians by the hundreds wrote in their rave reviews about this "quintessential New Orleans", "world-class Creole" restaurant that's like a "French restaurant of 100 years ago" and feels "like an old friend"; "this is an institution and a very good one" – it's worth the wait and the several Andrew Jacksons it will cost.

Gautreau's/M
| 25 | 19 | 22 | $29 |

1728 Soniat St. (Daneel St.), 504-899-7397

U – An old favorite that reopened with a new young chef and carpeting on the floor to cut the noise; delighted New Orleanians say this renovated old pharmacy is "a newcomer who's off to a superb start"; "outstanding", creative Nouvelle Creole cuisine in a unique, "fun" setting is attracting an avid Uptown following; dress smartly – you're sure to see someone you know.

Genghis Khan/S
| 23 | 17 | 21 | $21 |

4053 Tulane Ave. (bet. Gravier & Ulloa Sts.),
504-482-4044

U – "Chopsticks and Chopin" are both available at this very good, medium-priced Korean owned by a member of the New Orleans Symphony violin section; whole fried fish and the Genghis Khan shrimp are two of the favorite dishes which, when combined with the musical offerings, make this "a delight to both the palate and the ear."

NEW ORLEANS | F | D | S | C |

Grill Room/SM | 28 | 29 | 27 | $41 |
Windsor Court Hotel, 300 Gravier St. (bet. Magazine & Tchoupitoulas Sts.), 504-523-6000
U – Chef Kevin Graham and the Windsor Court management get raves for the "fabulous food and decor"; comments like "the ultimate dining experience", "best place in town", "in a class by itself" and "the grandest room in the city" leave no doubt about how New Orleanians feel about this stunning and regal dining room in one of America's great hotels; but overall, this is the place to come for that special-dining experience or power luncheon; and, yes, it is expensive, but worth every penny.

La Cuisine/S | 22 | 17 | 20 | $21 |
225 W. Harrison Ave. (bet. Fleur de Lis Ave. & Pontchartrain Blvd.), 504-486-5154
U – This wonderful, old-fashioned, middle-class, white-tablecloth Lakefront neighborhood place produces reliably good, traditional New Orleans dishes and seafood served by waiters who "call you 'honey'"; regulars say this "may be the best value in town" with "prices and food that can't be beat" for a generally older clientele that enjoys the dose of nostalgia.

Lafitte's Landing/S | 25 | 22 | 22 | $27 |
Hwy. 70, Donaldsonville, 504-473-1232
U – The "wonderful", "imaginative" Cajun-Creole cooking gets nothing but praise; if you're searching for "the real thing", make your way out to Donaldsonville, where talented chef John Folse guarantees that the long drive will be worthwhile; this restaurant is a great place for Sunday lunch and a perfect ending to a day of sightseeing in plantation country.

La Provence/LS | 27 | 25 | 24 | $34 |
Hwy. 190, Lacombe, 504-626-7662
U – If you want to "dine like a country squire" in the closest thing to a "French country inn" outside of France, this is the place; it's "perfect for a Sunday afternoon" and definitely worth the 45-minute drive across Lake Pontchartrain to enjoy chef Chris Kerageorgiou's rich and "divine" food; don't miss the wonderful game, veal and duck dishes.

La Riviera/M | 25 | 19 | 21 | $28 |
4506 Shores Dr. (bet. W. Esplanade Ave. & Bell St.), Metairie, 504-888-6238
U – The bad news is that the original chef-owner Goffredo Fraccaro is in semi-retirement; the good news is that the Italian kitchen is as good as ever, thanks to new owners who continue to pay loving attention to the food; crab meat–stuffed ravioli, osso bucco, great fried calamari and veal dishes are still evident and still winning raves; unfortunately, the restaurant is also still pretty noisy and, too often, you have to wait for a table even with a reservation.

NEW ORLEANS

| F | D | S | C |

L'Economie/M | 23 | 14 | 17 | $19 |

325 Girod St. (Commerce St.), 504-524-7405
U – This "underground surprise" in the heart of the Warehouse District "has the feeling of a small Parisian bistro"; now that there's air-conditioning, the legions of artsy and literary types who come to this trendy, "funky" spot to taste the coq au vin and fine mussels will be much more comfortable.

Le Jardin/SM | 21 | 26 | 20 | $29 |

Westin Hotel, 100 Iberville St., 11th fl. (Canal St.), 504-568-0155
U – An elegant hotel dining room on the 11th floor of Canal Place with "a striking river view"; new food and beverage management seems to be making a real effort to upgrade the menu – here's hoping that effort extends to the slow service; lunch and Sunday brunches are the best bet so far.

Little Greek, The/S | 22 | 14 | 17 | $20 |

2051 Metairie Rd. (bet. Beverly Gdn. Dr. & Helios), 504-831-9470
U – In a town that has hardly any Greek cuisine, this Old Metairie restaurant with "sparkling Mediterranean cuisine" is a winner; the great lamb that "melts in your mouth", grilled fish and shrimp, and delicious appetizers and pastries would be winners even in Athens; the only problems here are service, which even the devotees say "needs major improvement", and getting a table.

Little Tokyo/M | 23 | 15 | 19 | $18 |

1521 N. Causeway Blvd. (bet. 44th & 45th Sts.), Metairie, 504-831-6788
1612 St. Charles Ave. (Uterpe St.), 504-524-8535
U – Fans of Japanese restaurants seem to be like regular patrons of British pubs – their spot is "the best"; comments on the original, cozy Jefferson Parish location range from "best sushi in New Orleans" to "freshest fish this side of the Ginza"; the recently opened second location on St. Charles Avenue is fancier, but too new to rate; however, if past history is any indication, it will be affordable and fresh, with good Japanese cooked dishes.

Louis XVI/SM | 24 | 25 | 23 | $37 |

St. Louis Hotel, 730 Bienville St. (bet. Royal & Bourbon Sts.), 504-581-7000
M – Some feel that this elegant French Quarter classic in the Vieux Carre may have slipped a little over the years; loyalists, however, disagree, saying it's "making an impressive comeback" and is still "very romantic" and "always an experience"; though pricey, all agree it's at least very good and many say better.

NEW ORLEANS | F | D | S | C |

Mike's on the Avenue/M | – | – | – | VE |
628 St. Charles Ave. (Lafayette Sq.), 523-1709
One of the newest rising stars in town, this big, chic restaurant in the newly reopened Lafayette Hotel is the brilliant reflection of talented chef Mike Fennelly, formerly of Santa Fe's SantaCafe; featuring Eclectic dishes that successfully combine Southwestern influences with Oriental spices and ingredients, Fennelly and charming hostess Vicki Bayley have instantly garnered a tremendous and devoted following (despite the stiff tariffs), making this one of the really "in" spots in New Orleans.

Mosca's/X | 25 | 10 | 18 | $26 |
4137 Hwy. 90 (Bridge City Ave.), Jefferson, 504-436-9942
U – "You don't go there for the decor" say regulars, but for "wonderful" Creole Italian food; those who "really love garlic" don't mind driving all the way out of town to this no-frills roadhouse (if you blink your eyes, you'll miss it); the best way to experience this icon to garlic and pasta is to go with a group and order Chinese-style.

Mr. B's/SM | 25 | 24 | 23 | $26 |
201 Royal St. (bet. Iberville & Bienville Sts.), 504-523-2078
U – This is "New Orleans food with a twist" at what our surveyors boast to be one of the most "handsome" and "best restaurants in the Quarter"; from the spicy gumbo ya-ya to the pasta jambalaya to the wonderful daily specials, the innovative menu and appealing environment all reflect the creativity of the brother-and-sister team of Ralph and Cindy Brennan, the next generation of the Commander's Palace Brennans.

Palace Cafe/SM | – | – | – | E |
605 Canal St. (bet. Chartres & Royal Sts.), 523-1661
This new and highly successful Parisian-style grand cafe is the creation of a group of second-generation cousins of New Orleans's first restaurant family, the Brennans; located in a creatively redone Beaux-Arts music store in the heart of Downtown, it features traditional Creole dishes with a contemporary touch; the sophisticated setting combines the best of European and New Orleans cafe dining styles.

Ruth's Chris Steak House/LSM | 26 | 17 | 22 | $32 |
3633 Veterans Memorial Blvd. (bet. Edenborn Ave. & Hesper St.), Metairie, 504-888-3600
711 N. Broad St. (Orleans Ave.), 504-486-0810
U – If you're in the mood for a steak, "this is it"; the most popular steakhouse in town (especially the one on Broad Street) and the parent of a national chain, it serves "steaks fit for a king and his purse"; expensive, yes, but the secret here is to split one entree between the two of you, then order the great onion rings, matchstick potatoes or vegetables, and watch the power brokers at the surrounding tables.

NEW ORLEANS

| F | D | S | C |

Sal & Judy's/S | 26 | 14 | 20 | $23 |
U.S. Hwy. 190 (north of the Lake, off Hwy. 190),
Lacombe, 504-882-7167
U – This cramped, but friendly North Shore "down-home Italian" has many fans who say it's well worth the 45-minute drive across the Causeway; although Judy's gone now, Sal still keeps the "great paneed veal" coming; regulars come hungry because the portions are big and, by all means, ignore the decor.

Sazerac/SM | 24 | 25 | 24 | $37 |
Fairmont Hotel, University Pl. (bet. Common & Canal Sts.), 504-529-4733
U – Newly renovated, this upscale hotel dining room serves consistently good Continental food that draws the local power crowd for lunch, more so than for dinner; plush and ornate, it's definitely a "special-occasion place"; but what's the "most romantic spot in New Orleans" for some, is the "most overdone place" to others; dining deluxe, nevertheless.

Tony Angello's/M | 23 | 20 | 21 | $24 |
6262 Fleur de Lis Ave. (W. Harrison Ave.), 504-488-0888
U – "Forget the menu, have Mr. Tony feed you" is the advice of regulars in this Suburban Italian where unfortunately, "reservations don't mean a thing"; a dimly lit dining room with odd, heavy, turn-of-the-century "antiques" for decorating flavor, it's always crowded and always good; just don't be in a hurry and you won't get mad.

Trey Yuen/SM | 24 | 24 | 22 | $22 |
600 N. Causeway Blvd. (Hwy. 150), Mandeville, 504-626-4476
2100 N. Morrison Blvd. (Columbus St.), Hammond, 504-345-6789
U – "Try the Szechuan alligator or Mandarin crawfish for good, classic Chinese cooking with a local twist" is the advice of North Shore surveyors who frequent these excellent Chinese twins; upscale decor, good service and "fresh, creative dishes" keep customers coming from both sides of the lake; perhaps a little more expensive, but worth it.

Uglesich/MX | 23 | 6 | 12 | $11 |
1238 Baronne St. (bet. Erato & Thalia Sts.), 504-523-8571
U – "The best soft-shell crab in town", "great fried oysters", "wins the Holy Grail award for stuffed crabs and bell peppers" are a few of the endless raves regarding this run-down dive where it's "fun to watch lawyers in suits line up behind plumbers' helpers"; if you're smart, you'll leave your jacket in the car since "the smell lingers"; it's a terrible neighborhood, so park close by.

NEW ORLEANS

| F | D | S | C |

Upperline/SM
| 22 | 19 | 21 | $25 |

1413 Upperline St. (bet. Prytania & St. Charles Aves.), 504-891-9822

U – Under the stewardship of chef Tom Cowman, this modest bistro's food quality has definitely gone up; the largely Uptown clientele praises the "imaginative" Creole-influenced, contemporary menu; though service can be a problem here, this "lovely little restaurant" nestled on a residential side street off St. Charles Avenue has become a "reliable favorite" for many.

Versailles/M
| 26 | 25 | 24 | $38 |

2100 St. Charles Ave. (bet. Jackson Ave. & Josephine St.), 504-524-2535

U – This "special-occasion place" is the domain of chef Gunter Preuss, whose Franco–European-style creations "deserve more attention"; expensive, but worth it for the "old-world style" and "romantic" atmosphere; a few feel this place is a "bit pretentious", but most call it simply "outstanding."

Young's/X
| 25 | 14 | 19 | $22 |

850 Robert Blvd. (Gause Blvd.), Slidell, 504-643-9331

U – This North Shore steakhouse does so well that the owners don't have a sign out front; the crowds and long waits for tables haven't stopped the folks in Slidell or New Orleans, for that matter, from coming for what they say are the "best steaks for the money in the Metro area"; they feel the same way about the "excellent prime rib and fresh fish"; better call and get directions or you'll never find it.

NEW YORK

TOP 30 RESTAURANTS
(In order of food rating)

Restaurant	Cuisine Type
28 – Bouley	French
Aureole	Amer. Contemp./French
27 – Le Cirque	French
Lutece	French
Le Bernardin	French/Seafood
La Cote Basque	French
Peter Luger	Steakhouse
La Grenouille	French
Il Mulino	Northern Italian
26 – Gotham Bar & Grill	Amer. Contemp.
Chanterelle	French
Four Seasons	Continental
Union Square Cafe	Amer. Contemp.
Les Celebrites	French
25 – La Caravelle	French
Sushisay	Japanese
Lespinasse	French
Montrachet	French Bistro
Arcadia	Amer. Contemp.
Manhattan Ocean Club	Seafood
Patsy's Pizza (Bklyn)	Pizza
Le Regence	French
Le Perigord	French
La Reserve	French
Terrace	French
Da Umberto	Northern Italian
Primavera	Northern Italian
March	Amer. Contemp.
24 – Sparks Steak House	Steakhouse
River Cafe	Amer. Contemp.

OTHER TOP PLACES
(In alphabetical order)

Cafe des Artistes	French
Carnegie Deli	Deli
Hatsuhana	Japanese
Mesa Grill	Southwestern
Oyster Bar	Seafood
Palm	Steakhouse
Rainbow Room	Continental
Russian Tea Room	Russian
Shun Lee Palace	Chinese
Smith & Wollensky	Steakhouse
Tavern on the Green	Continental
"21" Club	Amer. Tradition.
Windows on the World	Continental
Zarela	Mexican

NEW YORK

| F | D | S | C |

Arcadia
| 25 | 22 | 22 | $58 |

21 E. 62nd St. (bet. 5th & Madison Aves.), 212-223-2900
U – This "stylish", "intimate" East Side "jewel box" with admireres who "can't get enough" of Anne Rosenzweig's American cuisine: "inventive and delicious", "as beautiful to look at as it is to eat."

Aureole
| 28 | 27 | 26 | $65 |

34 E. 61st St. (bet. Madison & Park Aves.), 212-319-1660
U – Chef Charlie Palmer's French-accented American ranks No. 2 for food our Survey and inspires paroxysms of praise: "luminous", "poetry in motion", "magical"; service gets high marks, and both the flowers and townhouse setting are "gorgeous"; in sum, "going to heaven should be this good."

Bouley
| 28 | 28 | 25 | $70 |

165 Duane St. (bet. Greenwich & Hudson), 212-608-3852
U – Again No. 1 for food in New York, this "divine" TriBeCa French organic leaves dazzled diners wondering "where do you go from here?" – chef David Bouley's cooking, best showcased by his $70 tasting menu, is "inspired" and the "beautiful" setting is as "romantic as the South of France"; all in all, it's an "intoxicating experience", sobered only by "slow" service and "waits"; P.S. don't miss the $32 lunch.

Cafe des Artistes/LS
| 23 | 26 | 22 | $49 |

1 W. 67th St. (bet. CPW & Columbus), 212-877-3500
U – This "perfect valentine" near Lincoln Center combines "crisp service", a "romantic" setting filled with lovely murals of gamboling nymphs, and Contemporary French cooking that keeps getting "better and better"; it's always among the most popular in our Survey.

Carnegie Deli/LSX
| 20 | 7 | 12 | $19 |

854 Seventh Ave. (bet. 54th & 55th Sts.), 212-757-2245
U – This "Hirschfeld cartoon come to life" is "just what a deli should be" – i.e. "seriously huge" sandwiches, theatrically "abusive" servers and elbow-to-elbow dining; expect lines at this "shrine" to pastrami.

Chanterelle
| 26 | 24 | 26 | $70 |

2 Harrison St. (Hudson St.), 212-966-6960
U – "Pure magic", "always a delight" and "sublime" typify reactions to David and Karen Waltuck's "austere but so elegant" TriBeCa French where both food and service are "top-notch"; only the high tab and "stark" setting give surveyors pause; the $30 prix fixe lunch is a good intro.

NEW YORK | F | D | S | C |

Da Umberto | 25 | 18 | 21 | $47 |
107 W. 17th St. (bet. 6th & 7th Aves.), 212-989-0303
U – "Sublime", "fabulous", "a winner", report satisfied surveyors of this amber-hued Chelsea Italian whose service is usually "impeccable" and whose ambiance is "unpretentious" and "laid-back"; expect crowds and noise at night – it's far more relaxed at lunch.

Four Seasons/L | 26 | 27 | 26 | $64 |
99 E. 52nd St. (bet. Park & Lexington), 212-754-9494
U – "World-class", "a great institution" and a "favorite any season", this "quintessential NYer" continues to "delight all the senses" with its "superb", if pricey, Continental-Eclectic cuisine, "grand architectural setting" and "impressive service"; the only real debate is whether the Grill Room (home to NYC's lunchtime power elite) or the Pool Room is more heavenly; all agree that the Grill Room's prix fixe at $26.50 is one of NYC's best deals.

Gotham Bar & Grill/S | 26 | 24 | 23 | $53 |
12 E. 12th St. (bet. 5th & University Pl.), 212-620-4020
U – "One of NYC's best", this "vibrant" Contemporary American cafe has over 2,200 surveyors spewing superlatives: "simply superb", "better and better", "chef Portale's a genius", "what NYC is all about", "a must"; don't miss the $19.93 lunch.

Hatsuhana | 24 | 16 | 19 | $38 |
17 E. 48th St. (bet. 5th & Madison Aves.), 212-355-3345
237 Park Ave. (46th St.), 212-661-3400
M – Those with a yen for "top-drawer" sushi head for these Japanese icons; although other sushi purveyors are also highly rated, fans feel "one of the first is still one of the best", with "fish you can trust."

Il Mulino/L | 27 | 18 | 22 | $54 |
86 W. 3rd St. (bet. Thompson & Sullivan), 212-673-3783
M – "Il Supremo"; once again our surveyors rate this Villager as NY's Numero Uno Italian; it's "the ultimate" for "delicious" garlic-ladened dishes, "warm" service and "superb people-watching"; long waits, "cramped tables" and high noise levels are the downside of its vast popularity; at lunch there's less hassle and more light.

La Caravelle | 25 | 24 | 25 | $62 |
33 W. 55th St. (bet. 5th & 6th Aves.), 212-586-4252
U – Enjoying a "renaissance", this French Classic is once again "superb in every regard", from "exquisite" haute cuisine and "gracious" service to its flower-filled setting; try it again for yourself.

NEW YORK | F | D | S | C |

La Cote Basque | 27 | 27 | 25 | $63 |
5 E. 55th St. (bet. 5th & Madison Aves.), 212-688-6525
M – A "timeless classic", this French standby's fervent fans find it a "favorite forever" for its "exceptional" haute cuisine ("give up on your cholesterol for tonight"), "superb" service and "ever-so-beautiful" setting, highlighted by murals of the Basque coast; critics call it "heavy", "stuffy" and "old."

La Grenouille/L | 27 | 27 | 25 | $66 |
3 E. 52nd St. (bet. 5th & Madison Aves.), 212-752-1495
U – "Exquisite in every way", this Classic French beauty is one of those rare "grand dames" that keeps improving with age; the "superb" cuisine is "better than ever", service exudes "charm and finesse", and the setting is forever a "flower-filled paradise"; most of its celebrated clientele consider it "one of NYC's treasures"; N.B. there's a charming studio upstairs for private parties.

La Reserve | 25 | 25 | 24 | $55 |
4 W. 49th St. (bet. 5th & 6th Aves.), 212-247-2993
U – NYers are unreserved in praising this "gracious and relaxing" Midtown French; what fuels their enthusiasm is the "outstanding" Classic cuisine, "impeccable" service, presided over by owner Jean-Louis Missud, and a lovely flower-filled setting that's "very impressive" for business or romance.

Le Bernardin | 27 | 26 | 25 | $69 |
155 W. 51st St. (bet. 6th & 7th Aves.), 212-489-1515
U – "Neptune himself couldn't do better" than this "phenomenal" but "pricey" French fish specialist; it draws oceans of praise for its "simply smashing" seafood, "comfortable" and "serene" setting and "perfect" service; the gates of this "seafood heaven" open most affordably at its $42 prix fixe lunch.

Le Cirque | 27 | 25 | 25 | $69 |
The Mayfair Hotel, 58 E. 65th St. (bet. Madison & Park Aves.), 212-794-9292
U – "One of the best shows in town", this "charged-up" electric circus is not only "the ultimate NY society restaurant", but a culinary "powerhouse" as well; fans of its "flawless" French cuisine report that chef Daniel Boulud's departure hasn't dimmed the luster of the food and they know nothing can dim the luster of NY's No.1 host, Sirio Maccioni; yes, it's "too damn crowded", but who cares when the people at your elbow are named Kissinger, Lauder or Jagger.

NEW YORK

| F | D | S | C |

Le Perigord | 25 | 22 | 24 | $59 |
405 E. 52nd St. (east of 1st Ave.), 212-755-6244
U – "Always wonderful", this "timeless" Classic French is regarded as "one of the best" for its "superb" food, "plush, quiet" setting, and "impeccable service with a smile"; "you're made to feel like an old friend here", and the prix fixe meals are a "best value among top gourmet places"; all in all, "you can't ask for more."

Le Regence/S | 25 | 27 | 26 | $65 |
Hotel Plaza Athenee, 37 E. 64th St. (bet. Madison & Park Aves.), 212-606-4647
M – "Versailles in NY"; this "luxurious" French Classic is rated "magnifique" by most diners for its "fine" food, "impeccable" service and sky-blue "baroque fantasy" decor plus a Sunday brunch fit for royalty; despite the above, it has never been adopted by NYers.

Les Celebrites | 26 | 28 | 25 | $74 |
Essex House, 160 Central Park So. (59th St.), 212-247-0300
U – "The Newcomer of the Year", this French Classic draws rave reviews that correspond to its high ratings; star chef Christian Delouvrier's "spectacular" creations are beautifully served in a small but "stunning" room dotted with paintings by Hollywood stars (i.e. the celebrities); some say the prices are hard to swallow, but most consider this "one of the very best", especially for that "special occasion."

Lespinasse/S | 25 | 27 | 25 | $66 |
St. Regis Hotel, 2 East 55th St. (5th Ave.), 212-339-6719
M – This "ultra-elegant" Louis XV room is a "plush" showcase for the "original" flavorsome cooking of chef Gray Kunz; to the majority, his Asian-accented French creations are backed up by "gorgeous" decor and "attentive" service; but a minority say "the pieces don't quite fit" and the place feels like 1950 redux.

Lutece | 27 | 24 | 26 | $71 |
249 E. 50th St. (bet. 2nd & 3rd Aves.), 212-752-2225
U – Like a long-time lover, Lutece can still arouse NYers' culinary passions even though it no longer holds exclusive reign over their affections; Andre Soltner "still has the touch", and his "pluperfect" French haute bistro food remains the "gold standard" against which all others are judged; yes, it has faults – service can be "less than superb" and the decor, though elegant, is "showing its age" – but to most it's still seductive.

Manhattan Ocean Club/LS | 25 | 22 | 22 | $53 |
57 W. 58th St. (bet. 5th & 6th Aves.), 212-371-7777
U – Popularly acclaimed for "the best seafood in the city" with fish "so fresh it's almost swimming", a "great wine list" and polished service, this "stylish" seafood house is "what dining in Manhattan should be."

NEW YORK | F | D | S | C |

March | 25 | 24 | 24 | $60 |
405 E. 58th St. (bet. 1st Ave. & Sutton Pl.),
212-838-9393
U – For a "romantic", "intimate" dinner in a "delightful townhouse", nearly everyone admires this "innovative" American that presents the "creations" of chef Wayne Nish; only a few complain: "steep prices", "too staid."

Mesa Grill/S | 23 | 20 | 18 | $40 |
102 Fifth Ave. (bet. 15th & 16th Sts.), 212-807-7400
U – "Originality abounds" at this "hip", upscale SW grill that draws rave reviews and "packs 'em in"; customers report that chef Bobby Flay "creates magic" daily; bright colors and a soaring ceiling help you endure the "incredible noise" at this "David Hockney" of restaurants.

Montrachet | 25 | 19 | 23 | $56 |
239 W. Broadway (bet. Walker & White Sts.),
212-219-2777
U – Hard to get to but worth it, this TriBeCa Nouvelle French rates "among the very best", thanks to chef Deborah Ponzek's "remarkable cooking"; most proclaim it a "gourmet's delight" with an "excellent wine list" too; the prix fixe menus are a real bargain.

Oyster Bar | 22 | 15 | 15 | $38 |
Grand Central Station, Lower Level (bet. Vanderbilt & Lexington Aves.), 212-490-6650
U – This huge animated seafood classic is called "the quintessential NY restaurant"; it's an international destination for its raw bar, pan roasts, "fresh fish of all types", "amazing" desserts and American white wine list; if noise gets to you, try the "much quieter" adjacent Saloon Room.

Palm/L | 24 | 13 | 17 | $50 |
837 Second Ave. (bet. 44th & 45th Sts.), 212-687-2953
Palm Too
840 Second Ave. (bet. 44th & 45th Sts.), 212-697-5198
U – "Brassy" and "abrasive", this NY "legend", with caricatures of its famous patrons on its walls, is for many "the city's best steakhouse", with "brontosaurus-sized portions"; for cost-control, try sharing or the $19.93 lunch.

Patsy's Pizza (Brooklyn)/LX | 25 | 10 | 14 | $16 |
19 Fulton St. (Water & Front Sts.), 718-858-4300
U – At this new Brooklyn pizzeria, brick-oven-baking and "the freshest ingredients" spell success; "Numero Uno" with our pizza partisans.

NEW YORK　　　　　　　　　| F | D | S | C |

Peter Luger Steak House　　| 27 | 15 | 19 | $49 |
(Brooklyn)/SX
178 Broadway (Driggs Ave.), 718-387-7400
U – "The gold standard" of steakhouses is "head and shoulders above the rest"; "mammoth", "melt-in-your-mouth" steaks, creamed spinach, fried potatoes and pecan pie ("love the schlag") make it "fabulous from start to finish"; despite the "earthy", "beer-hall" ambiance and service ("the waiters are aged to perfection"), it's "worth the trip."

Primavera/LS　　| 25 | 21 | 22 | $58 |
1578 First Ave. (82nd St.), 212-861-8608
U – A "classy crowd" gives this Upper East Side Tuscan "four stars" for "ingenious", "consistently excellent" food, for its "sophisticated", "clubby" wood-paneled setting, and service that makes you feel like "royalty"; N.B. *if owner-host Nicola Civetta recommends it, order it!*

Quilted Giraffe (CLOSED)　　| 25 | 24 | 24 | $73 |
Sony Plaza, 550 Madison Ave. (bet. 55th & 56th), 212-593-1221
U – Despite its reputation as NY's "most extravagant" restaurant, this Nouvelle American that some say is "turning Japanese" wins praise for chef Barry Wine's "exquisite" "creative" cooking; the extraordinary "21st-century" stainless-steel decor softened by flowers and artwork adds the right touch for dining that is truly "postmodern"; at $45, the prix fixe lunch is a bargain.

Rainbow Room/LS　　| 19 | 28 | 22 | $63 |
GE Bldg., 30 Rockefeller Plaza, 65th Floor (bet. 49th & 50th Sts.), 212-632-5100
U – For a "dinner and dancing extravaganza" or "for drinks and admiring the view", there's "nothing like it"; RR "lives up to all its notices" as "the perfect NY dream evening", "unequaled for glamour", with "the most romantic" art deco atmosphere; if the Continental menu falls a bit short, the "fab '40s" "Fred and Ginger fantasy" is sufficient compensation.

River Cafe (Brooklyn)/LS　　| 24 | 27 | 23 | $59 |
1 Water St. (East River), 718-522-5200
U – "One of NY's treasures", this "beautiful" barge cafe is "everything it's cracked up to be" – matching a "brilliant" New American menu with "breathtaking views" of Downtown Manhattan; regulars report "the tasting menu is a must" and suggest brunch, late lunch or drinks on the outdoor deck; for a "romantic" or "celebratory" evening, it's "magical."

NEW YORK

| F | D | S | C |

Russian Tea Room/LS | 17 | 23 | 17 | $49 |
150 W. 57th St. (bet. 6th & 7th Aves.), 212-265-0947
U – "Incomparable", this "glitzy" and "grand" Midtown landmark over the years has won the hearts of diners by offering "a Russian gala" of blinis, caviar, chilled vodka and other Romanov dishes; most love its "always festive" green, red and gold Christmas feeling, but a few say its food "needs perestroika."

Shun Lee Palace/S | 24 | 20 | 21 | $40 |
155 E. 55th St. (bet. Lexington & 3rd Ave.), 212-371-8844
U – The cream of the Chinese crop, this "sophisticated" Eastsider rates "first class" in all departments, from its "superb" food ("exquisite" Peking duck and seafood) to its "elegant" setting and service, if "pricey for Chinese"; for best results, "follow your captain's suggestions" or try the prix fixes.

Smith & Wollensky/LS | 22 | 16 | 18 | $50 |
201 E. 49th St. (3rd Ave.), 212-753-1530
U – Exactly "what a steakhouse should be"; with a "fine wine list" as a plus, this "big", "bustling" Midtowner has the formula down pat: it provides "excellent" "elephant"-sized steaks, chops, lobster and trimmings in a handsome "old-boys–club" setting; undoubtedly the most popular steakhouse in town – they've discovered a new way to print money.

Sparks Steak House | 24 | 18 | 21 | $54 |
210 E. 46th St. (bet. 2nd & 3rd Aves.), 212-687-4855
U – Besides steak "done exactly the way you want it", this "top-tier" Midtowner has "terrific lobster", "wonderful" wines, an "elegant, masculine" setting and "first-class" service; waits and noise are the price of popularity.

Sushisay | 25 | 16 | 20 | $40 |
38 E. 51st St. (bet. Madison & Park Aves.), 212-755-1780
U – "Afishonados" say this Midtown Japanese serves "without a doubt, the best sushi in NYC"; "friendly, helpful" service and a crisp, clean setting add to its appeal.

Tavern On The Green/S | 15 | 26 | 17 | $46 |
Central Park West & 67th St., 212-873-3200
U – Is "NY's quintessential wow" "still magical" or "strictly for the rubes"?; critics disdain the "banal food", but they don't get the point: this "Disneyland NY", with all its "gaudiness" and "glitz", its Crystal Room and "lovely" garden is simply "a must for celebrations"; even the food is "surprisingly good", if you keep it simple; P.S. its prix fixe lunch and pre-theater dinner can't be beat.

NEW YORK | F | D | S | C |

Terrace/S | 25 | 26 | 23 | $57 |
400 W. 119th St. (bet. Amsterdam & Morningside), 212-666-9490
U – A "360-degree view" and "heavenly" Classic French food are the top draws at this "very romantic", "much-ballyhooed" Columbia rooftop; it's "an island of civilization" in a locale where the valet parking after 6 PM is a necessity.

"21" Club/L | 19 | 22 | 20 | $56 |
21 W. 52nd St. (bet. 5th & 6th Aves.), 212-582-7200
M – A "NY landmark", this Midtown former speakeasy has a "vastly improved kitchen" that complements its "elegant", "clubby" four-story quarters; it also has "surprisingly pleasant service" for "a place known for its caste system"; the downstairs barroom is most popular with its "power-hitting celeb" regulars, but it also does "well-run parties" upstairs in a choice of rooms; for a bargain introduction, check out the $19.93 lunch.

Union Square Cafe/S | 26 | 22 | 23 | $48 |
21 E. 16th St. (bet. 5th Ave. & Union Sq.), 212-243-4020
U – Customers of Danny Meyer's "very civilized" cafe – and they are legion – praise this New American as a model of what "the restaurant of the '90s should be", citing its "marvelously creative" yet "consistently excellent" cuisine, "friendly and knowledgeable" staff, "extensive wine list" and "warm", "relaxed" ambiance; among NYC's top restaurants, it's a "great value."

Windows On The World/S | 16 | 27 | 19 | $52 |
1 World Trade Ctr., 107th fl., West St. (bet. Liberty & Vesey Sts.), 212-938-1111
M – The view and decor at this "Eighth Wonder of the World" get all raves: "breathtaking", "spectacular", "20 million sparkling lights", but the Continental food rates less well: "tourist fare", "doesn't measure up"; still, this elegant aerie is always "great for drinks", watching the sunset in the City Lights Bar or for Sunday brunch; the mimeoed wine list is an oenophile's dream.

Zarela/S | 22 | 16 | 17 | $35 |
953 Second Ave. (bet. 50th & 51st Sts.), 212-644-6740
U – Satisfied surveyors for the fourth year in a row have rated this colorful and cacophonous Eastsider "NYC's Best Mexican", citing "inventive" dishes with "flavors that explode off the plate"; a "fun crowd" fueled by potent margaritas makes for a "festive atmosphere."

ORANGE COUNTY, CA

TOP 10 RESTAURANTS
(In order of food rating)

Restaurant	Cuisine Type
28 – Pascal	French Bistro
27 – Antoine	French Classic
26 – Five Feet	Pacific New Wave
JW's	Continental
25 – Antonello	Northern Italian
Ritz	Continental
Gustaf Anders	Continental
Caffe Piemonte	Northern Italian
24 – Bistro 201	Californian
Ritz-Carlton	Continental

OTHER TOP PLACES
(In alphabetical order)

Bangkok IV	Thai
Chanteclair	French Bistro
Il Fornaio	Nuova Cucina Italian
Kachina	Southwestern
Kitayami	Japanese
Las Brisas	Mexican
Pavilion	Eclectic
Splashes	Mediterranean
Tutto Mare	Nuova Cucina Italian
Zov's Bistro	Mediterranean

F	D	S	C

Antoine | 27 | 26 | 26 | $47 |
Le Meridien Hotel, 4500 MacArthur Blvd. (across from John Wayne Airport), Newport Beach, 714-476-2001
U – This "elegant and excellent" high-end French in the Le Meridien Hotel's "superb" multimirrored and flower-filled dining room is "the best restaurant in Orange County to wear a tux"; while some feel there's a "fancy-schmancy" attitude, the exquisite contemporary cuisine ranks a remarkable No. 2 in Orange County; dinner only.

Antonello/M | 26 | 24 | 24 | $39 |
Southcoast Village Shopping Ctr., 3800 S. Plaza Dr. (bet. Sunflower Ave. & Bear St.), Santa Ana, 714-751-7153
U – The expansive menu of this grand Northern Italian across from South Coast Plaza receives high marks in every category, but respondents react mostly to the "warm, elegant" ambiance of muraled walls and low lights; "great service" suits the expense-account business and political crowds just fine.

ORANGE COUNTY, CA | F | D | S | C |

Bangkok IV/SM | 22 | 20 | 21 | $28 |
Crystal Court, 3333 Bear St., 3rd fl. (Sunflower St.), Costa Mesa, 714-540-7661
U – "Graciously run" Thai with delicate, airy decor, this South Coast Plaza location is "great for pre- or post-theater" dining; "go for the scene and the garlic chicken" plus a menu full of "subtle flavors"; go during the Thai New Year and the "gracious hostess" will sprinkle you with rose water.

Bistro 201/M | 24 | 23 | 22 | $35 |
18201 Von Karman Ave. (Michelson Dr.), Irvine, 714-553-9201
U – "Great people-watching" at this sleek yet warm high-end Contemporary Californian that not only is "yuppie central", but a comfortable hangout for older customers; fans go for "creative" dishes such as salmon wrapped in thinly sliced potatoes; owner David Wilhelm's flagship restaurant "does everything well" and so, some rate it their "No.1 spot to go on the Gold Coast."

Caffe Piemonte/S | 25 | 16 | 24 | $25 |
1835 E. Chapman Ave. (Tustin Ave.), Orange, 714-532-3296
U – "Wonderful Italian food in a strip mall" says it all: the cuisine at this tiny family-run Northern Italian rates second among all Italians in Orange County – no one goes for the ambiance; instead, regulars are rewarded with "moderate prices" and recognition from the "warm, attentive" staff.

Chanteclair/SM | 23 | 24 | 22 | $38 |
18912 MacArthur Blvd. (across from John Wayne Airport), Irvine, 714-752-8001
M – Traditionalists rely on this country-style French for its "romantic" corner tables and "elegant floral arrangements", but diners disagree on whether the rich food is "exquisite" or "outdated."

Five Feet/SM | 26 | 19 | 21 | $34 |
328 Glenneyre St. (Forest Ave.), Laguna Bch., 714-497-4955
U – "A tiny restaurant with big ideas" sums it up here; "often brilliant, always creative", this new age Asian's "spectacular food" – including the renowned whole catfish – holds its own as trends come and go; its diminutive size and bold decor help make it Laguna Beach's most popular restaurant.

Gustaf Anders/SM | 25 | 20 | 23 | $38 |
South Coast Plaza Village, 1651 Sunflower Ave. (Bear St. side), Santa Ana, 714-668-1737
U – This low-key, cosmopolitan Continental across from South Coast Plaza offers "a refreshing change from the ubiquitous" Californian cuisine, serving "exquisite" Swedish dishes that often surprise; respondents rave about the breads and special events such as holiday smorgasbords and Sunday jazz brunches.

ORANGE COUNTY, CA | F | D | S | C |

Il Fornaio | 22 | 24 | 20 | $30 |
18051 Von Karman Ave. (Michelson Dr.), Irvine,
714-261-1444
U – This Nouvelle Italian in the airport area with a "gorgeous", light-filled interior enthralls diners and draws a beautiful "see-and-be-seen" crowd; the "nice" rotisserie meats and simple pastas, however, don't seem to rise to the level of the "appealing", "unique" decor.

JW'S/M | 26 | 25 | 24 | $38 |
Anaheim Marriott Hotel, 700 W. Convention Way (next to Anaheim Convention Ctr.), Anaheim,
714-750-0900
U – The "five-star", "superb" Continental cuisine and "intimate" and "romantic" rooms elicit sighs from respondents and rate among the County's top; this is definitely the class act in the Disneyland area "for special occasions"; dinner only.

Kachina/SM | 25 | 21 | 20 | $31 |
222 Forest Ave. (P.C.H.), Laguna Beach,
714-497-5546
U – Laguna Beach's tiny Southwestern has a big following who "love the duck tamales" and call everything else on the menu "dynamite"; it's hard to get a seat at this "noisy" place where the "tables are too close together" and the decor is minimalist-modern, but when the "taste buds come alive", few seem to mind; dinner only.

Kitayama/M | 24 | 23 | 23 | $35 |
101 Bay View Pl. (Jamboree Rd.), Newport Beach,
714-725-0777
U – The setting of this lavish "traditional" Japanese is as it should be: "tranquil, serene, friendly", and the dishes, as beautiful as still lifes, can transport you to "another world"; "I felt like I was in Japan – what presentation!"; "cultured Japanese service" is a bonus.

Las Brisas/SM | 17 | 24 | 17 | $27 |
361 Cliff Dr. (North Coast Hwy.), Laguna Beach,
714-497-5434
U – The "stunning location" and "spectacular ocean view" above Laguna's Main Beach bring this upscale Mexican plenty of praise, and the "great guacamole" and frothy margaritas make it a "let's party place"; but locals skip the "ok food" suitable for a "tourist trap."

ORANGE COUNTY, CA | F | D | S | C |

Pascal/M | 28 | 22 | 26 | $39 |
1000 Bristol St. (MacArthur Blvd.), Newport Beach, 714-752-0107
U – Crowned the best restaurant in Orange County by respondents, this deceptively simple French is "outstanding", "sublime" and "exquisite" in a charmingly unpretentious way, and its strip-mall location hardly tarnishes its reputation; owners Pascal and Mimi Olhats offer "hard work and attention" to every detail, from the abundance of fragrant roses about the room to the "excellent" crudité basket that only launches the menu; it's "definitely worth a detour" for out-of-towners.

Pavilion, The/SM | 23 | 23 | 24 | $41 |
Four Seasons Hotel, 690 Newport Ctr. Dr. (Santa Cruz Dr.), Newport Beach, 714-759-0808
U – A refined Contemporary American in the Four Seasons Hotel that's not only "elegant and trendy", but more important "always good"; the menu changes seasonally and always includes imaginative low-cal cuisine; "the calming decor is augmented by the beautiful gardens"; but perhaps the biggest selling point is the civilized service that "leaves you feeling like you just had a massage."

Ritz-Carlton/M | 24 | 27 | 25 | $46 |
Ritz-Carlton Hotel, 33533 Shoreline Dr. (P.C.H.), Laguna Niguel, 714-240-2000
U – The dining room at this "stunning" hotel offers European elegance and "impeccable service"; respondents don't all feel, however, that the Modern Continental food always matches the gracious surroundings; even those pleased with their meals raise an eyebrow at the highest prices in the County.

Ritz, The/M | 25 | 25 | 25 | $42 |
Newport Fashion Island, 880 Newport Center Dr. (Santa Barbara Dr.), Newport Beach, 714-720-1800
U – The "old-fashioned luxury" of this plush, posh Newport Beach Continental always makes respondents "feel cherished" by both the knowledgeable staff and the skilled kitchen; it may be expensive, but looking at the contented customers filling the rooms; one respondent asks, "recession? what recession?"

Splashes/SM | 20 | 24 | 19 | $32 |
Surf and Sand Hotel, 1555 South Coast Hwy. (Bluebird Canyon Dr.), Laguna Beach, 714-497-4477
M – "Practically on the beach", this Contemporary Mediterranean works best at lunch or sunset, when the view creates a getaway atmosphere; otherwise, the food can be a lukewarm "good" or a cold "ok", and the staff tends toward "sophomoric."

ORANGE COUNTY, CA | F | D | S | C |

Tutto Mare/SM | 23 | 24 | 21 | $31 |
Newport Fashion Island, 545 Newport Center Dr. (San Miguel Dr.), Newport Beach, 714-640-6333
U – Bustling, "very slick" Contemporary Italian brimming with the "pretty people" of Newport Beach, who come for the "beautiful" "New York–bistro look" and the "terrific" pastas and seafood; the "whole Dover sole roasted in a wood oven is among the best dishes."

Zov's Bistro | 24 | 16 | 20 | $26 |
17440 E. 17th St. (Tustin Ave.), Tustin, 714-838-8855
U – This sweet little neighborhood Mediterranean is a "well-kept secret" among Central County customers; the menu runs from a parsley-flecked tabbouleh to a "great lamb sandwich" ("yum") and grilled swordfish; a new bakery now offers light breakfasts and delicious breads.

ORLANDO

TOP 20 RESTAURANTS
(In order of food rating)

Restaurant	Cuisine Type
28 – Dux	Amer. Contemp.
27 – Jordan's Grove	Amer. Tradition./Eclectic
26 – Le Coq au Vin	French Bistro
Hemingway's	Seafood
Park Plaza Gardens	Continental
Arthur's 27	International
Chatham's Place	Amer. Tradition.
Enzo's	N/S Italian
25 – La Cena	Northern Italian
La Scala	Northern Italian
La Normandie	French Classic
Le Cordon Bleu	French Bistro/Swiss
Maison et Jardin	Continental
24 – Pebbles	Amer. Contemp.
Empress Room	Continental
Palma Maria	N/S Italian
Boston's Fish House	Seafood
Straub's Fine Seafood	Seafood
Antonio's LaFiamma	N/S Italian
Ruth's Chris Steak House	Steakhouse

OTHER TOP PLACES
(In alphabetical order)

Bubbalou's Bar-B-Q	BBQ
Cafe de France	French Bistro
Chefs de France	French Classic
Christini's	N/S Italian
Forbidden City	Chinese
La Coquina	Californian/French
Linda's La Cantina	Steakhouse
L'Originale Alfredo di Roma	Northern Italian
Portobello Yacht Club	Seafood
Top of the World	Continental

ORLANDO | F | D | S | C |

Antonio's Lafiamma | 24 | 23 | 20 | $27 |
611 S. Orlando Ave. (Maitland Ave.), Maitland, 407-645-5523
M – "This restaurant bends over backwards to get it right" and succeeds most of the time, say fans of this elegant but "inconsistent" young Italian on the shores of Lake Lilly; many cheer the "beautifully presented", "very creative" food and "refined" decor; others say the experience is diminished by "snooty" waiters; lunch is served downstairs in an incongruously laid-back Italian deli that many pronounce "excellent."

Arthur's 27 | 26 | 27 | 26 | $52 |
Buena Vista Palace Hotel, 1900 Buena Vista Dr. (near Disney Village), Lake Buena Vista, 407-827-3450
U – A lofty spot that offers International cuisine from high atop one of Central Florida's tallest hotels, this place gets just about everything right; location, quality and price are all high (it's one of the most expensive restaurants surveyed), but for such a "grand", "perfect" "class act", few critics find the cost excessive; a minority deem it "uppity" and "pompous", but it's a must-go on the night "you give her the diamond."

Boston's Fish House/SX | 24 | 13 | 16 | $11 |
7325 Aloma Ave. (Palmetto), Winter Park, 407-678-2107
U – A Red Sox pennant and some lobster-boat paintings are all the decor you'll get, but the throngs who crowd this diner-style Winter Park seafood spot couldn't care less; they're in those endless lines for an "excellent value" on "great seafood" cooked by a Back Bay family; takeout is an option for those who are impatient or picky about atmosphere.

Bubbalou's Bodacious Bar-B-Q | 23 | 11 | 17 | $9 |
1471 Lee Rd. (near Hwy. 17-92), Winter Park, 407-628-1212
U – This dumpy, bargain wayside stand gets such rave comments as "best BBQ in Orlando", "excellent Brunswick stew" and "best baked beans and corn bread anywhere"; the people who run it are so nice you won't even mind the long lines or lack of table service.

Cafe de France | 23 | 21 | 21 | $26 |
526 S. Park Ave. (near Fairbanks), Winter Park, 407-647-1869
U – French expatriates and statesiders alike sing the praises of this petite Park Avenue bistro; the "great French food" at this "lovely nook" is served in a "down-home atmosphere" with matching prices; despite somewhat "snooty service", this qualifies as a "hidden treasure"; BYO.

ORLANDO

| F | D | S | C |

Chatham's Place/S | 26 | 22 | 23 | $31 |
Phillips Pl., 7575 Dr. Phillips Blvd. (Hinson St.), Orlando, 407-345-2992
U – Right outside Universal Studios, this "watering hole for movie folks" really delivers, with "great gourmet cooking", American style, as well as "sophisticated charm" and "friendly" staff; all in all, it's a "delicious, casual, fun" place that might be "Orlando's most underrated."

Chefs de France/S | 23 | 22 | 20 | $31 |
Epcot Center, French Pavilion, Lake Buena Vista, 407-824-4321
U – The chefs are, of course, world-famous Paul Bocuse, Roger Verge and Gaston LeNotre, who, with their imported French staffs, take turns dazzling Epcot visitors and locals alike with superbly executed regional French cuisine; some menus work better than others, and the upstairs bistro is usually the best bet, but the friendly ("I wish the waiters in Paris were this nice") service and the accessible atmosphere make it "magnifique."

Christini's/L | 24 | 23 | 22 | $33 |
7600 Dr. Phillips Blvd. (Sand Lake Rd.), Orlando, 407-345-8770
M – Love it or hate it, this "clubby" Italian enclave for the rich and pseudo-rich always causes a stir; a favorite of Disney and Universal execs, the "elegant" food, "snooty" but love-'em-anyway waiters and omnipresent owner add up to a "New York Continental" experience – with Manhattan prices to match; the jacket requirement doesn't sit well in this casual town.

Dux | 28 | 27 | 27 | $45 |
Peabody Hotel, 9801 International Dr. (opposite Convention Ctr.), Orlando, 407-345-4550
U – "Always a treat", this Nouvelle American at the Peabody Hotel – top-rated for food in Orlando – will make you "feel pampered" with its "elegant and delightful" surroundings, "fantastic food" and service that's equally first-rate, even though there is occasionally "too much presentation"; the stratospheric prices are worth it, say our surveyors, but they tend to make this a place for special occasions and expense accounts.

Empress Room/S | 24 | 27 | 24 | $36 |
Empress Lilly, Disney Village, Lake Buena Vista, 407-828-3900
U – "Intimate" and "romantic" aren't words you associate with Disney, but this longtime anchor of the Disney Village food operation earns them; the haute Continental cuisine on a riverboat has held up well, thanks to the "super menu" and "impeccable staff"; no Mickey Mouse here – this is pure Snow White.

ORLANDO

| F | D | S | C |

Enzo's | 26 | 23 | 21 | $30 |
1130 S. Hwy. 17-92 (bet. SR 434 & Dog Track Rd.), Longwood, 407-834-9872
U – "Everybody's favorite" is this "Orlando classic" Italian housed in a converted lakefront home; the most popular restaurant in Orlando proper got that way by dishing up "earnestly prepared" Italian food that's "always superb"; "bustling and far from intimate", it "needs to get its reservations act together" and teach its waiters a few manners, but all criticisms pale in light of food that makes it "the place you dream of going to when you're dieting."

Forbidden City | 23 | 16 | 18 | $15 |
948 N. Mills Ave. (Weber St.), Orlando, 407-894-5005
University Park Plaza, 141 University Park Dr. (Hwy. 436), Winter Park, 407-678-5005
U – "Wonderful" Szechuan and Hunan wins out over "sloppy" service and a setting that still recalls its gas-station predecessor at these siblings; it's the "tastiest, most varied" Chinese around, but "eat blindfolded" – the decor leaves everything to be desired.

Hemingway's/S | 26 | 27 | 25 | $29 |
Hyatt Regency Grand Cypress Hotel, One Grand Cypress Blvd., Orlando, 407-239-1234
U – This "excellent but pricey" bastion of resort dining is among Central Florida's elite; first and foremost, it's a "great looker", the place to watch a sunset while dining, but there's a lot more to it than that; its Florida seafood menu is "top-notch – it always impresses", and the "elegant but casual" setting and "attentive service" are up to the food.

Jordan's Grove/S | 27 | 26 | 25 | $31 |
1300 S. Orlando Ave. (1/2 mile north of Lee Rd.), Maitland, 407-628-0020
U – One of Central Florida's most highly rated spots is "delectably eclectic", using local fruits, vegetables, meat and seafood to create an "inventive, always different" American menu with a regional twist; owner Mark Rodriguez "does a superb job" with his rotating team of chefs in this handsome mansion surrounded by oak trees, and the "great help" and "good wine list" contribute to an "all-around great restaurant."

La Cena | 25 | 18 | 22 | $23 |
Longwood Village Shopping Ctr., 1811 W. SR 434, Longwood, 407-834-3994
M – Pasta is the thing at this Italian hot spot, and most surveyors are enthusiastic about the "wonderful" and "fresh" cooking; the "casual atmosphere" is considered "bland" and even "cold" by some, but the service is "friendly" and solicitous, and prices are "reasonable" for what you get.

ORLANDO

| F | D | S | C |

La Coquina | – | – | – | E |
Hyatt Regency Grand Cypress, One Grand Cypress Blvd., Orlando, 407-239-1234
This new Hyatt dining room mixes French, Continental and Californian cooking in a somewhat formal setting that draws tourists and occasional locals; Sunday brunch is popular, as is the mellow music from the harpist.

La Normandie | 25 | 20 | 22 | $25 |
2021 E. Colonial Dr. (near Bumby Ave.), Orlando, 407-896-9976
U – "Vive la France", say respondents about this "stately" Country French landmark that, though "classic", is "not pretentious"; the "country-style" dining room rates well, but strikes some as "depressing"; however, the "great quality", "wonderful people" and good-value early-bird specials all make this a respected "standby."

L'Originale Alfredo di | – | – | – | E |
Roma Ristorante/S
Epcot Center, Italian Pavilion, Lake Buena Vista, 407-824-4321
Rome meets Epcot at this Northern Italian, and the result is "excellent food and service", the "best fettuccine and bread" and "good atmosphere", with strolling musicians adding a nice touch; authenticity is not a strong point, but it doesn't need to be.

La Scala | 25 | 24 | 24 | $29 |
430 Loraine Dr. (Douglas St.), Altamonte Springs, 407-862-3257
U – It's "romantic and quiet – except for when the owner breaks into song" at this "definition of fine Italian dining"; some like his voice, some don't, but the "outstanding" cooking, classy surroundings and the "best help" all are deserving of an encore.

Le Coq au Vin/S | 26 | 19 | 22 | $24 |
4800 S. Orange Ave. (Holden Ave.), Orlando, 407-851-6980
M – "Consistently well-prepared" Country French food with an American regional twist is the forte at this "comfortable little place", whose "welcoming atmosphere" and unstuffy attitude all sit well with our respondents; even if the decor "doesn't match the food" and the place "needs soundproofing", the "honest" cooking and low tab make these complaints unimportant.

ORLANDO

| F | D | S | C |

Le Cordon Bleu | 25 | 19 | 23 | $27 |
537 W. Fairbanks Ave. (Orange Ave.), Winter Park, 407-647-7575
M – For years Winter Park's most fashionable restaurant, this Swiss–French bistro may be starting to show its age; while fans insist "the tradition continues", foes say it's "living on its reputation"; the famous Caesar salad still has its partisans, as do the "amiable service" and "classic elegance of the decor", but one surveyor may have pinpointed the true reason for its continuing popularity: "I go there because it's there."

Linda's La Cantina | 23 | 15 | 18 | $21 |
4721 E. Colonial Dr. (bet. Bennett & Humphries Sts.), Orlando, 407-894-4491
M – This red-blooded, red-tableclothed roadhouse serves a steak that most "sophisticated beefeaters applaud"; love 'em or hate 'em, people seem willing to sit in the "lounge-lizard" bar for up to an hour to get at the beef and Italian side dishes; heaven knows they're not there for the "smoky, noisy" room and too-close tables.

Maison et Jardin/S | 25 | 25 | 23 | $32 |
430 Wymore Rd. (¼ mile south of Hwy. 436), Altamonte Springs, 407-862-4410
M – The "standard for all others", this haute Continental in Altamonte Springs is an "elegant" setting for that special occasion; while most concur that the decor works best "if you get the garden room", a few surveyors find it "stuffy" and sometimes "uneven", which is hard to believe at the price; still, when the place is on, it's "romantic" and "wonderful."

Palma Maria | 24 | 19 | 21 | $22 |
Summit Plaza Shopping Ctr., 1015 E. Semoran Blvd. #8 (near Red Bug Lake Rd.), Casselberry, 407-339-2856
U – This "intimate" shopping-center Italian with a "family atmosphere" is "not as popular as it used to be", but you'll still find lots of folks lined up to get into the "tiny, cramped" room for the "best calamari around", "great eggplant Florentine" and other much-appreciated Italian basics.

Park Plaza Gardens/S | 26 | 26 | 24 | $29 |
319 S. Park Ave. (bet. Lyman & New England Aves.), Winter Park, 407-645-2475
U – This gem of a "patio garden" restaurant captures top honors in popularity thanks to its "top-quality" Continental cooking, "impeccable" service, "serenity" and, most of all, "location, location, location"; even if it could be more imaginative, the menu's always "well-prepared", and that's probably why this "jet-set landing pad" has vanquished all local competition for the past 20 years.

ORLANDO

| F | D | S | C |

Pebbles/LS | 24 | 23 | 22 | $19 |
2110 W. SR 434 (near Douglas St.), Longwood, 407-774-7111
2516 Aloma Ave. (near Lakemont), Winter Park, 407-678-7001
Crossroads, 12551 SR 535, Lake Buena Vista, 407-827-1111
17 W. Church St. (Orange Ave.), Orlando, 407-839-0892
U – Judging from the number of responses, many locals are making the journey to "Yuppieville" for the "creative" Contemporary American fare with heavy Californian and Floridian influences offered at this "consistently reliable" group of restaurants; while this minichain "doesn't soar, it rarely disappoints", and the "interior decorator's dream" of a setting and personable staff make it a consistent, affordable "favorite."

Portobello Yacht Club/S | 23 | 20 | 19 | $23 |
Pleasure Island, 1650 Buena Vista Dr., Lake Buena Vista, 407-934-8888
M – This seafooder with a Pleasure Island view is "typical of a Disney operation" in both the good and bad senses – "fun", "loud" and "a bit expensive"; it's loaded with tourists, but the kitchen manages not only to keep up but, as its ratings show, frequently to shine.

Ruth's Chris Steak House/S | 24 | 24 | 23 | $33 |
Interior Decor Center, 999 Douglas Ave. (bet. 434 & 436), Altamonte Springs, 407-682-6444
M – Even though it's a national chain, the "great steaks" "you can cut with a fork" and "club atmosphere" make it a welcome local player; maybe it's "too expensive for what you get", but the private booths ("ask the waiter to knock first") are a kick.

Straub's Fine Seafood/S | 24 | 20 | 20 | $18 |
512 E. Altamonte Dr. (1 mile east of I-4), Altamonte Springs, 407-831-2250
5101 E. Colonial Dr. (1 mile east of Fashion Sq. Mall), Orlando, 407-273-9330
M – These twin seafood houses get top marks for their "great fresh fish at great prices"; though some call the environment "depressing" and "plastic" with tables so close you'd better be "fascinated by your dinner partners", "friendly young servers" and "unbeatable early-bird specials" are definite pluses.

Top Of The World/S | 20 | 25 | 20 | $32 |
Contemporary Resort, 4600 N. World Dr., Lake Buena Vista, 407-824-3611
U – The nightly best-of-Broadway show is what drives this Disney-resort Continental – the food's good enough, but it's not the star attraction; just make sure you get good seats and be somewhere else when the check comes; still, it's "well worth the experience."

PALM BEACH

TOP 10 RESTAURANTS
(In order of food rating)

Restaurant	Cuisine Type
26 – La Vieille Maison	French
Gazebo Cafe	French
25 – Maxaluna	Nuova Cucina Italian
Cafe Chardonnay	Amer. Contemp.
Cafe L'Europe	Continental/French
St. Honore	French
24 – L'Auberge le Grillon	French Bistro
Morada Bar & Grill	Amer. Contemp.
Ruth's Chris	Steakhouse
23 – Renato's	N/S Italian

OTHER TOP PLACES
(In alphabetical order)

Arturo's	Northern Italian
Charley's Crab	Seafood
Explorers	Amer. Contemp.
La Finestra	Northern Italian
Mark	Amer. Contemp.
Max's Grille	American/Californian
Ocean Grand Hotel	Florida Regional
Prezzo	Northern Italian
Tom's Place	Southern
Uncle Tai's	Chinese

F	D	S	C

Arturo's/S | 22 | 22 | 21 | $34 |
6750 N. Federal Hwy. (1 mile north of Yamato Rd.), Boca Raton, 407-997-7373
M – This large, "pricey" Boca Northern Italian earns high marks for its "fresh" pasta, "great presentation" and lovely setting, but not everyone is enchanted – some are "unimpressed" by the food and say that service "can be spotty"; still, the ayes are clearly in the majority, as ratings reflect.

Cafe Chardonnay/S | 25 | 21 | 23 | $33 |
Garden Sq. Shoppes, 4533 PGA Blvd. (Military Trail), Palm Beach Gardens, 407-627-2662
U – "Wow! California here we come"; this colorful Contemporary American is "highly recommended" for its "inventive" (some say too inventive) lighter fare and "colorful decor"; "like a great New York restaurant", this "class act" is "loud but good"; its summer prix fixe special menus merit a try.

PALM BEACH

| F | D | S | C |

Cafe l'Europe/S

| 25 | 26 | 24 | $41 |

Esplanada Shopping Ctr., 150 Worth Ave. (bet.
S. Ocean Blvd. & County Rd.), Palm Beach,
407-655-4020

U – As haute as the haute couture on Worth Avenue, this French-Continental is where the "beautiful people" gather for "stellar food" and "romantic atmosphere"; the "Parisian ambiance", complete with the "most beautiful floral decor", combines with "refined service" and "classic" cooking for an experience that's well worth the price.

Charley's Crab/S

| 22 | 20 | 22 | $31 |

1000 N. U.S. 1 (3 blocks north of Indiantown Rd. on Intracoastal), Jupiter, 407-744-4710
456 S. Ocean Blvd. (1 block south of Worth Ave.), Palm Beach, 407-659-1500

U – This "comfortable", publike minichain is "a longtime front-runner" for its "excellent seafood", "friendly, solicitous service" and the Jupiter location's "view of the water"; especially appealing for "brunch or lunch", these places are usually "crowded"; if a few reviewers "don't understand their popularity", the majority feel they "rise above chain status."

Explorers, The*/S

| 22 | 22 | 22 | $39 |

PGA National Resort Hotel, 400 Ave. of the Champions (PGA Blvd.), Palm Beach Gardens, 407-627-2000

U – You may want to "discover" this "good-looking" American in the PGA National Resort Hotel; it's filled with maps and explorer memorabilia, the menu runs to the likes of Caesar salad and venison chops, and the staff is "attentive."

Gazebo Cafe/S

| 26 | 22 | 22 | $37 |

4199 N. Federal Hwy. (bet. Yamato Rd. & Spanish River Blvd.), Boca Raton, 407-395-6033

M – Watch the chefs in action in the open kitchen at this excellent Boca French cafe, which features "one of the best kitchens in Palm Beach County"; despite a "very interesting menu" and "beautiful presentations", an occasional "failure to honor reservations" and "stuffy" service leave some customers feeling "poorly treated."

La Finestra

| 23 | 21 | 23 | $36 |

171 E. Palmetto Park Rd. (Mizner Blvd.), Boca Raton, 407-392-1838

U – "Dress for dinner" and enjoy "superb", "imaginative food", "impeccable service" and "great ambiance" at this "outstanding, undiscovered" Northern Italian; though some consider it "pricey" for the "small portions" served, most customers "can't wait to go back."

PALM BEACH | F | D | S | C |

L'Auberge le Grillon/S | 24 | 21 | 22 | $37 |
6900 N. Federal Hwy. (1 mile north of Yamato Rd.), Boca Raton, 407-997-6888
U – At this "quiet epitome of a French bistro", diners have found "consistently superb" traditional fare and "personalized service"; it may be "too dark" and "too small" for some, but "superior" cooking makes it a "longtime favorite" with fans who have no regrets – not even about the prices.

La Vieille Maison/S | 26 | 28 | 26 | $46 |
770 E. Palmetto Park Rd. (bet. Intracoastal Bridge & A1A), Boca Raton, 407-391-6701
U – A "culinary extravaganza" is how our respondents feel about Leonce Picot's "fabulous" Boca French, set in an old Mediterranean-style mansion filled with antiques; the classic cuisine is "consistently superior in all respects", as are the waiters (though you "can feel rushed in season"); a minority "don't understand all the fuss", but the prevailing view is that this "sets the gold standard for South Florida."

Mark, The | 23 | 22 | 20 | $36 |
Esperante Bldg., 222 Lakeview Ave. (Chase St.), W. Palm Beach, 407-835-8686
M – What some call the "best lunch in West Palm Beach" is available at this Contemporary American in a high-rise office building (though dinner's not nearly so well liked); the "unusual", "creative food", which strikes many as "light and delicious", "misses the mark" for others; nonetheless, if you're out to impress a yuppie client, it's "expensive" but a good investment.

Maxaluna Tuscan Grill/S | 25 | 23 | 22 | $36 |
Crocker Ctr., 21150 Military Trail (½ mile north of Palmetto Park Rd.), Boca Raton, 407-391-7177
U – "The best of Dennis Max's" productions brings foodies from all over to Boca's Crocker Center for "wonderfully innovative" "Contemporary Italian" cooking, served in a stylish, airy setting with a centerpiece oak-fired Tuscan grill; "friendly service" and a "hip Euro-scene" put this one "on the cutting edge", though it's inevitably "too noisy" and trendy for some; there's an "excellent selection of wines by the glass" and pleasant outdoor tables.

Max's Grille/LS | 22 | 21 | 20 | $28 |
156 Mizner Park (bet. Palmetto Pk. & Glades Rds.), Boca Raton, 407-368-0080
M – "The epitome of casual elegance", this "marvelous offering by Dennis Max" serving a "creative Californian pop menu" is a "welcome addition" to Mizner Park; the "bistro" atmosphere, featuring an "open kitchen", and "good, everyday" American cooking keep this "fashionable food mill" crowded and noisy.

PALM BEACH

| F | D | S | C |

Morada Bar & Grill/S | 24 | 21 | 19 | $37 |
Crocker Ctr., 5100 Town Ctr. Circle (1 mile north of Palmetto Pk. Rd.), Boca Raton, 407-395-0805
M – *Recently relocated, this architecturally striking Contemporary American, with its floor-to-ceiling windows allowing passersby to see the open kitchen, has been well received in the Boca dining scene; chef Andrew Swersky's "creative and tantalizing menu" and gorgeous presentations please most diners; however, on prices: "everything was great, but I'm glad I wasn't paying"; P.S. a hip mezzanine bar offers live jazz and cocktails until 5 AM on the weekends.*

Ocean Grand Hotel/S | 22 | 29 | 24 | $40 |
2800 S. Ocean Blvd. (Southern Blvd. Bridge), Palm Beach, 407-582-2800
M – *There's imaginative Contemporary regional Florida cuisine to be had at the casual Ocean Bistro, but most report being more impressed by The Restaurant, the "elegant but comfortable" dining room in the "world-class" Ocean Grand Hotel; the food is "innovative" and the "presentation great", but "grandioso prices" may make you do a double take; dissenters say "fancy-schmancy, but nothing to eat."*

Prezzo/S | 22 | 22 | 21 | $25 |
Arvida Parkway Ctr., 7820 Glades Rd. (Arvida Pkwy.), Boca Raton, 407-451-2800
U – *The ubiquitous Dennis Max is also the force behind this "very Californian", "very attractive" Northern Italian "winner"; the focal point of the decor – and the menu – is a "great wood-fired brick oven" turning out moderately priced, "consistently good food", especially the pizzas and "divine complimentary baked garlic"; "bring out-of-town guests" but expect to wait at this "always-fun" place.*

Renato's/S | 23 | 23 | 22 | $40 |
Via Mizner Arcade, 87 Via Mizner (Worth Ave.), Palm Beach, 407-655-9752
M – *"A local favorite", this "consistent" and "friendly" Italian with its "beautiful Worth Avenue setting" is "romantic on a rainy night", but many of our correspondents prefer the food at lunch; the kitchen's efforts can vary from "fair-to-good" to "superb", but prices remain "expensive."*

Ruth's Chris Steak House/S | 24 | 19 | 21 | $35 |
661 U.S. 1 (bet. N. Lake & PGA Blvds.), N. Palm Beach, 407-863-0660
M – *The consensus on the Palm Beach branch of this national chain: big steaks and big prices; fans adore what they call "the best steak in town", with "portions so large they require sharing"; critics of the cooked-in-butter approach dismiss it as a "typical steakhouse" with "outrageous prices"; solid numbers suggest that if you enjoy red meat, you'll do well here.*

PALM BEACH | F | D | S | C |

St. Honore/S | 25 | 24 | 22 | $46 |
Harbour Shops, 2401 PGA Blvd. (Prosperity Farm), Palm Beach Gardens, 407-627-9099
U – "Très French" and "très good", this lovely auberge overlooking the harbor is terrific for a leisurely meal – "make sure you have five hours to dine"; its "very fattening" Classic-Contemporary menu pleases nearly all of our diners, as does the "great setting" and professional service, but don't be surprised by the stiff bill.

Tom's Place/X | 23 | 12 | 17 | $18 |
7251 N. Federal Hwy. (bet. Linton Blvd. & Yamato Rd.), Boca Raton, 407-997-0920
M – "Hog heaven" to many, this "Boca tradition" dishes up "down-home barbecue" and "the best Southern trimmings around", though a few find the sauce "too sweet" and the ribs "greasy"; service is famously "surly" (the high number suggests it doesn't matter a bit) and the crowds make it imperative to "get there early", but once you try the ribs, "you'll never go anywhere else."

Uncle Tai's | 23 | 24 | 22 | $31 |
Crocker Ctr., 5250 Town Ctr. Circle (1 mile north of Palmetto Pk. Rd.), Boca Raton, 407-368-8806
U – "A refined refuge from chop suey joints", this top-rated, "creative" Boca Chinese is undeniably "expensive", but the "luxurious decor" and "superb service" help justify the cost; while many find the Hunan-Szechuan specialties "in a class by themselves", a few Sinophobes say it's "much ado about nothing."

PHILADELPHIA

TOP 30 RESTAURANTS
(In order of food rating)

Restaurant	Cuisine Type
29 – Le Bec-Fin	French Classic
28 – Fountain	International
26 – Ciboulette	French Nouvelle
Dmitri's	Mediteranean
Swann Lounge	Amer. Tradition.
Tacconelli's Pizza	Pizza
Le Bar Lyonnais	French Bistro
Gaetano's	Northern Italian
Green Hills Inn	Continental
Jean-Pierre's	French Classic
Susanna Foo	Chinese
Alisa Cafe	French/Thai
Napoleon Cafe	Desserts
25 – Deux Cheminees	French Classic
Evermay on Delaware	Amer. Contemp./French
Joe's Restaurant	Amer. Contemp.
La Truffe	French Classic
Osteria Romana	N/S Italian
Frenchtown Inn	Continental
Restaurant 210	Continental
La Famiglia	N/S Italian
24 – Harrow Inne	Continental/French
La Bonne Auberge	French Classic
Mainland Inn	Amer. Contemp.
Sagami	Japanese
La Fourchette	French Classic
Saloon	N/S Italian/Steakhouse
Chez Robert	French Nouvelle
Monte Carlo Living Rm.	Northern Italian
Coventry Forge Inn	French Classic

OTHER TOP PLACES
(In alphabetical order)

Braddock's Tavern	Amer. Tradition.
Dilullo Centro	N/S Italian
Inn at Phillips Mill	French Bistro
Jake's Restaurant	Amer. Contemp.
La Campagne	French Bistro
Morton's of Chicago	Steakhouse
Odeon	French Bistro
Reading Term. Mkt.	Eclectic
Roller's	Amer. Contemp.
Vietnam Restaurant	Vietnamese

PHILADELPHIA | F | D | S | C |

Alisa Cafe/S | 26 | 14 | 22 | $30 |
109 Fairfield Ave. (Garrett Rd.), Upper Darby,
215-352-4402
U – This "tiny gem" in Upper Darby is a "great find" and the "best BYO bargain in town", winning raves for its "excellent", "fresh, original French-Thai cuisine"; a handful of dissenters feel it has "gone downhill" in the last few years, and more than a few find the tables "too close for comfort", but its food ratings continue to be among the highest in the area.

Braddock's Tavern/S | 22 | 22 | 21 | $32 |
39 S. Main St. (Rtes. 70 & 541), Medford, NJ,
609-654-1604
M – The "quaint" setting of this restored 19th-century South Jersey American earns high marks from most diners, though some call it "coldly correct" and others deem it "country kitsch"; while the Early American food pleases the majority ("try the game pie"), some think it "could use a little innovation."

Chez Robert | 24 | 24 | 22 | $51 |
329 Haddon Ave. (Kings Hwy. & Cuthbert Blvd.),
Westmont, NJ, 609-854-5727
M – South Jersey's fanciest French restaurant is either a "superior" experience with "plentiful" quantities of "great" food (especially the "heavenly" seafood buffet) or a "pretentious", "très cher" "Le Bec-Fin wannabe", depending on whom you ask; lunch is a relative bargain.

Ciboulette | 26 | – | 24 | $51 |
200 S. Broad St. (13th St.), 215-790-1210
U – The understated decor at the relatively new site of this Contemporary Provençal French pleases those who want "no distractions" from the "well-conceived", "exquisitely presented" food, which ranks with "the best in town"; there's no question that the food is "incredible", even "awesome", and that the service is excellent, but past surveyors hope the new room merits the stiff tab.

Coventry Forge Inn | 24 | 23 | 22 | $44 |
Coventry Forge Inn, Pottstown-Coventryville Rd.
(1½ miles west of Rtes. 100 & 23), Coventryville,
215-469-6222
M – Owner Wallis Callahan may well be "the patron saint of the Philadelphia restaurant renaissance", but whether the French cooking is still sublime at his "lovely country estate" in northern Chester County is a matter of debate; most (supported by high ratings) report it's "still tops", while a few suggest it's "in decline"; almost everyone thinks the overnight rooms (reserve ahead) make it "the perfect romantic getaway."

PHILADELPHIA

| F | D | S | C |

Deux Cheminees/S | 25 | 26 | 24 | $55 |
1221 Locust St. (bet. 12th & 13th Sts.), 215-790-0200
U – The "most beautiful room in Philadelphia" may well be in this 19th-century Center City townhouse, where dining can be a "celestial experience" – though more than a few lament the "unreal" prices; when it's good, which is almost always, the food is "masterfully prepared", and the "warm", "theatrical" setting works well with service that's "impeccable" if a bit "stuffy."

Dilullo Centro | 23 | 26 | 21 | $43 |
1407 Locust St. (bet. Broad & 15th Sts.), 215-546-2000
M – "Gorgeous murals" and lush appointments make this "romantic, sensuous" restaurant near the Academy of Music "one of the most beautiful in the city", but the Italian food, though very good, doesn't rate quite as well; some consider it "very rich", "fancy" and "superb", but others subtract points for "microscopic" portions from a kitchen that produces "more flash than substance."

Dmitri's/S | 26 | 15 | 20 | $21 |
795 S. 3rd St. (Catharine St.), 215-625-0556
U – The lines outside this tiny Queen Village Mediterranean every night tell it all: "by far the best new kid on the block", with "excellent everything"; despite some irritation with the "havoc-creating" no-reservations policy and the fact that it's "cramped and uncomfortable", most say the "fresh, simply and skillfully prepared" seafood ("who'd ever have thought I'd dream of octopus?") and excellent value make it "worth the minor inconvenience"; BYO.

Evermay On The Delaware/S | 25 | 26 | 25 | $48 |
Evermay on the Delaware Hotel, River Rd. (13½ miles north of New Hope), Erwinna, 215-294-9100
M – A "treasure" of a "beautiful country house", "simply delicious" French-American cooking and "attention to detail" make this Bucks County hotel the sort of place that kindles romance; "stay the night – breakfast is lovely on the porch"; a very few nitpickers say they "don't see why this place gets such great reviews."

Fountain, The/S | 28 | 28 | 28 | $48 |
Four Seasons Hotel, Logan Sq. (bet. 18th St. & Ben Franklin Pkwy.), 215-963-1500
U – For "the best fancy meal in town", with "excellent, inventive food in a beautiful setting" and the "most attentive service short of being burped", don't miss this International overlooking the Parkway in the "classiest hotel in the city"; universal raves greet everything from the "orgasmic brunch" to the "beautifully rich dessert cart."

PHILADELPHIA | F | D | S | C |

Frenchtown Inn/S | 25 | 22 | 22 | $40 |
7 Bridge St. (Rte. 29), Frenchtown, NJ, 908-996-3300
U – *This "rural romantic" small-town inn is "one of the most all-around charming" restaurants in the Philadelphia area; its mostly "fantastic" Continental cooking features "inventive combinations", but there's less enthusiasm for its usually good but at times "offhanded service."*

Gaetano's | 26 | 24 | 24 | $47 |
705 Walnut St. (bet. 7th & 8th Sts.), 215-627-7575
U – *Inez Gaetano, hostess and co-owner (with her husband, Tommy), is "the heart and soul" of this "very romantic" townhouse near Washington Square, which serves "the absolute best Northern Italian food in Philadelphia"; there's no telling whether you'll find her "warm" or "overbearing", but you're almost sure to approve of the "homey", "gracious" atmosphere and the "superb" "old-style" cooking.*

Green Hills Inn, The | 26 | 23 | 24 | $41 |
Exit 2, Rte. 10, Green Hills (near Reading), 215-777-9611
U – *"An honest welcome is followed by a great meal" at this "consistently good" Berks County country inn; most proclaim the Continental food, starring the "best meats in the area", to be "superb in every way"; though some surveyors say the decor is getting "a little shabby", it's still well "worth the trip."*

Harrow Inne, The/S | 24 | 22 | 24 | $43 |
Rtes. 611 & 412, Ottsville, 215-847-2464
U – *This handsome Bucks County inn is "worth the trip" for its "wonderful" French-Continental fare, "incredible wine cellar" and "congenial host" in the person of owner Klaus Reinecke; sure, it's expensive, but this is "hospitality at its warmest" – probably the reason why it's a "favorite on cold nights."*

Inn at Phillips Mill, The/SX | 23 | 25 | 21 | $35 |
The Inn at Phillips Mill, North River Rd. (Rte. 32), New Hope, 215-862-9919
U – *The "grand Colonial setting" and "timeless" French menu of this Bucks County inn are quintessentially "romantic", especially in the garden ("sigh"); though some say the food is "unimaginative", most of our participants say it's a "favorite" "jewel" in the country; P.S. book early for a table in the garden or for overnight stays.*

Jake's Restaurant/S | 23 | 20 | 22 | $34 |
4365 Main St. (Levering St.), 215-483-0444
U – *The "artsy decor" of this "hopping Manayunk eatery" – both the building and its interior are decorated with orginal artwork – keeps up with the "artful" New American food, which fans praise as "consistent" and "innovative"; the wine list is "fine", and there's "great service" and even greater people-watching.*

PHILADELPHIA

| F | D | S | C |

Jean-Pierre's/S | 26 | 21 | 23 | $47 |
101 S. State St. (Centre St.), Newtown, 215-968-6201
U – The "best French restaurant in the 'burbs'" is this "wonderful", "elegant and romantic" 18th-century stone house in Newtown in the Delaware Valley, where excellent service complements "superb", if not always consistent, Classic French fare.

Joe's Restaurant | 25 | 17 | 21 | $39 |
450 S. 7th St. (Laurel St.), Reading, 215-373-6794
U – Mushroom lovers flock to Reading, and no wonder: wild and tame, "mushrooms like you never imagined" – handpicked by the Czarnecki family – distinguish an American menu that "still manages to be original after all these years"; though phobes say it's "a long drive for some mushrooms", philes say it's "worth a detour" to dine on "excellent" (if "pricey") food – don't miss the mushroom soup – in a "relaxed, European atmosphere" featuring solid service and a "spectacular" wine list.

La Bonne Auberge/S | 24 | 26 | 24 | $46 |
Village 2, Mechanic St., New Hope, 215-862-2462
U – "The most romantic French restaurant this side of Paris", this "elegant" stone farmhouse in the Bucks County countryside is "worth the trip even in a snowstorm" say our surveyors; a few dissenters think only the prices are extraordinary, but most say "if you can afford it, it can't be beat" for its "beautiful dining room", polished service and "fabulous food."

La Campagne/S | 23 | 21 | 21 | $39 |
312 Kresson Rd. (Brace Rd., 2 miles from Rte. 70), Cherry Hill, NJ, 609-429-7647
M – Set in a farmhouse overlooking a garden in Cherry Hill, this "absolutely charming" Country French is under new ownership, but most think it's still "good for the suburbs"; doubters grouse about prices, close tables and the corkage fee, but there's universal praise for the "incredible" desserts.

La Famiglia Ristorante/S | 25 | 22 | 22 | $43 |
8 S. Front St. (bet. Market & Chestnut Sts.), 215-922-2803
U – The "best Italian restaurant in town", period, say the myriad fans of this Old City landmark, with "glorious food" and a cool, formal setting, plus a wine list that's "the Bible of Italian wine"; the service, though "impeccable", strikes some as haughty, and the food is "seriously high-priced", but no one is complaining at this "Italian answer to Le Bec-Fin"; "mangia, mangia."

PHILADELPHIA | F | D | S | C |

La Fourchette/S | 24 | 22 | 23 | $40 |
110 N. Wayne Ave. (Rte. 30, Lancaster Pike), Wayne, 215-687-8333
U – Pretty-in-pink and "wonderfully elegant", this French restaurant in Wayne is "tops on the Main Line", offering "classic food" and "beautiful decor", with "attentive" service to match, according to its many devotees; the worst anyone can find to say is that the menu could be "more innovative", but then again, this is the Main Line.

La Truffe | 25 | 24 | 24 | $50 |
10 S. Front St. (bet. Market & Chestnut Sts.), 215-925-5062
M – "A joy forever" is how delighted diners describe this "elegant" Old City favorite, "one of Philadelphia's best for French Classic" and "second only to Le Bec-Fin" (and "not as pricey"); some worry that it's "tattered around the edges" and starting to slide, but the clear majority say "superb", "imaginative" – a "must for a special occasion."

Le Bar Lyonnais | 26 | 26 | 26 | $29 |
1523 Walnut St. (15th St.), 215-567-1000
U – The "fanciest snack-and-dessert spot in town" and a "wonderful idea that's long overdue" is how fans describe this basement bistro beneath Le Bec-Fin; it's "fun" anytime and especially "great after the theater" for its pleasing "light fare"; drinks are "very expensive", but the food is "wonderful and reasonably priced."

Le Bec-Fin | 29 | 28 | 28 | $73 |
1523 Walnut St. (15th St.), 215-567-1000
U – When chef-owner Georges Perrier is in the kitchen, Philadelphia's most famous shrine to French cuisine is "heaven", "the best French restaurant in the country" and "one of the premier restaurants on the planet" according to its many, many admirers; they admonish that "if you don't love this restaurant, you don't understand haute French food"; though it's undeniably expensive, most say they'd "rather eat one meal here than four anywhere else" and that it's "worth every C-note"; as with all great restaurants, there are a few who complain of laurel-resting and pomposity, but for almost everyone else, it's "first class all the way"; N.B. the $31 prix fixe lunch is a steal.

Mainland Inn | 24 | 22 | 24 | $35 |
17 Main St. (Rte. 163), Mainland, 215-256-8500
U – "Montgomery County's best-kept secret" is this "beautiful restored Colonial inn" near Lansdale, which gets raves for its "very consistent", "imaginative and well-prepared" seasonal American food; the "friendly but professional" service and "hands-on" management convince our surveyors that "these people really know what they're doing"; kudos also go to the wine list, with its emphasis on local wines.

PHILADELPHIA | F | D | S | C |

Monte Carlo Living Room/S | 24 | 24 | 23 | $45 |
150 Second St. (South St.), 215-925-2220
U – The "exquisite" Northern Italian fare at this elegantly "baroque" restaurant/lounge off Headhouse Square is "an all-time favorite", with enthusiastic reviewers reporting that it's "as good as Italy" or at least New York; it carries too hefty a price tag for some, however, while others disparage the "Mediterranean glitz" and staff "with an attitude problem"; all praise the "romantic" upstairs lounge where you can "dance off the calories."

Morton's of Chicago/S | 23 | 19 | 21 | $40 |
19th & Cherry Sts. (Ben Franklin Pkwy.), 215-557-0724
U – For beef lovers, this dark and sort of "stuffy" City Center outpost of a Chicago-based steakhouse chain really "delivers when you crave red meat at its best", serving up "huge great steaks exactly as ordered", along with gigantic lobsters; fans rave over the porterhouse ("not to be believed!") and cauliflower soup, but beefs include the noise level and "attentive but very pushy" waiters; P.S. this one's expensive, but "worth it."

Napoleon Cafe/SX | 26 | 27 | 25 | $12 |
2652 E. Somerset St. (bet. Richmond & Aramingo Sts.), 215-739-6979
U – It's "unparalleled for dessert" and coffee, say the unrestrained admirers of this "unexpectedly beautiful" place in the working-class neighborhood of Port Richmond; besides "exquisite", "amazing desserts" from the "emperors of cream", all served up in a European atmosphere, it's swell for lunch too; N.B. a decent pasta restaurant called Upstairs at Napoleon opened recently.

Odeon | 23 | 21 | 21 | $36 |
114 S. 12th St. (bet. Chestnut & Sansom Sts.), 215-922-5875
M – This "exquisite French bistro right in Center City" serves "wonderful" French-Mediterranean fare accompanied by an "exceptional", "well-priced" wine list; the balcony tables are perfect for people-watching, but a few of our surveyors say the "staff needs to loosen up"; fans consider it "an oasis of civility" in a chaotic world.

Osteria Romana/S | 25 | 19 | 22 | $44 |
935 Ellsworth St. (bet. 9th & 10th Sts.), 215-271-9191
U – "The tops in a city filled with Italian restaurants" is this "authentically Roman" ristorante in South Philly, serving "inventive", "intriguing", "tantalizing", but far-from-cheap food in an "intimate yet convivial setting"; though critics say it's "inconsistent" and the service is "too macho", most of our surveyors are convinced that there is "really something special here."

PHILADELPHIA

| F | D | S | C |

Reading Terminal Market/X | 23 | 16 | 17 | $11 |
12th & Arch Sts., 215-922-2317
U – "One of the best things about Philadelphia" is this "giant food circus" of fresh produce, fish, meat and poultry stands, as well as a plethora of inexpensive ethnic and Amish lunch counters and even the Down Home Diner; though a few gadflies say it's "dirty", to hundreds of our surveyors it's "an irreplaceable treasure", bordering on a "religious experience" of "ethnic and epicurean diversity", not to mention "the greatest value in town."

Restaurant 210 | 25 | 26 | 25 | $50 |
The Rittenhouse Hotel, 210 W. Rittenhouse Sq. (19th St., bet. Walnut & Locust Sts.), 215-790-2534
U – "Elegant – quite simply elegant", this new Continental restaurant in the Rittenhouse Hotel offers "outstanding" food and "superb light sauces", as well as a "beautiful view" of Rittenhouse Square; the consensus, borne out by high ratings across the board, is that this newcomer is "trying very hard to be the best and doing very nicely" in approaching its goal.

Roller's/SX | 23 | 12 | 19 | $27 |
8705 Germantown Ave. (Bethlehem Pike), 215-242-1771
M – "If you can take the hustle-bustle" and the "out-of-sight noise level", this popular ("crowded!") bistro in Chestnut Hill is a "great neighborhood restaurant", with a display kitchen that serves "delicious", "fresh", "consistently tasty and stylish" Contemporary American food at "great prices"; critics contend that it's a "zoo" and the food's "nothing to write home about"; N.B. brunch is your best bet.

Sagami/S | 24 | 17 | 20 | $25 |
37 Crescent Blvd. (Rte. 130), Collingswood, NJ, 609-854-9773
U – "Worth the drive" to New Jersey for "great sushi" and "good basic Japanese home cooking" (including the "best yosenabe" and macrobiotic specialties), this is "the No. 1 Japanese in the area"; fans say it also it has the "most efficient service in the Delaware Valley", even though customers are "packed in like sardines."

Saloon | 24 | 21 | 20 | $38 |
750 S. 7th St. (bet. Fitzwater & Catharine Sts.), 215-627-1811
M – This crowded and noisy, "masculine" South Philly power spot is a favorite of many, who praise its "great decor", "gorgeous antiques", "consistently outstanding" steaks and Italian fare, and "nice waitresses"; dissenters think it's "overpriced" and the "wait for tables is ridiculous."

PHILADELPHIA | F | D | S | C |

Susanna Foo/S | 26 | 21 | 22 | $37 |
1512 Walnut St. (bet. 15th & 16th Sts.), 215-545-2666
U – Susanna "takes Chinese food to new heights" at this "sleek and elegant" Center City spot; typical reactions to her French-influenced fare include: "exquisite and progressive", "the best Chinese ever" and a "memorable experience"; the few complaints registered center on "aloof" service, "tiny portions" and prices that seem high for Chinese food, but most of Susanna's myriad admirers report that her tab is well "worth it."

Swann Lounge & Cafe/LS | 26 | 27 | 25 | $33 |
Four Seasons Hotel, 1 Logan Sq. (bet. 18th St. & Ben Franklin Pkwy.), 215-963-1500
U – This "wonderful", "elegant" lounge in the Four Seasons Hotel provides "very creative" American cuisine in a "romantic" atmosphere that's perfect for a light meal, "exquisite" afternoon tea, late-night drink or "super" Sunday brunch; with its wonderful view of the Parkway, excellent service and overall feeling of luxury, "why go anyplace else?"

Tacconelli's Pizza/X | 26 | 9 | 14 | $12 |
2604 E. Sommerset St. (bet. Richmond & Aramingo Sts.), 215-425-4983
U – Surveyors debate whether the pizza from this brick-oven shrine in Port Richmond is the "best in Philly", the "best this side of the Tiber", or the "best in the universe", but virtually no one says that it's anything less than "great" (especially the white pizza); hour-long waits help sharpen the appetite; BYO and don't expect much in the way of decor.

Vietnam Restaurant/S | 23 | 9 | 19 | $16 |
221 N. 11th St. (bet. Race & Arch Sts.), 215-592-1163
U – "Never before have so many eaten so well for so little" could be the motto of this "excellent" – and "crowded" – Chinatown Vietnamese; it's a "real value", and the "friendly" staff will gladly guide you through the exotic menu that's so good it's hard to make a mistake; N.B. a recent renovation addresses the complaints many of our surveyors had about the decor – or lack thereof.

PHOENIX/SCOTTSDALE

TOP 30 RESTAURANTS
(In order of food rating)

Restaurant	Cuisine Type
29 – Vincent Guerithault	Amer. Tradition./SW
27 – Franco's Trattoria	Northern Italian
Yamakasa	Japanese
Marquesa	Spanish
Christopher's/Bistro	French Nouvelle/Amer.
26 – Palm Court	Continental
Ruth's Chris	Steakhouse
Latilla Room	Amer. Contemp.
Mary Elaine's	Mediterranean
Restaurant	Continental
Golden Swan	Southwestern
Voltaire	French Classic
25 – La Hacienda	Mexican
Roxsand	Amer. Contemp.
Gourmet House	Chinese
Greekfest	Greek
Grill/Ritz-Carlton	Amer. Tradition.
Eliana's	Salvadoran
Christo's	Continental/No. Italian
24 – Nina L'Italiana	N/S Italian
Malee's on Main	Thai
Chapparal Room	Continental
Mrs. White's Golden Rule	Soul Food
Shogun	Japanese
T.C. Eggington's	Amer. Tradition.
23 – House of Joy	Continental
L'Ecole	Eclectic
Havana Cafe	Cuban
Arizona Kitchen	Southwestern
Indian Delhi Palace	Indian

OTHER TOP PLACES
(In alphabetical order)

Different Pointe of View	Continental
Fajitas	Tex-Mex
Horny Toad	Amer. Tradition.
Houston's	Amer. Tradition.
Jean Claude's	French Bistro
Mancuso's	Continental
Steamer's	Seafood
Top of the Rock	Southwestern
Z'Tejas Grill	Southwestern

PHOENIX/SCOTTSDALE

| F | D | S | C |

Arizona Kitchen | 23 | 22 | 23 | $26 |

Wigwam Resort, 300 E. Indian School Lane (bet. Litchfield Rd. & Indian School Rd.), Litchfield Park, 602-935-3811

U – It's "worth the drive" out to the boonies to try the "top-shelf" "brilliantly inventive regional creations"; a cozy Southwestern-accented room with an open-to-view kitchen and "excellent service" make this "a gem."

Chapparal Room/S | 24 | 24 | 25 | $30 |

Camelback Inn, 5402 E. Lincoln Dr. (Tatum Blvd.), Scottsdale, 602-948-1700

M – Long "one of the Valley's best hotel restaurants", this "first-class" Continental is perfect for a "romantic Southwestern-style dinner" and "servers are real pros"; the cuisine, though not adventurous, is "always a treat"; all this adds up to a delightful dining experience.

Christopher's and The Bistro/S | 27 | 27 | 25 | $34 |

Northern Trust Bank Bldg., 2398 E. Camelback Rd. (24th St.), Phoenix, 602-957-3214

U – Two separate standout restaurants sharing a single kitchen and "the best wine cellar in town" under the aegis of nationally known chef-owner Chris Gross; The Bistro features Mediterranean-influenced American food, while the fancier Christopher's is Contemporary French; both "stylish spots" have "great decor", "cosmopolitan elegance" and "first-rate people-watching"; both are deemed "pricey", however, and service while generally first-class, can be "snobbish and inconsistent."

Christo's | 25 | 20 | 23 | $22 |

6327 N. 7th St. (bet. Bethany Home Rd. & Glendale Ave.), Phoenix, 602-264-1784

U – At this "friendly", "warm", North Central Italian-Continental, the fare is "consistently excellent in quality and value"; what some call "small" and "intimate", others say is "noisy" and "crowded", but the crowd has plenty of good reasons to be here.

Different Pointe of View/S | 22 | 25 | 22 | $27 |

Pointe Hilton Resort, 11111 N. 7th St. (Thunderbird Rd.), Phoenix, 602-863-0912

M – This mountaintop Continental is "high-up and high-priced"; while most surveyors call the interior "elegant" and like the "award-winning view", others say it's "tired"; all agree that Sunday brunch is "great" but the Continental food may be "inconsistent" and service, usually "professional", may be "attitudinal."

PHOENIX/SCOTTSDALE | F | D | S | C |

Eliana's/SX | 25 | 10 | 21 | $11 |
2401 N. 32nd St. (4 blocks south of Thomas Rd.),
Phoenix, 602-957-9442
U – Owned and operated by a "charming family", this friendly, centrally located Salvadoran restaurant is nothing to look at, but is universally adored for "delicious home-cooked food and great values"; every city needs an Eliana's.

L'Ecole | 23 | 20 | 23 | $19 |
8100 E. Camelback Rd. (Hayden Rd.), Scottsdale,
602-990-7639
U – This working classroom of the Scottsdale Culinary Institute serves student-prepared fare which is "uneven but interesting" at "the most reasonable cost anywhere"; the service is "impeccable" and the "new accommodations in East Scottsdale are terrific."

Fajitas/S | 23 | 17 | 18 | $14 |
9841 N. Black Canyon Hwy. (bet. Dunlap & Peoria),
Phoenix, 602-870-4030
U – As the name suggests, this high-energy Westside Tex-Mex serves "the best fajitas in town"; the "to-die-for flour tortillas", "killer" margaritas and "fast service" also receive thumbs up, but the no-reservation policy (read: long waits) and bad ventilation (read: smoky) get thumbs down.

Franco's Trattoria | 27 | 15 | 23 | $24 |
Mountain View Plaza, 9619 N. Hayden Rd. (Mountain View), Scottsdale, 602-948-6655
U – Chef-owner Franco (ex NYC's Cent'Anni) has brought his "fabulous" if "pricey" Florentine food to the Southwest, and diners say it's "the best in Phoenix", with matching service; it's ever-popular despite a hard-to-find, "less-than-lovely" strip-mall location that survyeors report as "small, crowded and noisy."

Golden Swan/S | 26 | 28 | 25 | $32 |
Hyatt Regency Scottsdale, 7500 E. Doubletree Ranch Rd. (south of E. Shea Blvd.), Scottsdale, 602-483-5572
U – "Lovely setting and lovely food" describe this "wonderfully romantic" hotel restaurant serving "innovative" and "excellent" but "pricey" Southwestern-inspired food; "feed the swans while eating" on the beautiful patio and don't forget the "fantastic Sunday brunch"; all in all, a "treat."

Gourmet House of Hong Kong/S | 25 | 9 | 17 | $10 |
1438 E. McDowell Rd. (15th St.), Phoenix, 602-253-4859
U – Located near Downtown, this "authentic" bargain spot wins the title "best Chinese in the area" from its many fans; it's "truly a back alley bonanza" that has recently expanded and redecorated (the decor rating may not reflect the change); try the "five-spice shrimp" or Peking duck.

PHOENIX/SCOTTSDALE | F | D | S | C |

Greekfest | 25 | 19 | 22 | $19 |
1940 E. Camelback Rd. (20th St.), Phoenix, 602-265-2990
U – "Upscale Greek" recently relocated to Midtown that's "possibly the best in Phoenix"; "wonderful management and service" and "great Greek goodies" (gyros, moussaka, etc.) make this "a delightful food fest."

Grill at The Ritz-Carlton/S | 25 | 27 | 26 | $30 |
Ritz-Carlton Hotel, 2401 E. Camelback Rd. (24th St.), Phoenix, 602-468-0700
U – A clubby and "ritzy" dining room tucked away in a centrally located Phoenix hotel, this American grill has a "wonderful classy atmosphere", high-priced "excellent fare" and "very good service."

Havana Cafe | 23 | 18 | 21 | $19 |
4225 E. Camelback Rd. (44th St.), Phoenix, 602-952-1991
U – The Eastside is home to this "busy, crowded Cuban" that's as "real as Fidel" but forget the cigar – "no smoking allowed"; the "excellent food" ("super" Cuban steak, "great" plantains) is a "value" and the staff likes to make everyone happy.

Horny Toad/S | 17 | 18 | 17 | $15 |
6738 E. Cave Creek Rd. (north of Carefree Hwy.), Cave Creek, 602-997-9622
M – All surveyors agree that this "very rustic" American is "fun", and a "must" when in Cave Creek – especially for visitors; on the downside, the "no-frills" fried chicken and burger fare is "nothing special", and this spot is "so noisy" you can't hear yourself chew.

House of Joy/SX | 23 | 22 | 23 | $24 |
Hull Ave., Jerome, 602-634-5339
U – This "former brothel" in "ghost town–like" Jerome is a joy for our survey participants; the "cozy and unusual" decor, homestyle Continental dinners and the "friendliest" service earn high marks across the board; "a favorite" that's "worth the trip."

Houston's/S | 21 | 19 | 21 | $16 |
The Esplanade Complex, 2425 E. Camelback Rd. (24th St.), Phoenix, 602-957-9700
M – This moderately priced Eastside "yuppie boy-meets-girl" watering hole is always crowded and "very noisy"; some like the fast service, but others complain about "Gestapo-like hostesses" who "turn tables too fast"; the straightforward American food (especially the burgers and salads) is "always good."

PHOENIX/SCOTTSDALE | F | D | S | C |

Indian Delhi Palace/S | 23 | 14 | 18 | $15 |
5050 E. McDowell Rd. (51st St.), Phoenix, 602-244-8181
U – Delhi meets Phoenix at this "choice bit of India in the Valley"; some grumble about the "odd Eastside location" and the "disgusting restrooms", but all agree that the reasonably priced "authentic" fare is "amply portioned" and "wonderfully hot and spicy."

Jean Claude's Petit Cafe | 23 | 20 | 22 | $24 |
7340 E. Shoeman Ln. (southeast of Scottsdale & Camelback Rds.), Scottsdale, 602-947-5288
M – The pricey "petite portions" at this old-town Scottsdale "Country French favorite" bother some critics, as does the all-alleged "pretentious attitude", but most diners laud the "lovely, romantic" ambiance and "consistently excellent food."

La Hacienda/S | 25 | 26 | 24 | $25 |
Scottsdale Princess Resort, 7575 E. Princess Dr. (Scottsdale Rd., north of Bell Rd.), Scottsdale, 602-271-9000
U – Elegant upscale Far North Scottsdale Mexican that rings the bell with "fabulous food, service and decor"; try the signature roast suckling pig or the "delicious black bean dip"; it's "fun, fun, fun", especially the wandering mariachi players; "pricey" by local standards, this would be a big bargain in NYC or LA.

Latilla Room/S | 26 | 27 | 26 | $34 |
Boulders Resort, 34631 Tom Darlington Rd. (Carefree Hwy.), Carefree, 602-488-9009
U – The main dining room of this "superb resort" wins unanimous praise: "most beautiful", "elegant", "romantic" and "wonderful"; the "innovative" New American fare is expensive but first-class all the way – "close to perfection"; ditto: service.

Malee's on Main Street/S | 24 | 18 | 22 | $17 |
7131 E. Main St. (west of Scottsdale Rd.), Scottsdale, 602-947-6042
U – "Crowds and noise" are the price of popularity at this upscale Midtown Thai where a "wonderful and knowledgeable" staff serves "spicy", "creative" and "authentic" dishes that surveyors say are the "best in town"; this is the place to Thai one on.

Mancuso's | 22 | 25 | 22 | $27 |
Borgotta Shopping Ctr., 6166 N. Scottsdale Rd. (south of Lincoln Dr.), Scottsdale, 602-948-9988
M – No question about it, this Northside Italian-Continental's "elegant" "old-world" European decor wins unanimous praise, but surveyors are divided on the very expensive food – some say it's "magnificent", while others say it's "disappointing"; the staff, while generally attentive and professional, strike some as "stuffy " and "pretentious."

PHOENIX/SCOTTSDALE | F | D | S | C |

Marquesa/S | 27 | 27 | 26 | $31 |
Scottsdale Princess Resort, 7575 E. Princess Dr. (Scottsdale Rd., north of Bell Rd.), Scottsdale, 602-271-9000
U – Not your usual resort dining room, this "wonderful" cream-toned special-occasion stunner serves "fantastic" Catalan-style food in an "elegant" yet "unpretentious" manner; it's expensive, but worth every dime, and to top it off, the "Sunday brunch is the best in the U.S."

Mary Elaine's | 26 | 28 | 27 | $41 |
The Phoenician Resort, 6000 E. Camelback Rd. (60th St.), Scottsdale, 602-941-8200
U – Another "special-occasion place", this "elegant" Mediterranean with a "gorgeous view" has "first-class", "very expensive" food and a "fabulous wine list"; the only sour note is an occasional service lapse, but as its ratings show, lapses here are exceedingly rare.

Mrs. White's Golden Rule Cafe/X | 24 | 11 | 17 | $9 |
808 E. Jefferson St. (8th St.), Phoenix, 602-262-9256
U – The "home-cooked Soul Food" is "perfect" at this quintessential "hole-in-the-wall" near Downtown; the name refers to the fact that no bills are presented, the customers tell the cashier what they ate – "do unto others..."

Nina L'Italiana/S | 24 | 16 | 22 | $19 |
Laguna Palms Shopping Ctr., 3625 E. Bell Rd. (36th St.), Phoenix, 602-482-6167
U – Northside Italian newcomer that wins kudos for its "made-from-scratch" fare, particularly the "excellent pastas" and "mouth-watering" ravioli; some "overpriced" dishes and "slow" but "attentive" service are the only glitches that need to be ironed out at this sure to be a winner.

Palm Court/S | 26 | 26 | 25 | $32 |
Scottsdale Conf. Resort, 7700 E. McCormick Pkwy. (east of Scottsdale Rd.), Scottsdale, 602-991-3400
U – The "Sunday brunch is especially wonderful" at this "elegant" "first-class" Continental tucked away in East Scottsdale; it's "worth the cost" for full pampering despite what some call "pretentious" service.

Restaurant, The/S | 26 | 27 | 26 | $34 |
Ritz-Carlton Hotel, 2401 E. Camelback Rd. (24th St.), Phoenix, 602-468-0700
M – "Prick your finger and if it comes out blue you belong" at this "luxurious" Midtown Continental; this is first-class "celebration dining in a rich European atmosphere" with "lovely service" and "class without pretense" – but do "bring money", it's expensive.

PHOENIX/SCOTTSDALE | F | D | S | C |

Roxsand/S | 25 | 23 | 23 | $27 |
Biltmore Fashion Park, 2495 E. Camelback Rd., 2nd fl. (24th St.), Phoenix, 602-381-0444
M – "If smug New Yorkers are visiting, take them here" for the "most imaginative cooking in town" (owner Roxanne Scocos calls it "New American Fusion cuisine") and sharp, contemporary decor; some critics take exception to the "noise", "uncomfortable chairs" and what they call "spotty service", but the food, if a little pricey, gets an unqualified "sublime."

Ruth's Chris Steak House/S | 26 | 21 | 22 | $30 |
2201 E. Camelback Rd. (22nd St.), Phoenix, 602-957-9600
M – A branch of a national chain, this top-dollar red-meat sibling packs in the carnivores for butter-flavored, melt-in-your-mouth steaks; the "sterile surroundings" and "servers filled with their own self-importance" don't win special praise, but solid ratings for decor and service should make you discount such criticism, and if great steak is your goal this is the place.

Shogun/S | 24 | 15 | 20 | $17 |
12615 N. Tatum Blvd. (Cactus Rd.), Phoenix, 602-953-3264
U – "The best all-around Japanese food in the Valley", not to mention "impeccably fresh sushi", is dished up at this "cozy", "appealing" Northside restaurant; it's "always packed", but the food is reasonably priced and the service is casual and friendly; N.B. the "peanut and chicken salad" at lunch gets extra votes.

Steamer's Genuine Seafood/S | 22 | 21 | 20 | $21 |
Biltmore Fashion Park, 2576 E. Camelback Rd., 2nd fl. (24th St.), Phoenix, 602-956-3631
M – "Good fresh fish" and plenty of noise are the specialties at this popular Midtown yuppie fish house; although a few complain of inconsistency and high prices, most praise the "excellent seafood", "pleasant setting" and "great staff."

T. C. Eggington's/S | 24 | 18 | 21 | $11 |
1660 S. Alma School Rd. (Superstition Fwy.), Mesa, 602-345-9288
U – "Henhouse delicacies" are the name of the game at this "clean", attractive breakfast-and-lunch spot adjacent to the freeway; our surveyors love it, citing "huge" portions of "superior" food at moderate prices and "wonderful service."

PHOENIX/SCOTTSDALE | F | D | S | C |

Top of the Rock/S | 22 | 25 | 21 | $28 |
The Buttes Resort, 2000 Westcourt Way (48th St.),
Tempe, 602-225-9000
M – The "beautiful view of the city" from this great-looking mountain-topper gets more plaudits than the Southwestern-influenced menu, which is nonetheless very good and "unusual"; "great big prices" bother a few, but service is top-notch, and the Sunday brunch "awesome", making this a good "place to take visitors."

Vincent Guerithault on Camelback | 29 | 26 | 28 | $36 |
3930 E. Camelback Rd. (40th St.), Phoenix,
602-224-0225
U – Clearly "the best in town", Guerithault's "creative" Southwestern-American cuisine is the "ultimate", "comparable to any great restaurant anywhere"; service is "impeccable", the wine list exceptional, the decor "elegant and comfortable" and the ambiance "classy" but "not snobby"; yes, it's expensive, but it's also worth every penny for an experience that our respondents say is "as good as it gets."

Voltaire | 26 | 23 | 27 | $28 |
8340 E. MacDonald Dr. (bet. Hayden & Granite Reef Rds.), Scottsdale, 602-948-1005
M – Consistency is the hallmark of this Eastside Scottsdale Traditional French, a highly rated favorite with folks who "couldn't afford the Concorde but could afford Voltaire's"; though some complain that it's "boring and unimaginative", most appreciate the "pleasant" surroundings, "reliable" fine food and "personal service" – "a real treasure."

Yamakasa | 27 | 17 | 21 | $20 |
9301 E. Shea Blvd. (92nd St.), Scottsdale, 602-860-5605
U – This Far Northeast Scottsdale Japanese looks "a bit sterile" but delivers an outstanding product; the food is "excellent", with sushi so "very fresh" and fairly priced, that it's almost "always crowded" – still, the "excellent" staff manages to keep up.

Z' Tejas Grill/S | – | – | – | M |
Scottsdale Fashion Sq. Mall, 7014 E. Camelback Rd.,
Scottsdale, 602-946-4171
Good Southwestern-style cuisine served in a pretty setting draws crowds to this mall-located newcomer; "interesting" dishes, "casual" friendly service and moderate prices make this spot worth a try before you get to the end of the alphabet.

PORTLAND, OR

TOP 10 RESTAURANTS
(In order of food rating)

Restaurant	Cuisine Type
28 – Cafe des Amis	French Classic
27 – Genoa	Northern Italian
26 – Indigene	Indian
25 – Winterborne	Seafood
L'Auberge	French Classic
24 – Yen Ha	Vietnamese
Heathman Hotel	Northwest Regional
Papa Haydn	Amer. Contemp.
23 – Couch Street Fish House	Seafood
Chen's Dynasty	Chinese

OTHER TOP PLACES
(In alphabetical order)

Atwater's	Amer. Contemp.
Bijou Cafe	Eclectic
Delphina's	N/S Italian
Esplanade	Cajun/Creole
McCormick & Schmick's	Northwest Regional
McCormick's Fish House	Seafood
Obi	Japanese
Opus Too	Seafood
Plainfield's Mayur	Indian
Ringside	Amer. Tradition.

| F | D | S | C |

Atwater's/S | 22 | 27 | 22 | $32 |
U.S. Bancorp Tower, 30th Floor, 111 SW Fifth Ave. (Burnside St.), 503-275-3600
M – "Top of the city – top of the line" with elegant decor and a view of Mount Hood on a clear day sets the stage for a dining experience atop the U.S. Bancorp Tower that many find "close to heaven in all respects", but others say is "not worth the price" for risking "poor service" and an "uneven kitchen"; save it for a special occasion, stop by after work for a drink in the "beautiful bar" or go for the "total-indulgence" Sunday brunch.

PORTLAND, OR | F | D | S | C |

Bijou Cafe/SX | 21 | 15 | 17 | $11 |
132 SW Third Ave. (Pine St.), 503-222-3187
U – Breakfasts are busy and there's "always a line" for weekend brunch despite the no-frills decor and service at this popular "morning place"; "new-fashioned taste" – wholesome, close to organic and locally produced – means menu highlights of hash, buckwheat pancakes, fresh-squeezed carrot juice and curried turkey salad; casual, funky and fun for both "yuppies and artists."

Cafe des Amis | 28 | 23 | 26 | $26 |
1987 NW Kearney St. (20th St.), 503-295-6487
U – For "consistently rewarding" Northwest dining featuring excellent seasonal dishes, our surveyors recommend this cafe in a residential area of Victorian houses; they report it has "understated elegance in a renovated old house" and attentive service, plus wonderful soups, homemade breads, "classic entrees with innovative twists" and an alluring dessert tray; quite simply "the best", and a real bargain; dinner only.

Chen's Dynasty/S | 23 | 20 | 21 | $18 |
622 SW Washington St. (6th Ave.), 503-248-9491
U – "Uncle Chen" introduced the Northwest to the fiery cuisines of northern China in the late '70s and the love affair continues at this large plush, peach-toned Downtowner that features small and large booths in several dining areas, a popular bar and banquet facility; the large booklike menu is "an education – you'll never live long enough to try it all."

Couch Street Fish House, The/S | 23 | 22 | 23 | $28 |
105 NW Third Ave. (bet. Couch & Davis Sts.),
503-223-6173
M – Expense-account and older diners will be comforted by "solicitous, sometimes pretentious" service, elegant surroundings and Northwest seafood judged "good but not great"; the Old Town neighborhood is "a terrible location", but says one critic, it's "someone's idea of what an elegant restaurant looked like in the '50s"; dinner only.

Delphina's/S | 22 | 19 | 19 | $17 |
2112 NW Kearney St. (bet. 21st & 22nd Aves.),
503-221-1195
U – Everyone in town seems to come to this deservedly popular, "no pretensions" Contemporary Italian spot; bare floors and an open kitchen add to the crowd's noise, but the staff is nice if harried and the food is "consistent" and "well prepared"; superfresh salads and pastas, great pizza and focaccia nicely balanced by a small wine list, attract everyone from lovers to families to with-it seniors.

PORTLAND, OR | F | D | S | C |

Esplanade/S | 22 | 26 | 22 | $29 |
Riverplace Alexis Hotel, 1510 SW Harbor Way (bet. Market St. & Front Ave.), 503-295-6166
U – This upscale hotel restaurant perched aside the Willamette River marina close to Downtown boasts "gracious service", an ambitious, "unique menu" featuring seafood, Northwest products, some Cajun-Creole dishes and fancy sauces, and "lovely decor" in pastels; still, the majority of our surveyors are not altogether overwhelmed – "falls just short of being wonderful."

Genoa | 27 | 19 | 25 | $36 |
2832 SE Belmont St. (bet. 28th & 29th Sts.), 503-238-1464
U – "Good, true Northern Italian cuisine" and "very gracious staff" characterize this universally loved, longtime Portland star; its leisurely multicourse, fixed price Classical Italian dinners are served in a "soft and warm atmosphere" that's "in a class by itself"; dim lights and a less-than-ideal neighborhood are the only complaints heard about "this very special place"; dinner only.

Heathman Hotel Restaurant/S | 24 | 23 | 24 | $29 |
Heathman Hotel, 1009 SW B'dway (Salmon), 503-241-4100
U – This small, "elite" and pricey Downtown hotel dining room is known for "elegant", "innovative" Northwest cuisine (a few say "boring" and "formula") served in a crowded but quiet setting brightened with Andy Warhol paintings and efficient service; a "power-eating establishment", it also offers a popular bar and tea time with piano music adjacent to the lobby.

Indigene | 26 | 14 | 21 | $23 |
3725 SE Division St. (bet. 37th & 38th Aves.), 503-238-1470
U – Portlanders tolerate this restaurant's setting (a bare little house in a neighborhood close to Laurelhurst) for its warm service and "imaginative and well-executed menu" of Indian-influenced cuisine dished out in "gigantic" portions at "a good value"; Friday and Saturday nights feature a popular fixed price, multicourse Indian dinner, other nights look for "eclectic" offerings from around the world; so "unique and creative", only the adventurous need enter; dinner only.

L'Auberge/S | 25 | 21 | 22 | $34 |
2601 NW Vaughn St. (26th Ave.), 503-223-3302
M – Split personality problems occur at this romantic Classic French restaurant (downstairs) and crowded, noisy bar (upstairs) found in a renovated house stuck out in an old manufacturing district in the Northwest area; it's no wonder that despite friendly staff, a "dramatic fireplace" and outside patio, our surveyors have mixed feelings; the three- and six-course fixed price menu downstairs is "pricey for Portland", but also "one of the best"; the popular upstairs bar menu is Eclectic and cheaper; dinner only.

PORTLAND, OR | F | D | S | C |

McCormick & Schmick's/S | 23 | 19 | 21 | $23 |
235 SW First Ave. (Oak St.), 503-224-7522
U – Portland's Downtown business people keep this rendition of a Northwest restaurant chain "noisy" and "usually crowded"; they especially appreciate the "good bar", helpful staff and "long fresh sheet" of "reliable", "but overpriced", seafood in what some feel to be "a man's bar."

McCormick's Fish House/S | 22 | 18 | 21 | $23 |
9945 SW Beaverton Hwy. (bet. 96th & 99th Aves.), Beaverton, 503-643-1322
U – A "good family restaurant", this casual Suburban seafood place has "consistent middle-of-the-road" food, better-than-average service and a noisy wood-and-tile interior; the bar is popular and business is brisk, so they may "rush you"; despite almost equal ratings, some say it's a "lesser rendition" of its Downtown sibling.

Obi* | 27 | 13 | 18 | $17 |
101 NW Second Ave. (Couch St.), 503-226-3826
M – "Rock 'n' roll meets sushi" at this Old Town Japanese restaurant where service is personable, sushi "highly imaginative" and ambiance is provided by the music, not decor; busy lunch hours make takeout a viable option while in this neighborhood, courage – and luck with parking – are needed at dinner; if you're not a rock fan, bring earplugs, valium or both; dinner only.

Opus Too/S | 23 | 19 | 20 | $22 |
33 NW Second Ave. (Couch St.), 503-222-6077
U – "The best fish place in the Northwest" cooks on a mesquite grill in an open kitchen before your very eyes; select the freshest, then sit in your choice of attractive dining areas; despite a "lousy location" in Old Town, problems with noise and a limited menu, this upscale eatery is justifiably popular at lunch and dinner; the bar pipes in excellent jazz to set the mood.

Papa Haydn/S | 24 | 16 | 17 | $16 |
5829 SE Milwaukie Blvd. (Bybee St.), 503-232-9440
701 NW 23rd Ave. (Irving St.), 503-228-7317
U – "See and be seen" for lunch or a light supper at this "chichi" Contemporary American restaurant with two locations – one in a residential area and one in Northwest; save room for "heavenly" or "sinful" (depending on your orientation) desserts – a huge case full of sweet toothsome beauties invites indulgence, and few resist despite lines, noise, functional decor and uneven service.

PORTLAND, OR | F | D | S | C |

Plainfield's Mayur | 23 | 23 | 20 | $24 |
852 SW 21st Ave. (Burnside St.), 503-223-2995
M – In a beautiful old home near Downtown, this "posh", "romantic and very classy" Indian restaurant offers "true North Indian cuisine" from a tandoor-show kitchen; the 1,000-degree clay ovens make air conditioning and the patio's umbrella tables especially welcome in summer; beware of "slow" service and high prices; dinner only.

Ringside, The | 23 | 16 | 20 | $23 |
East, 14021 NE Glisan St. (122nd Ave.), 503-255-0750
West, 2165 W. Burnside Blvd. (20th Ave.), 503-223-1513
M – There's "red meat and plenty of it" and "pretentious waiters" to make everyone feel at home in both the Downtown and Suburban locations (locals consider Burnside the better of the two); the menu highlights "steak and potatoes", prime rib and "superior onion rings"; dim lights are the decor and all Portland's good ol' boys eat here, which may be why some dub it "male chauvinist headquarters"; dinner only.

Winterborne | 25 | 15 | 22 | $26 |
3520 NE 42nd Ave. (Fremont St.), 503-249-8486
U – "Magic with seafood" happens in this small Beaumont neighborhood storefront where a "stark plain interior" is the backdrop and the "knowledgeable and attentive" service focuses attention on the "small menu" with "the best seafood in town"; P.S. no smoking; dinner only.

Yen Ha/S | 24 | 13 | 20 | $13 |
6820 NE Sandy Blvd. (68th Ave.), 503-287-3698
8640 SW Canyon Rd. (8th Ave. & Hwy. 217), Beaverton, 503-292-0616
U – Vietnamese cuisine reaches new heights at these popular bargain siblings, one on each side of the Willamette River, where decor and functional (if sometimes language-hampered) service are secondary to the 130-item menu; authentic hot-pot cooking at the table, crisp, rice-paper spring rolls and "tenderly prepared fish" are relished by the quality- and cost-conscious clientele – in a word, "yummy."

SAN DIEGO

TOP 10 RESTAURANTS
(In order of food rating)

Restaurant	Cuisine Type
27 – WineSellar/Brasserie	Californian/French
Mille Fleurs	Californian/French
El Bizcocho	French Classic
Marius	French Nouvelle
26 – Belgian Lion	Belgian/French
25 – George's at Cove	Californian/Seafood
Cindy Black's	French Bistro
24 – Pacifica Grill	Southwestern
Cafe Pacifica	Californian/Seafood
Grant Grill	Continental

OTHER TOP PLACES
(In alphabetical order)

Anthony's Star of the Sea	Seafood
Celadon	Thai
Dobson's	French Bistro
Fio's	Northern Italian
Fish Market	Seafood
French Side of the West	French Bistro
Rainwater's	Amer. Tradition.
Scarlett Loco	Southwestern
Thee Bungalow	Amer. Tradition.
Top O' The Cove	Continental

F	D	S	C

Anthony's Star of the Sea/SM | 22 | 21 | 20 | $35 |
1360 N. Harbor Dr. (Ash St.), 619-232-7408
M – A dressy, waterfront institution that's praised for its always good, elaborate seafood dishes; critics insist it's "touristy", "stuffy and pretentious" but the "elegant decor" makes it ideal for special occasions; jackets and ties are required at this dinner-only spot.

Belgian Lion | 26 | 22 | 25 | $33 |
2265 Bacon St. (West Point Loma Blvd.), 619-223-2700
U – "Charming European atmosphere and consistently excellent food" sum up the many charms of this family-owned and -operated Ocean Beach restaurant; the "top-quality ingredients and creative presentations" of the Belgian-French menu merit raves as does the "very personal service"; prix fixe weeknight dinners are among the best values in town; dinner only.

SAN DIEGO

| F | D | S | C |

Cafe Pacifica/SM | 24 | 19 | 22 | $30 |
2414 San Diego Ave. (off I-5 Frwy., 2 blocks north of Old Town Ave.), 619-291-6666
M – There's Contemporary California–style seafood and a "very romantic setting" at this Old Town casita, but even its biggest fans decry the Cafe's inconsistent service and frequent changes in kitchen staff; though the focus remains fixed on seafood, Mexican or Italian specialties are spotlighted, depending on the kitchen's whim; the atmosphere is "casual" and comfortable.

Celadon/M | 23 | 21 | 19 | $24 |
3628 Fifth Ave. (bet. Brooks St. & Pennsylvania Ave.), Hillcrest, 619-295-8800
M – "Good Thai food" in a dressier setting than one expects of a Southeast Asian eatery; fans focus on the "beautiful decor"; foes, on the "too mild" "for average tastes" food and the "unknowledgeable waiters"; the edge-of-Hillcrest location makes it a possibility for dinner before Balboa Park theater curtains.

Cindy Black's/S | 25 | 19 | 21 | $37 |
5721 La Jolla Blvd. (Birdrock Ave.), La Jolla, 619-456-6299
M – The hearty Country French food at this La Jolla restaurant earns high marks from most of our respondents, who praise "superb" dishes such as chicken bouillabaisse, roasted tomato soup and duck confit; however, some grouse about the "slightly seedy" and "antiseptic" setting and "spotty service"; nonetheless, reasonable prices and the "personal touch" of the celebrity chef-owner pack 'em in; prix fixe Sunday nights are a special bargain; lunch on Fridays only.

Dobson's/M | 24 | 20 | 22 | $36 |
956 Broadway Circle (2nd Ave.), 619-231-6771
U – This Downtown "big-city" bar combines charming turn-of-the-century decor with "reliable" French bistro food and some of the city's best people-watching; "power lunches and pampered dining" are trademarks; though a few grumble about the prices and noise level, the signature sourdough bread and "fantastic" mussel bisque win everybody over in the end.

El Bizcocho/SM | 27 | 24 | 26 | $44 |
Rancho Bernardo Inn, 17550 Bernardo Oaks Dr. (Rancho Bernardo Rd.), 619-277-2146
U – "Classic French with a pinch of Californian" describes the food at what surveyors call one of the region's "best hotel restaurants"; the "early California elegance" of the Rancho Bernardo dining room and polished service are icing on the cake; though prices are way up there, the uniformly "excellent" experience makes it a good value, especially if part of a golf-weekend package; dinner only.

SAN DIEGO | F | D | S | C |

Fio's/SM | 23 | 22 | 21 | $29 |
801 Fifth Ave. (F St.), 619-234-3467
U – A "comfortable, casual, chic" staff personality teams up with "innovative" Northern Italian fare to make this stylish Gaslamp Quarter trattoria one of San Diego's hardest-to-get reservations; entertainment is provided by the bustling open kitchen, the "hip" pizza bar and the trendy crowd in the lively bar/lounge; the wine list is a plus; noise and crowded tables are minor negatives.

Fish Market, The/SM | 21 | 18 | 18 | $23 |
750 N. Harbor Dr. (1½ blocks south of Broadway), 619-232-3474
640 Via de la Valle (Jimmy Durante Blvd.), Del Mar, 619-755-2277
U – With its "wide variety of fish", "simple, unadorned" preparations and "marvelous view", these mid-priced seafooders are "geared to tourists but good enough to bring locals back on a regular basis"; no reservations are accepted so there's often a crush; however, the elaborate sushi and oyster bars make the wait tolerable, and service comes from a "friendly" staff.

French Side of the West/SM | 23 | 21 | 22 | $25 |
2202 4th Ave. (Ivy St.), 619-234-5540
M – Initially prized for its hearty Country French food and rock-bottom prices, this "nice neighborhood restaurant" has slipped, say respondents; nonetheless, for every comment of "just fair" or "nothing special", there's someone who loves its "unique charm", "outstanding" food and convenience to Balboa Park.

George's at the Cove/SM | 25 | 25 | 23 | $36 |
1250 Prospect St. (bet. Ivanhoe & Cove Sts.), La Jolla, 619-454-4244
U – Diners find La Jolla's "'in' spot" a perfect combination of "terrific food", "luxurious surroundings" and service that's "very supportive of the customer"; the chef's "creative flair" shows up in "superb" soups, seafood, salads and rotisserie chicken; regulars praise the "great view", especially from the hip, casual rooftop cafe; in sum, "a restaurant that lives up to its reputation."

Grant Grill/SM | 24 | 24 | 23 | $37 |
U.S. Grant Hotel, 326 Broadway (bet. 3rd & 4th Aves.), 619-239-6806
M – The setting is "old-fashioned formal", but the food in this Downtown landmark hotel dining room is "superb" and "exciting", thanks to a young French chef with big ideas; some find the ambiance "a bit stuffy and rushed"; others call it "elegant" and "cozy"; notoriously high prices have dropped in response to the recession, and the elaborate buffet lunch is a bargain.

SAN DIEGO | F | D | S | C |

Marius/S | 27 | 27 | 26 | $47 |
Le Meridien Hotel, 2000 Second St. (Glorietta Blvd.),
Coronado, 619-435-3000

M – "Pretentious and stuffy" but "enchanting", this elegant resort dining room specializes in stylish presentations of the boldly flavored cuisine of Provence; "outstanding" food and "great old-style service" are worth its stratospheric price tags; dinner only.

Mille Fleurs/SM | 27 | 26 | 26 | $48 |
6009 Paseo Delicias (5 miles east of I-5 Frwy., Loma Santa Fe exit), Rancho Santa Fe, 619-756-3085

U – This "perfect special-occasion place" wraps up "the best French food in San Diego", "divine service" and a "romantic Moorish atmosphere" into one of the county's most attractive dining experiences; the "creative menu", which marries French and Californian cuisines, makes the trip to Rancho Santa Fe worthwhile; prices are high, "but so is the quality."

Pacifica Grill/SM | 24 | 21 | 22 | $31 |
1202 Kettner Blvd. (bet. A & B Sts.), 619-696-9226

U – With "fabulous Southwestern dishes" and a "sophisticated decor", this very comfortable Downtowner is "never a disappointment"; don't miss the takoshimi (flash-grilled ahi in a crispy won ton skin "taco" shell with Chinese salsa); service, though usually good, is the restaurant's one noticeable flaw.

Rainwater's | 22 | 20 | 21 | $34 |
1202 Kettner Blvd. (B St.), 619-233-5757

M – There's "top-quality" food, a "clubby atmosphere" and an "upper-class clientele" at this Downtown chop house where a "variety of seating options makes it a great place to watch the trains come in"; "don't expect originality", say respondents, who also decry "inconsistent" service; if a bit pricey, "large portions of hearty food" are the norm.

Scarlett Loco*/M | 23 | 13 | 19 | $29 |
1400 Front St. (Ash St.), 619-234-2000

U – "One of the best chefs in town" turns out very good "Southwest bistro–style food" in this tiny Downtown eatery, but even fans decry the rather "crummy" decor and "dead-corner" location; go for lunch.

Thee Bungalow/SM | 24 | 20 | 24 | $27 |
4996 West Point Loma Blvd., Ocean Beach,
619-224-2884

U – Voters love the "innovative" American food as well as traditional fare at this slightly seedy Ocean Beach cottage; "the best duck in town" and a "spectacular list of California wines" receive praise and top billing; a management that's "eager to please" and "terrific mid-week specials" are icing on the cake; dinner only.

SAN DIEGO

| F | D | S | C |

Top of the Cove | 23 | 24 | 23 | $41 |
1216 Prospect St. (Herschel Ave.), La Jolla,
619-454-7779
M – While most surveyors rave about the "dramatic view", "innovative" food and "elegant, romantic" environment, a few pan the food as "overpriced" and the setting as "ostentatious" at this La Jolla village bungalow.

WineSellar & Brasserie, The/S | 27 | 17 | 24 | $36 |
9555 Waples (1¾ miles east of 805 Frwy., off Mira Mesa Blvd.), 619-450-9557
U – Its location in an out-of-the-way industrial park makes this French-Californian "difficult to find" (call ahead for directions), but the "ingenious" cooking of "brilliant young chef Doug Organ" and a "phenomenal wine list" make it "impossible to forget."

SAN FRANCISCO

TOP 30 RESTAURANTS
(In order of food rating)

Restaurant	Cuisine Type
28 – Masa's	French Nouvelle
Fleur de Lys	French Classic/Nouvelle
La Folie	French
27 – Chez Panisse	Californian
Cafe at Chez Panisse	Californian
L'Avenue	Californian
26 – Fresh Cream	French Nouvelle
Terra	Californian
Le Mouton Noir	French Nouvelle
Lark Creek Inn	Amer. Contemp.
Domaine Chandon	French Nouvelle
Flying Saucer	Eclectic
Campton Place	Amer. Contemp./Calif.
25 – Kabuto Sushi	Japanese
Stars	Californian
Swan Oyster Depot	Seafood
Aqua	Seafood
Helmand	Afghan
Postrio	Californian
Acquerello	Nuova Cucina Italian
Square One	Eclectic/Mediterranean
Rodin	French/Japanese
Downtown Bakery	Desserts
La Taqueria	Mexican
House of Nanking	Chinese
Sherman House	French Nouvelle
Tra Vigne	Northern Italian
24 – Bay Wolf	Meditteranean
Ristorante Ecco	N/S Italian
231 Ellsworth	French Classic

OTHER TOP PLACES
(In alphabetical order)

Cafe Macaroni	Southern Italian
Cypress Club	Californian
Flower Lounge	Chinese
Green's	Vegetarian
Harris' Restaurant	Steakhouse
Khan Toke Thai House	Thai
Kyo-Ya Restaurant	Japanese
L'Escargot	French Classic
Pane e Vino	Italian
Ritz-Carlton Dining Rm.	Amer. Contemp.
Vivande Porta Via	N/S Italian

SAN FRANCISCO | F | D | S | C |

Acquerello | 25 | 23 | 24 | $41 |
1722 Sacramento St. (bet. Polk & Van Ness Aves.),
415-567-5432
U – Enter this Polk/Van Ness Northern Italian and be prepared for "a romantic adventure in an epicurean Xanadu"; some diners dislike "eating in a cramped tunnel" as well as a "snooty reception", but overall, the consensus is that this is "serious eating" prepared by people who are "committed and passionate about food"; buon viaggio!

Aqua/M | 25 | 27 | 22 | $41 |
252 California St. (Battery St.), 415-956-9662
U – This trendy Downtown seafood palace has made a big splash: "yummy tuna tartar", superb foie gras/tuna combination; chef George Morrone is a culinary genius who produces food that's said to "rival Le Bernardin in NYC"; the "wonderful flower-filled" setting and "incredible food" suffers only from the self-absorbed staff" and high-end prices.

Bay Wolf/SM | 24 | 20 | 23 | $31 |
3853 Piedmont Ave. (Rio Vista), Oakland, 510-655-6004
U – This long-standing "Mediterranean hideaway in Downtown Oakland" features "clever combinations" of "wonderful, fresh California cuisine" with "the best duck" and "awesome salmon and pâtés"; sure, it "can be schizophrenic depending on who's cooking", but comments such as "Chez Panisse without the high prices" explains why it's so well liked; P.S. surveyors wish the portions were bigger.

Cafe at Chez Panisse/LSM | 27 | 21 | 22 | $28 |
1517 Shattuck Ave. (bet. Cedar & Vine Sts.), Berkeley,
510-548-5049
M – This East Bay Californian is "paradise by any measure", though a few feel it's paradise lost – an "overpriced victim of its success"; as its 27 food rating shows, most agree this is "Californian cuisine done to perfection" with "healthy, tasty food", but you'd better expect long waits for tables, and service that can be "haughty."

Cafe Macaroni/SM | 22 | 13 | 19 | $24 |
59 Columbus Ave. (Jackson St.), 415-956-9737
M – This "fun, tasty circus" (with cramped "low-ceilinged" "homey" quarters "not for claustrophobes") in North Beach draws mixed comments for its generally well-liked Italian food that some argue lacks zest; the personal service is wonderful – "let Mario order for you" – but still be prepared for an occasional flop.

SAN FRANCISCO

| F | D | S | C |

Campton Place/SM | 26 | 26 | 25 | $47 |
Campton Place Kempinski Hotel, 340 Stockton St. (Sutter St.), 415-781-5555
U – *Downtown American-Californian popular with visitors who don't mind the usually excellent – sometimes "snotty" – service, but universally love the "great frutti de mare with polenta" and other well-crafted dishes; the austere hotel dining room "is a bit of a temple" with the faithful worshipping the "elegant, serious food" of chef Jan Birnbaum; it's a great special-occasion place.*

Chez Panisse/S | 27 | 23 | 25 | $56 |
1517 Shattuck Ave. (bet. Cedar & Vine Sts.), Berkeley, 510-548-5525
U – *"God bless Alice Waters", founder of this East Bay Californian mecca where she originated California cuisine; though a few nonbelievers call it "overrated" and "somewhat more food religion than enjoyment", the majority say it's "an ethereal experience"; call ahead to check the menu since there's a fixed, no-substitutions menu each night; despite high prices, "very good" service and the freshest-of-fresh ingredients make this an all-time favorite.*

Cypress Club/SM | 21 | 25 | 21 | $41 |
500 Jackson St. (Montgomery St.), 415-296-8555
M – *"A bulbous Freudian vision" that reminds one woman "of breast feeding my son", this Downtown Californian is lauded for its exotic decor – "Fred Flintstone on acid" – stellar wine list, great social scene and "orgasmic" desserts; the fare is good, not great, ditto: service, but this is "nirvana for the pretentious ponytail set"; come and see how one spends $3 million on a restaurant.*

Domaine Chandon/SM | 26 | 26 | 25 | $44 |
California Dr. (Hwy. 29, Veterans Home exit), Yountville, 707-944-2892
U – *It's "worth a special journey" to this "dreamlike" Napa Valley French, which serves "elegant" cuisine prepared by chef Philippe Jeanty; enjoy "great tomato soup", superb duck and "one of the prettiest terraces" anywhere; there's also "excellent, gracious" service; it all comes with a steep bill, but it's "worth every penny."*

Downtown Bakery and Creamery/SMX | 25 | 12 | 16 | $12 |
308A Center St. (on the Plaza), Healdsburg, 707-431-2719
U – *This Sonoma bakery/creamery is "not a restaurant really", but may very well be your "new addiction"; superb bread, "great" cinnamon rolls and "the best wild raspberry sherbet in the world" make it a "sinful" must-stop along Highway 101.*

SAN FRANCISCO | F | D | S | C |

Fleur de Lys/M | 28 | 28 | 26 | $59 |
777 Sutter St. (bet. Taylor & Jones Sts.), 415-673-7779
U – The Classic and Contemporary French fare at this posh "treasure" is as "close to heaven" as you can get and what's more, many consider this "the most romantic restaurant in SF"; such praise comes at a cost, but "save those pennies" because the world-class cuisine prepared by superstar chef Hubert Keller is "the finest around."

Flower Lounge/SM | 23 | 16 | 17 | $22 |
1671 El Camino Real (Park Pl.), Millbrae, 415-588-9972
51 Millbrae Ave. (El Camino Rd.), Millbrae, 415-878-8108
5322 Geary Blvd. (bet. 17th & 18th Aves.), 415-668-8998
M – These Peninsula and Richmond District siblings serve "authentic" Hong Kong cuisine with the "freshest" ingredients that lead fans to call them "the best Bay Area Chinese"; however, their decor is "typical Chinese restaurant" (read: nonexistent) and too few of the staff speak English.

Flying Saucer/SX | 26 | 16 | 16 | $32 |
1000 Guerrero St. (22nd St.), 415-641-9955
M – "Out-of-this-world" "funky" Mission Eclectic with "hefty" portions of innovative and unusually presented fare; "reservations are a must" to get into this "weird little place" even though some feel it's in a "terrible area" and complain about "spaced-out" service; if you are fewer than four, be prepared to share a table with strangers.

Fresh Cream/SM | 26 | 23 | 24 | $43 |
Heritage Harbor, 99 Pacific St., Ste. 100F (Scott St.), Monterey, 408-375-9798
U – The only problem with this Monterey French Contemporary is deciding what to order; though the menu has no weak spots, "try the tart tatin" or the "super soft-shell crab"; it's worth the trip down from SF for memorable, extra-special dining, but dissenters (a tiny minority) feel it's "pretentious" and "overrated"; fans (the majority) consider Fresh Cream "a dream", "a religious experience."

Green's/S | 24 | 23 | 20 | $28 |
Fort Mason, Bldg. A (bet. Marina & Buchanan Sts.), 415-771-6222
U – This "Vegetarian Valhalla" in the Marina serves "very good vibes" plus creative, interesting food that will charm even the most ardent carnivore with its freshness and healthy taste; the waterfront location offers a "wonderful" view of the Golden Gate, but precious pricing (for veggies) and "pompous" waiters may be turnoffs; great wine list.

SAN FRANCISCO | F | D | S | C |

Harris'/SM | 22 | 21 | 22 | $36 |
2100 Van Ness Ave. (Pacific Ave.), 415-673-1888
U – This Van Ness/Polk standout steakhouse serves "excellent steaks in a clubby atmosphere"; quiet and elegant, it's "a restaurant for grown-ups" at grown-up prices; indulge in a NY prime but, even though service is generally good, don't be surprised by a "snobby" waiter.

Helmand/M | 25 | 20 | 23 | $24 |
430 Broadway (Kearny St.), 415-362-0641
U – At this North Beach Afghan "sleeper", the food's "scrumptious", the service "gracious" and fortunately, the parking is validated; you'll enjoy a "wonderful Afghan experience" – "get it while it's cheap."

House of Nanking/SMX | 25 | 3 | 10 | $14 |
919 Kearny St. (bet. Jackson St. & Columbus Ave.), 415-421-1429
M – Even Greg Louganis couldn't make a more perfect dive than this "classic" Chinatown Chinese; expect inexpensive "awesome" food in a smelly, "dumpy room that's small and crowded", with "pushy" service; but dishes such as shrimp in beer sauce and Nanking mixed vegetables make up for all deficiencies; P.S. "let Peter Fang order for you."

Kabuto Sushi/MS | 25 | 12 | 19 | $27 |
5116 Geary Blvd. (15th Ave.), 415-752-5652
M – The top-rated Asian in the Bay area offers a "great manic sushi master" but "depressing decor"; many sushi lovers say this Richmond-area location is the "best in town" for "large portions" and a "great show at the counter" as well as being a late-night meeting place.

Khan Toke Thai House/SM | 24 | 23 | 21 | $23 |
5937 Geary Blvd. (bet. 23rd & 24th Aves.), 415-668-6654
U – You have to limber up for this "excellent" Richmond District Thai because you may end up sitting without shoes on the floor, however, "exquisite decor", "fabulous art work" and "wonderful flavors" make it worth the exercise; this SF institution is "always fun" and "a great introduction to Thai food."

Kyo-Ya Restaurant/M | – | – | – | VE |
Sheraton Palace Hotel, 2 New Montgomery St. (Jessie St.), 415-392-8600
This Downtown spot is "very Japanese – perhaps too much"; most respondents say it's the "best in the city" with a "varied" menu and "supreme" sushi, but prices are higher than Mt. Fuji and nonclimbers say "boring."

SAN FRANCISCO

| F | D | S | C |

La Folie/M
| 28 | 22 | 25 | $48 |

2316 Polk St. (bet. Union & Green Sts.), 415-776-5577
U – Wunderkind chef Roland Passot prepares creative French cuisine "par excellence" at this Van Ness/Polk star; "sublime and unforgettable" if a "tad heavy", his "wonderful food and "beautiful, artistic" presentations are equaled only by his warm hospitality; the "relaxed, casual" ambiance and fine wine list add to one of San Francisco's premier dining experiences.

Lark Creek Inn, The/SM
| 26 | 26 | 23 | $37 |

234 Magnolia Ave. (Madrona Canyon Rd.), Larkspur, 415-924-7766
U – This Marin American, tucked among the redwoods, is an idyllic setting for celebrated chef Brad Ogden to prepare his "robust, mouth-watering American classics"; according to the "very-California crowd", he proves "American fare can reach great heights" and note "huge" portions; only inconsistent service sobers this intoxicating experience; N.B. brunch in the garden can be heavenly.

La Taqueria/SMX
| 25 | 10 | 14 | $9 |

2889 Mission St. (25th St.), 285-7117
U – The "incredible" burritos at this Mission Mexican plus "heavenly carnitas", "great chorizo" and excellent fresh fruit drinks make it "the best traditional taqueria in SF"; it has "all the ambiance of Taco Bell", but go for "quick, cheap and good" north-of-the border food.

L'Avenue/SM
| 27 | 19 | 23 | $38 |

3854 Geary Blvd. (3rd Ave.), 415-386-1555
U – Nancy Oakes's Californian cuisine is "impeccable – always different" at this Richmond District phenomenon; the small, but "cozy" and "warm" space is usually crowded (it's best to reserve) with patrons who laud her "wonderful" food and service which is "informal but caring"; many dread the day Nancy moves this great restaurant to a new Downtown location.

Le Mouton Noir/SM
| 26 | 25 | 24 | $44 |

14560 Big Basin Way (bet. 4th & 5th Sts.), Saratoga, 408-867-7017
M – "This black sheep of the South Bay" breaks away from the herd with "memorable", "delicious" lamb and duck dishes served with care, though some feel the "seating is too close" and the portions are "petite", all agree it's "not a typical French menu", but "elegant, excellent" food and a "great" wine list make this "romantic" Victorian "the best in the South Bay" with prices to match.

SAN FRANCISCO | F | D | S | C |

L'Escargot/S | 24 | 21 | 23 | $36 |
1809 Union St. (Octavia St.), 415-567-0222
U – *"France on Union Street", this tellement Français has been "very good for years"; in its "quiet, elegant" setting, you're "not rushed" and "always made to feel special"; the "good escargot and wild boar" are best buys when the $20 special is offered.*

Masa's | 28 | 26 | 28 | $69 |
Vintage Crt. Hotel, 648 Bush St. (Powell St.), 415-989-7154
U – *"The best in SF" and most expensive describes this "heavenly" Downtown French Contemporary "food temple"; the vast majority (and there are many) of our surveyors say it's "worth every penny" for chef Julian Serrano's "first-class" fare, at what they simply describe as "the greatest"; to a tiny minority, "the decor is drab" and the service "snotty", but a "26" and "28" rating, respectively, shows they're outvoted.*

Pane e Vino/M | 23 | 19 | 20 | $30 |
3011 Steiner St. (Union St.), 415-346-2111
M – *"Wow, I thought I was in Italy"; this Union Street trattoria has diners raving over its "authentic pasta", risotto, grilled fish, veal chop – "you could live on the bread and wine" – and "dynamite desserts"; a few (the minority) say "overrated", "success has taken its toll."*

Postrio/SM | 25 | 26 | 23 | $45 |
Prescott Hotel, 545 Post St. (Mason St.), 415-776-7825
M – *Any restaurant with as many laurels as this Downtown Wolfgang Puck creation is bound to generate incredibly high expectations; regularly named as one of the top three restaurants in town, Postrio either wows diners with its haute Californian cuisine or horrifies them with its haute prices; as high ratings show, most people find chefs Annie and David Gingrass's fare to be "uniformly wonderful" and Pat Kuleto's decor "stunning."*

Ristorante Ecco/M | 24 | 20 | 20 | $28 |
101 South Park (2nd St.), 415-495-3291
U – *"Brand spanking new" SOMA Italian that most agree is hearty and refined, with "food that's great and incredibly low priced"; lunch is particularly good, with "intelligent combinations"; try it for yourself!*

Ritz-Carlton Dining Room/SM | 24 | 26 | 25 | $53 |
Ritz-Carlton Hotel, 600 Stockton St. (California St.), 415-296-7465
U – *SF is abuzz over the brilliant New American creations of talented chef Gary Danko; moreover, the handsome decor of this Nob Hill dining room and "great service" match the dazzling food; some claim sommelier Emmanuel Kemigi is one of "the best in SF" and others laud the presence of a cheese course; at these prices, puttin' on the Ritz can only be a "now-and-then" experience.*

SAN FRANCISCO | F | D | S | C |

Rodin/M | 25 | 21 | 23 | $45 |
1779 Lombard St. (bet. Laguna & Octavia Sts.),
415-563-8566
M – It doesn't take a great Thinker to realize this Marina French-Japanese mix is "very romantic", with "excellent food" and "reasonable" prices; those who complain about it limit their grievances to the "lousy location" and the "stuffy" atmosphere that's "just too quiet."

Sherman House/SM | 25 | 28 | 26 | $53 |
The Sherman House, 2160 Green St. (Fillmore St.),
415-563-3600
U – The French Nouvelle cuisine with a Californian accent receives raves, as does just about everything else at this small, exclusive Pacific Heights hotel; it's a "secret-special spot" with "elegant food, decor and service" as its hallmarks; even those few left unimpressed by the cooking find the overall experience "so overwhelming you don't care that much."

Square One/SM | 25 | 19 | 23 | $39 |
190 Pacific Ave. (Front St.), 415-788-1110
M – Celebrity Joyce Goldstein's subdued Eclectic-Mediterranean cooking ("lovely creations, lovingly prepared") more than satisfies most of her Downtown customers; the delicious desserts, breathtaking breads and special menu on Jewish holidays all win applause; however, some find the "dinerlike" interior "cold" and "sterile"; detractors, a small minority, "don't understand why it's so highly touted", and complain that it's just "dressed-up home cooking", but they obviously don't understand – this is the '90s.

Stars/SM | 25 | 23 | 22 | $41 |
150 Redwood Alley (bet. Polk & Van Ness Aves.),
415-861-7827
U – While owner Jeremiah Tower stars, chef Mark Franz stays at his stove insuring that this landmark Civic Center Californian remains one of the country's most renowned restaurants; his consistently "stellar" riffs on American fare are matched with Emily Lucchetti's "heavenly desserts" in an ambiance that's "absolutely alive"; a few curmudgeons complain that this place is "too noisy" and "overrated", but, despite high prices, celestial people-watching, a handsome airy setting and top-notch service leave virtually everyone starry-eyed.

Swan Oyster Depot/MX | 25 | 15 | 22 | $18 |
1517 Polk St. (California St.), 415-673-1101
U – This family-run Van Ness/Polk seafood–oyster bar is a SF classic which is a "must see" and "must taste" with extremely fresh fish, superb chowder and "the best shellfish in the city"; go and find out what has all these old-timers flocking to the counter at this tableless well-priced favorite.

SAN FRANCISCO | F | D | S | C |

Terra/SM | 26 | 24 | 24 | $41 |
1345 Railroad Ave. (bet. Hunt & Adams Aves.), St. Helena, 707-963-8931
U – Surveyors unanimously praise this "flawless" Napa Valley Californian run by chef Hiro Sone (ex Spago) and his charming wife Lissa, and voted it the "the best wine country restaurant", as a result of its "marvelous creative food", "beautiful", "romantic" setting (the terrace is "wonderful") and "cordial welcoming service"; reserve well in advance, this place has been discovered.

Tra Vigne/SM | 25 | 26 | 22 | $34 |
1050 Charter Oak St. (Hwy. 29), St. Helena, 707-963-4444
U – To find this popular Napa Valley Northern Italian, just follow your nose to the "good smells of olive oil, sharp cheese and garlic"; Michael Ciarello's "truly fine, high-quality" fare tastes as good as it smells – "magnifico", "terrific" and "soooo good" are just a few of the many superlatives of this "must-stop in the wine country"; though inside has "a good feeling", eat outdoors if possible.

231 Ellsworth/M | 24 | 21 | 23 | $40 |
231 S. Ellsworth Ave. (bet. 2nd & 3rd Aves.), San Mateo, 415-347-7231
U – Heading down the Peninsula? – try this citified French Classic in San Mateo; "sublime" preparations, "the best service anywhere" and an up-to-date wine list make it possibly the best haute cuisine on the Peninsula; while some turn their heads at the pink-and-beige decor, none turn away from the food that's "never a disappointment."

Vivande Porta Via/SM | 23 | 17 | 18 | $24 |
2125 Fillmore St. (bet. California & Sacramento Sts.), 415-346-4430
U – Though the Italian fare is a little pricey considering the deli-like setting, most of our surveyors can't get enough of chef Carlo Middione's "delicious pastas and salads" and wish it was "open for more than just lunch"; sit at the counter and "watch the show" or takeout and turn it into a party at home.

SANTA FE

TOP 10 RESTAURANTS
(In order of food rating)

Restaurant	Cuisine Type
27 – SantaCafe	Southwestern
24 – Old Mexico Grill	Mexican
Cafe Pasqual's	Southwestern
23 – Coyote Cafe	Southwestern
22 – Pink Adobe	Continental
21 – Pranzo Italian Grill	N/S Italian
20 – Shed	New Mexican
El Farol	Spanish
La Casa Sena	Mexican
Rancho de Chimayo	New Mexican

OTHER TOP PLACES
(In alphabetical order)

Bishop's Lodge	Amer. Contemp.
Compound	Continental
Guadalupe Cafe	Amer. Tradition.
Inn of the Anasazi	Amer. Contemp.
Lambert's	Amer. Contemp.
La Tertulia	Amer. Tradition.
La Traviata	Northern Italian
Palace Restaurant	Continental
Staab House	Southwestern
Zia Diner	Amer. Tradition.

F	D	S	C

Bishop's Lodge/LS | 17 | 19 | 19 | $28 |
N. Bishop's Lodge Rd. (Washington Ave., 3 miles north of Santa Fe Rd.), 505-983-6377
U – *Though this famous old lodge was once Santa Fe's best, that was long ago; today despite having a "pleasant" atmosphere and a "good view from the terrace", it's called "old-fashioned" by some; to others it's "still wonderful" and as for its food, Sunday brunch receives the main praise on an otherwise standard American menu.*

Cafe Pasqual's/S | 24 | 16 | 19 | $18 |
121 Don Gaspar (Water St.), 505-983-9340
U – *If you can endure the "impossible wait" and "shoulder-to-tastebud seating", "the food and atmosphere will reward"; tiny, "funky" and "too crowded", this cafe is worth trying for its "innovative", "excellent" SW food and fair prices.*

SANTA FE

| F | D | S | C |

Compound/LS | 19 | 24 | 20 | $35 |
653 Canyon Rd., 505-982-4353
M – Despite good grades, especially for its "magical" decor, this pricey Continental suffers slings and arrows: "what a snooze", "ridiculously pretentious", "overpriced for underwhelming food"; still, though a little formal for Santa Fe – some grumble about the jacket and tie policy – it provides "a beautiful setting" for "gourmet" fare.

Coyote Cafe/S | 23 | 21 | 18 | $30 |
132 W. Water St. (bet. Don Gaspar & Galisteo), 505-983-1615
M – New Mexico's best-known chef, Mark Miller, has fans who like his "spicy, adventurous SW cuisine" and people-watching of "Ralph Lauren cowboys"; though most people say it "lives up to its reputation", high expectations lead to occasional disappointment, especially when Miller is away: "rude", "pretentious", "noisy", "uneven", "long waits", "cliche SW decor"; for best results eat at the counter – "the cooks are a lot of fun."

El Farol/S | 20 | 17 | 18 | $22 |
808 Canyon Rd. (Camino del Montezol), 505-983-9912
U – This "local hangout" near the top of Canyon Road is "a bit like the '70s before Santa Fe was chic"; the ancient building lacks ambiance, but the "very personable" staff and the moderately priced, "excellent and unusual" tapas make for a good meal and a "relaxing evening"; but "watch out for loud bands."

Guadalupe Cafe | 19 | 12 | 18 | $14 |
313 Guadalupe (Downtown), 505-982-9762
U – Tiny and always crowded, this "informal" Downtown cafe is "best for breakfast" but "cheap and good" anytime; green chili and stuffed sopaipillas are a nice "extra touch" on the Northern New Mexican menu.

Inn of the Anasazi/S | – | – | – | M |
Inn of the Anasazi, 113 Washington Ave. (bet. Palace & Marcy), 505-988-3030
Hot new American cuisine contender near the Plaza with elegant and authentic Southwestern decor; seafood is a specialty and they offer three vegetarian (sometimes organic) specials each evening; for sophisticated travelers and diners, this outstanding inn is worth a detour in spite of disorganized service.

La Casa Sena/S | 20 | 23 | 18 | $24 |
125 E. Palace Ave. (Washington), 505-988-9232
The ultimate Santa Fe tourist restaurant, this American Nuevo Mexicano in a lovely historic house (circa 1860), has a large outdoor garden and an interesting wine selection; singing waiters in the adjoining cantina are not to everyone's taste.

SANTA FE

| F | D | S | C |

Lambert's*/S | 24 | 25 | 27 | $30 |
309 Paseo del Pueblo Sur (south of the Plaza), Taos, 505-758-1009
U – With innovative Contemporary American food that contends for "the best in Taos", with "an extraordinary wine list at very reasonable prices" and top-notch service and decor, it's no surprise that Lambert's gets such high ratings.

La Tertulia/S | 19 | 21 | 19 | $21 |
416 Agua Fria (Guadalupe), 505-988-2769
M – This historic adobe restaurant is "pretty good on the right night" with its "safe New Mexican" fare that's for everyone from opera-goers to "tourists"; a not-so-hefty tab adds to the appeal, but a few unsatisfied diners claim it's "gone downhill."

La Traviata/S | – | – | – | E |
95 W. Marcy (Washington), 505-984-1091
Perhaps the best Northern Italian in town, though it can be pricey, LT delivers the goods in seafood, game and veal specialties as well as top-notch pastas and the "best soup"; renovated to accommodate the crowds, it's "still intimate" and feels like a "slice of time warp Italy"; P.S. the restaurant has recently added a few Sicilian dishes to the menu; reservations are a must.

Old Mexico Grill/S | 24 | 16 | 20 | $19 |
2434 Cerrillos Rd. (St. Michael's Dr.), 505-473-0338
U – "A favorite of locals" with an open-to-view kitchen and sizzling grill which turns out "superb Mexican food at a superb price"; though some squawk about waits even with reservations and "no atmosphere", most "never tire of eating here"; they make "terrific margaritas" too.

Palace Restaurant, The | 18 | 21 | 21 | $27 |
142 W. Palace (Museum of Fine Art), 505-982-9891
M – "Mae West would have eaten" at this "old-time favorite" with lots of local color and where politicos and lawyers stop off-season – still, some critics wonder "why are they still in business?"; the Continental food rates "ordinary" to "good" with "the desserts the best part of the meal"; "the red velvet and brocade is a bit much", but fans think the outdoor patio is "lovely."

Pink Adobe, The/S | 22 | 23 | 21 | $25 |
406 Old Santa Fe Trail (bet. Paseo de Peralta & Alameda), 505-983-7712
M – "Absolutely Santa Fe" – some say this local legend is "living on its reputation" with Continental food that runs the gamut from "excellent" to "bland and overcooked"; few complaints arise, however, about the solid service and "quaint" setting – "low ceilings, wooden floors and tiny fireplaces"; lunch is a real bargain; the adjoining Dragon Bar is the spot for "great" margaritas; watch out for dinnertime waits.

SANTA FE

| F | D | S | C |

Pranzo Italian Grill/S | 21 | 18 | 20 | $21 |
540 Montezuma (Guadalupe), 505-984-2645
U – Among the "best Italians in Santa Fe", the "great pizza" and other "good" food elicit locals' praise as "exciting" and "very affordable"; management and service get thumbs up at this "very noisy" grill, but, it's not quite unanimous – one critic cites it as "spam carbonara."

Rancho de Chimayo/S | 20 | 25 | 20 | $18 |
Rancho de Chimayo, State Rd. 520, Chimayo, 505-351-4444
M – Epitomizing fine Northern New Mexican cuisine", this inn and restaurant are "lovely", "romantic" and "worth a short trip" as an "international stopping point"; prices have remained moderate but a few grumble it gets "too crowded."

SantaCafe/S | 27 | 25 | 23 | $32 |
231 Washington Ave. (Paseo de Perlata & Marcy), 505-984-1788
U – Rated No. 1 for food in NM, this Asian-influenced Southwestern is the place to rub elbows with the rich and famous in a who's-who "celeb-watching", "NY investment-banking" crowd; this "elegant" restaurant offers "excellent" "creative" dishes "artistically" presented by a "caring" "attentive" staff; the only gripes are "highish prices" and "noise"; eat on the patio and be sure to reserve.

Shed, The/X | 20 | 19 | 19 | $14 |
113½ E. Palace Ave. (1 block from Square), 505-982-9030
U – It's "worth the wait" (no reservations) for the inexpensive and "incredibly consistent" prototypical New Mexican food at this "major tourist spot" in a historic 1692 adobe home near the Plaza; it's reported to be "a must" for lunch and for its "extraordinary" desserts.

Staab House/LS | – | – | – | E |
La Placada, 330 Palace Ave. (Placada), 505-986-0000
In this classic adobe hotel, the elegant Victorian surroundings house some of the best roadhouse Southwestern fare (some disagree: "I've never had a good meal here") around; the outdoor patio is nice in season and the margaritas all year round.

Zia Diner/S | 17 | 18 | 18 | $15 |
326 Guadalupe, 505-988-7008
U – On the register of historic places with a fine art deco interior, this is a "casual to the max" kind of place; the "wide-ranging menu" features good meat loaf, fish and chips and deep-dish fruit pies at prices that are a "rare bargain"; some complain about the service, but, overall this is worth a try "pre-movie" or on a night out with the kids.

SEATTLE

TOP 20 RESTAURANTS
(In order of food rating)

Restaurant | **Cuisine Type**

- **27** – Fullers — Continental/Northwest
- Gerard's Relais — French Classic
- **26** – Saleh al Lago — Northern Italian
- Labuznik — Middle European
- Cafe Juanita — Nuova Cucina Italian
- Chez Shea — Northwest Regional
- **25** – Al Boccalino — Southern Italian
- Nikko's — Japanese
- Le Gourmand — French Classic
- Georgian Room — Continental
- Le Tastevin — French Classic
- Il Terrazzo Carmine — Southern Italian
- **24** – Cafe Sport — Amer. Contemp.
- Andre's Gourmet — French/Vietnamese
- Adriatica — Greek/Italian
- Thai Restaurant — Thai
- Fountain Court — French/Northwest
- Il Bistro — N/S Italian
- **23** – Metropolitan Grill — Steakhouse
- Wild Ginger — SE Asian

OTHER TOP PLACES
(In alphabetical order)

- Botticelli Cafe — Italian
- brusseau's — Deli
- Cafe Sophie — International
- Campagne — French Bistro
- Dahlia Lounge — Amer. Contemp.
- El Puerco Lloron — Mexican
- Le Provencal — French Nouvelle
- Lobster Shop — Seafood
- Ray's Boathouse — Seafood
- Space Needle — International

SEATTLE | F | D | S | C |

Adriatica/S | 24 | 22 | 22 | $30 |
1107 Dexter Ave. N. (2 blocks north of Mercer St.),
206-285-5000
U – The Greek-Yugoslav-Italian cuisine "sparkles like the namesake sea" at this longtime Seattle favorite known for its top-of-the-line food, "lovely" service and great view of Lake Union; fried calamari, fresh seafood and good desserts are "simply orgasmic", but too garlicky ("I reeked for weeks") for a few; the loooong stairway up the hillside is a real obstacle, especially when there's no guarantee of a table by the windows; dinner only.

Al Boccalino | 25 | 21 | 20 | $27 |
1 Yesler Way (Western Ave.), 206-622-7688
M – This "tiny" Southern Italian newcomer in Pioneer Square took the city by storm with authentic, but light, modern and imaginative "tastes I want to remember forever"; the food (with many ingredients imported from Italy) is the draw – "makes getting fat worthwhile"; long lead time is needed for weekend reservations, but weeknights and lunches are good alternatives; service gets mixed reviews.

Andre's Gourmet/S | 24 | 14 | 18 | $17 |
14125 NE 20th St. (148th Ave. NE), Bellevue,
206-747-6551
U – "Unusual yet delicious" French-Vietnamese cuisine in an Eastside strip mall is "very good all around", although the food out-performs the subdued setting; people report the food is "always good", "very fresh" and "best for the money."

Botticelli Cafe | 23 | 15 | 16 | $8 |
101 Stewart St. (1st Ave.), 206-441-9235
U – Superlatives abound for this ten-seat hole-in-the wall, limited-menu Italian sandwich spot located Downtown near the Pike Place Market; espresso, cold drinks, desserts and sandwiches are "just like Italy", while the high tables and matching stools lend "wonderful great feel and personality"; service can be slow – "bring along your patience" – but the Italian men behind the counter make any woman's day; mostly takeout and lunch only.

brusseau's/S | 21 | 15 | 15 | $13 |
117 S. 5th St. (Dayton Ave.), Edmonds, 206-774-4166
U – For "simple, homemade food", try this gourmet deli in a converted, old-time filling station with "friendly", cafeteria-line service and renowned baked goods; breakfasts, brunches and lunches are often crowded with loyal locals, and sunny weather brings outdoor seating, bike riders and those on the way to the Kingston ferry.

SEATTLE

| F | D | S | C |

Cafe Juanita/S | 26 | 20 | 23 | $27 |
9702 NE 120th Place (97th Ave. NE), Kirkland, 206-823-1505
U – This Suburban Modern Italian in a converted house dragged Seattle dining into a new era a few years back and is still well-loved ("five-star! any excuse to go there!", "consistently excellent", "makes everyone feel special", "very friendly"); lamb, simple pastas, bread and pollo pistachio are "worth a trip across the lake"; the only complaint: "they've mastered the art of consistency – some change would be refreshing"; dinner only.

Cafe Sophie/S | 20 | 25 | 18 | $21 |
1921 First Ave. (bet. Stewart & Virginia Sts.), 206-441-6139
M – Problems plague this Downtowner whose small kitchen, uneven Continental-Italian food and "surly" service are offset by an elegant, romantic atmosphere; it can't quite carry off the creative and innovative menu, but most respondents love the desserts and the Victorian-baroque decor.

Cafe Sport/S | 24 | 20 | 21 | $23 |
2020 Western Ave. (Virginia St.), 206-443-6000
U – An immensely popular cafe near the Pike Place Market with smallish rooms, no-fault service and bright New Northwest cuisine (i.e., an imaginative American-Southeast Asian mix); the food wins praise ("gifted hand with seafood", "ingenious recipes cooked perfectly" and "consistently good") with such signature dishes as kasu black cod, black bean soup and good breakfasts and desserts; some surveyors feel it lost its "zing" since founding chef Tom Douglas' exit.

Campagne/S | 23 | 22 | 22 | $30 |
Pike Place Market, 86 Pine St. (Stewart St.), 206-728-2800
M – Despite generally high ratings, our surveyors' comments reflect a real love/hate affair ("wow food" vs. "worst ever") with this stark, white-tablecloth, pseudo-French bistro serving homey cuisine at the Pike Place Market; "excellent" say some, while others find "food does not come up to tableware" and get the feeling that the servers may hate them.

Chez Shea/S | 26 | 23 | 24 | $34 |
Pike Place Market, 94 Pike Place (1st Ave. & Pike St.), 206-467-9990
U – "The most romantic room in town", whose French food with a Northwest flair "can rank with the best in the country", has attentive, some say "snooty", service in small quarters overlooking the Pike Place Market; after a long, featureless climb to the top floor, it's "like stepping into Europe" with imaginative, fixed price, multicourse dinners; some complain that the menu choices are limited and portions too small, but a 26 food rating is a definitive answer; dinner only, completely smoke-free – "good place for footsies."

SEATTLE

| F | D | S | C |

Dahlia Lounge | 22 | 20 | 19 | $26 |
1904 Fourth Ave. (bet. Stewart & Virginia), 206-682-4142
M – Not everyone appreciates the "weird and wonderful" East-West fusion cuisine that chef-owner Tom Douglas puts out at this Downtown show-stopper (some find it "bizarre" and "affected"); the decor furthers the unease – the structural art deco interior has been painted red ("feels like I'm in a box" complains one); but enough people like this "fun place" to make it a Seattle "hot spot."

El Puerco Lloron | 21 | 15 | 12 | $10 |
1501 Western Ave. (Pike Place Hill climb), 206-624-0541
U – "The absolute best, junky, eat-with-your-fingers" Mexican food ("good, cheap, authentic") induces the local faithful to stream through this cafeteria line to the folding-metal card tables perched on the hillclimb between the Waterfront and the Pike Place Market; "great pork taquitos" (or chicken or shredded beef), "hottest fresh salsa" and freshly grilled, homemade tortillas make one exclaim, "Tijuana revisited."

Fountain Court, The/S | 24 | 21 | 21 | $28 |
22 103rd Ave. NE (Main St.), Bellevue, 206-451-0426
U – A real following has developed for the "beautifully presented", "elegant" French-accented Northwest cuisine in this small restaurant in old Bellevue; seafood and game highlight the menu, complemented by a good wine list; "impeccable service" adds to the "pricey" but "pleasant atmosphere", enhanced by romantic outdoor seating; "child-size portions" is the one complaint – otherwise, "it's a great restaurant."

Fullers | 27 | 26 | 25 | $38 |
Seattle Sheraton Hotel and Towers, 1400 Sixth Ave. (Union St.), 206-447-5544
U – With Seattle's highest food rating from our surveyors, "magic" abounds at this Downtown hotel dining room that "can compete with the best from any city" and consistently wins raves for its Northwest-style Continental cuisine, excellent wines, artful plates, tony service and museum-quality decor; "lots of thought all the way" pays off with "consistent, class" dining experiences that many wish they could afford more often; in sum, Seattle's "ultimate."

Georgian Room, The/S | 25 | 28 | 26 | $34 |
Olympic Four Seasons Hotel, 411 University St. (bet. 4th & 5th Aves.), 206-621-7889
U – You'll "feel like King George" with "wonderful pampering" in "Seattle's grandest room" where "impeccably prepared and presented" Continental cuisine and a renowned wine list provide (at a price) "the ultimate elegance"; our survey participants acclaim weekend brunch and holiday buffets, as well as quiet and solicitous business lunches; in sum, "always first class"; "to impress and be impressed."

SEATTLE | F | D | S | C |

Gerard's Relais de Lyon | 27 | 23 | 25 | $33 |
17121 Bothell Way NE (south of NE Ballinger Way), Bothell, 206-485-7600
U – The 30-minute drive from Downtown Seattle doesn't daunt those looking for a classic "taste of France" in this "quaint", "multiroomed country house"; although some complain that Gerard's "now rarely in the kitchen", "carefully prepared" sauces, lamb and the Grand Marnier soufflé make it all worthwhile; in sum, "a true special-occasion place"; dinner only.

Il Bistro | 24 | 21 | 19 | $29 |
93-A Pike St. (bet. 1st Ave. & Post Alley), 206-682-3049
U – This romantic, Pike Place Market Italianate bistro may "feel like Paris" as you duck into a dark cavern off a sloping, stone-paved alley, but it serves Classic Italian cuisine; "food is simple but sophisticated", with lamb, morels and prawns praised; the active bar scene in a "smoke-filled den" may be "very noisy", but it's "perfect for an affair", given the fact that it's often "so dark you can hardly see your plate"; dinner only.

Il Terrazzo Carmine | 25 | 24 | 22 | $30 |
411 First Ave. S. (near King Dome), 206-467-7797
U – All Seattle loves this Pioneer Square Southern Italian with its country inn ambiance, "great service" and "food for the gods"; "palate-tingling aromas" and the antipasto display set the stage for highly praised venison ravioli, fried calamari and fresh fish; noise may be a problem due to the crowds, but it's a perfect impress-your-client or woo-your-lover spot and, for foodies, ITC's "vibrant tastes leave no taste bud unchallenged."

Labuznik | 26 | 21 | 23 | $32 |
1924 First Ave. (Virginia St.), 206-441-8899
M – Many still look to this small Downtown Middle-European restaurant ("Seattle's best for over 10 years") for a "special-occasion" meal and not a light meal, either; it offers hearty portions of meat in a clubby "male atmosphere" that turns off as many as it turns on; service, generally good, can also cause problems – "I don't like to be the one taking orders when I go out."

Le Gourmand | 25 | 15 | 23 | $32 |
425 NW Market St. (4th Ave. NW), 206-784-3463
U – "One of the very best in the city" offers wonderful cuisine using Classic French techniques and the best local Northwest ingredients to overcome such disadvantages as a small storefront with "barren decor" and an out-of-the-way Ballard location; "a pioneer in fresh, local cuisine", chef-owner Bruce Naftaly makes the "best vegetables in town", "creative triple-reduction sauces" and "fine meats and fish"; a few find the lack of corporate restaurant glitz disconcerting, but most say this "accommodating" restaurant is a "regional gourmet paradise"; dinner only.

SEATTLE

| F | D | S | C |

Le Provencal/S | 23 | 18 | 22 | $27 |
212 Central Way (Lake St.), Kirkland, 206-827-3300
M – Provincial French cuisine and comforting bistro food have been pleasing Eastsiders for nearly two decades (although some feel it's "really gone downhill") at this "inviting and warm", small Kirkland eatery with classically prepared food and caring service; "especially good for romantic evenings" say some, others chime in, "closer than France – and just as good."

Le Tastevin | 25 | 23 | 24 | $31 |
19 W. Harrison St. (1st Ave. W.), 206-283-0991
M – Large Queen Anne establishment where Classic French cuisine and an award-winning, "fabulous wine list" are impeccably served in the grand manner in a comfortable, tranquil ambiance; special pre- and post-theater suppers, lunches and a "terrific happy hour" feature lighter cuisine; food faddists see it as "old-fashioned" and "outdated", others as the "most civilized place around"; although pricey for Seattle, it's always a "good setting for romance" and wowing business associates.

Lobster Shop, The/S | 23 | 22 | 21 | $26 |
4015 Ruston Way (McCarver St.), Tacoma, 206-752-2991
6912 Soundview Dr. NE (Dash Point), Tacoma, 206-927-1513
U – The Ruston Way sibling of this popular piscatorial pair is modern, sterile and filled with singles looking to mingle, while the original site at Dash Point is a "wonderful and quaint" "hideaway with a water view"; chowder, grilled seafood and, of course, lobster are "consistently good" at both locations – ergo, don't be surprised if there's a crowd; dinner only.

Metropolitan Grill, The/S | 23 | 20 | 19 | $25 |
820 Second Ave. (Marion St.), 206-624-3287
U – "The best steaks in town" get "good trimmings" at this Downtown eatery – "good wine list", "service to boot", "beautiful, woodsy, warm" setting with a "clubby" feel patronized by those with "power and money"; as for the ambiance – "I feel special here", but "be ready for crowds and suits" that are de rigueur at "this 'in' place."

Nikko's | 25 | 18 | 21 | $24 |
1306 S. King St. (Rainier Ave. S.), 206-322-4641
M –"Without a doubt, Seattle's best" sushi/sashimi is served by "a great showman" in an out-of-the-way southern location; the "clubby, cliquish" ambiance and "dark and dingy" decor remind some of "a '40s movie set"; others complain of high prices and "only ok" table service; still, it can be "lots of fun", especially since "people-watching and listening are unavoidable"; dinner only.

SEATTLE

| F | D | S | C |

Ray's Boathouse/S | 22 | 23 | 21 | $26 |
6049 Seaview Ave. NW (near Shilshole Marina), 206-789-3770
U – "The gold standard" of Seattle seafood restaurants boasts a "billion-dollar view" (where the ship canal meets Puget Sound) "unparalleled at sunset" that's so popular during tourist season that "reservations are impossible"; however, "excellent service", "good, simple food" – chowder, cracked Dungeness crab, oysters, smoked black cod and salmon – and that view win the day; naysayers find it "not all it thinks it is, but better than most."

Saleh Al Lago | 26 | 22 | 23 | $30 |
6804 E. Green Lake Way N. (bet. 1st & 2nd Sts. NE), 206-524-4044
U – "Intimate", "sophisticated", "first-class", "consistently excellent" "attention to all details" and "worth the price" typify our surveyors' comments about this small Green Lake Italian, one of Seattle's finest and most popular; the Classic Italian menu features fresh-made pastas, "the best veal in town", good seafood and good wine-by-the-glass selections; most leave "so satisfied" and "mellow."

Space Needle Restaurant, The/S | 16 | 25 | 17 | $29 |
Seattle Center Grounds (5th Ave. & Broad St.), 206-443-2100
M – "Every city needs an overpriced, revolving eatery high in the sky" – this is Seattle's, with "the panorama of the Northwest"; many find the standard American menu "has improved", although service is still "slow" and prices evoke an "ouch! only for tourists"; try it for out-of-town guests, brunch or a special occasion.

Thai Restaurant, The/S | 24 | 16 | 20 | $15 |
101 John St. (1st Ave. N.), 206-285-9000
U – "Very, very good Thai food" that "never disappoints" is the draw at this small and "a little too popular", Seattle Center neighborhood spot with limited decor but a "personable owner" and "great service"; "hotter than others", "they don't compromise for wimpy palates."

Wild Ginger/LS | 23 | 22 | 21 | $21 |
1400 Western Ave. (near Pike Place Market), 206-623-4450
M – This "gorgeous", "stark modern", Southeast Asian restaurant (with the only satay bar in town) gets generally positive reviews from our surveyors: "beautiful, delicious, reasonable", "very courteous service", "a refreshing mix of Asian cuisines" with "sharp, clean flavors"; but some say its "menu reads better than what shows up on your plate" and is "overpriced" for the genre.

ST. LOUIS

TOP 30 RESTAURANTS
(In order of food rating)

Restaurant	Cuisine Type
28 – Tony's	Continental/N/S Italian
Fio's La Fourchette	French Classic
27 – Cafe de France	French Classic
26 – Andria's	Steakhouse
25 – Giovanni's	Northern Italian
Malmaison	French Classic
Kemoll's	Northern Italian
Pueblo Nuevo	Mexican
Faust's Restaurant	Continental
Seventh Inn	Continental
24 – Lorusso's	N/S Italian
Nobu's	Japanese
Cardwell's	Amer. Contemp./SW
Al's Restaurant	Steakhouse
Gianpeppe's	Southern Italian
Benedetto's	N/S Italian
Westerfield House	Amer. Tradition.
Chez Louis	French Classic
Mineo's	N/S Italian
Farotto's	N/S Italian/Pizza
DaBaldo's	N/S Italian
Giovannia's Little Place	Northern Italian
Balaban's	Californian
St. Louis Bread Co.	Sandwiches/Desserts
23 – Al Baker's	Steakhouse
Kreis' Restaurant/Bar	Steakhouse
Mai Lee	Vietnamese
L'Auberge Bretonne	French Classic
Cafe Renee	American/French Bistro
Agostino's Colosseum	N/S Italian

OTHER TOP PLACES
(In alphabetical order)

Bevo Mill	German
Bruno's Little Italy	Nuova Cucina Italian
Cunetto House of Pasta	N/S Italian
Damon's	BBQ
Giuseppe's	Southern Italian
Hunter's Hollow	French Bistro
La Patisserie	French
Lee's	Chinese
O'Connell's Pub	Hamburgers
Tornatore's	N/S Italian

ST. LOUIS

| F | D | S | C |

Agostino's Colosseum | 23 | 20 | 21 | $28 |
12949 Olive Blvd. (Fee Fee Rd.), Creve Coeur, 314-434-2959
M – Agostino Gabriele was the first restaurateur to leave the Hill for West County, where he has built "the best high-end Italian restaurant" – "like you've died and gone to Roman Heaven"; curmudgeons say "Renaissance Bronx" and "pompous, plastic, pretentious", but perhaps the final words are "she loved it!"

Al Baker's | 23 | 21 | 23 | $31 |
8101 Clayton Rd. (Brentwood Blvd.), Clayton, 314-863-8878
M – Posh, landmark Clayton steakhouse with Continental overtones; its many fans rave over its "fantastic wine list", "best steaks" and "great veal chop", but others cry "gaudy", "too red-flocked" and "19th-century bordello", and say it attracts "the aging-singles set"; dinner only.

Al's Restaurant | 24 | 20 | 23 | $36 |
1200 N. 1st St. (Biddle St.), 314-421-6399
U – On a dark corner just off Downtown, Al Baroni pioneered a display of the evening's fare instead of a menu, and built a most popular, rather formal steakhouse; typical comments include "consistently great", "never been disappointed" and "one of the best in the U.S."; in sum, well worth a try – unless you're a menu collector; dinner only.

Andria's | 26 | 12 | 19 | $23 |
6805 Old Collinsville Rd. (east of Hwy. 64), Fairview Heights, IL, 618-632-4866
M – East Side steakhouse that gets raves for beef ("could convert a vegetarian", "fabulous", "best in town"), but poor marks for overcrowding ("intimate dining – on someone else's lap") and worse ones ("ridiculous", "too long") for waits of two to three hours on weekends; dinner only.

Balaban's/S | 24 | 20 | 20 | $27 |
405 N. Euclid Ave. (McPherson Ave.), 314-361-8085
M – Despite a high rating for its Californian-style cuisine, the Bay Area wannabe crowd, "swishy service" and eclectic menu, this stylish Central West End restaurant bothers some diners – "too hip for its own good" and "pretentious"; the majority insists it has "creative" food, "very romantic" atmosphere, "best brunch" and a "great wine list."

ST. LOUIS

| F | D | S | C |

Benedetto's

| 24 | 22 | 21 | $25 |

12240 Manchester Rd. (1 mile east of Ballas Rd.), Des Peres, 314-821-2555

U – *Hiding its soft lights and tuxedo-clad waiters in a West County strip-shopping center, this quietly elegant Sicilian restaurant receives mostly applause: "improves every time", "great Traditional Italian", "unlikely location for a grand evening"; the worst anyone has to say is "a little inconsistent."*

Bevo Mill

| 18 | 22 | 18 | $17 |

4749 Gravois Ave. (Morganford Rd.), 314-481-2626

M – *This South Side landmark, once owned by Augustus Busch and famed for German food, has joined the Hanon-Gallardo group, and draws comments from "ya, das ist wonderful" to "ach, nein"; despite some high marks for prime rib ("the best"), comments such as "boring menu" and "just so-so" are more prevalent; a new menu offers more German dishes.*

Bruno's Little Italy

| 23 | 19 | 21 | $23 |

5901 Southwest Ave. (59th St.), 314-781-5988

M – *This impressive Italian restaurant recently moved to larger, more elegant quarters; it continues to get generally high marks for food, "superb sauces", "value" and higher ones for the "best Italian wine list in St. Louis"; but you can't please everyone – "better before they went upscale"; dinner only.*

Cafe de France

| 27 | 25 | 26 | $36 |

410 Olive St. (bet. 4th St. & Broadway), 314-231-2204

U – *The city's No. 2–rated French restaurant, this formal, elegant, Downtown dining room draws enthusiastic praise in every respect, from a simple "the best" to "Escoffier lives" to "what a way to treat yourself"; chef-owner Marcel Keraval is lauded for "dedication" and "desserts"; dinner only.*

Cafe Renee

| 23 | 16 | 19 | $18 |

403 Lafayette Ctr. (Manchester & Baxter Rds.), Manchester, 314-394-6445

M – *Mostly applause for this small, Franco-American bistro in a West County shopping center; "our basic weeknight outing" say regulars who praise the "best-kept secret in West Country" for soups, duck and "salmon cheesecake, ah!"; others criticize service and the limited menu.*

ST. LOUIS

| F | D | S | C |

Cardwell's | 24 | 23 | 21 | $28 |
8100 Maryland Ave. (Brentwood Blvd.), Clayton,
314-726-5055
U – The place where people in the know in the Clayton area lunch and dine; this attractive, modern American-Southwestern restaurant wins universal accolades – "the best of the best", "one of a kind", "most creative", "sensational" and "brilliant", to mention a few; the only source of complaint is the "killing noise level" that accompanies extraordinary popularity.

Chez Louis | 24 | 22 | 21 | $32 |
Seven Gables Inn, 26 N. Meramec Ave. (bet. Forsyth Blvd. & Maryland Ave.), Clayton, 314-863-8400
M – Located in the intimate Seven Gables Inn in Clayton, this crisp French restaurant enjoys high favor for "best cuisine in St. Louis", "charming European atmosphere" and "traditional, well-prepared" food; recent management changes both applauded ("very good new chef") and rapped ("declining since Bernard left"); the recent arrival of chef Michael Holmes from Balaban's may presage improvement.

Cunetto House of Pasta | 23 | 16 | 19 | $15 |
5453 Magnolia Ave. (Southwest Ave.), 314-781-1135
U – Excellent Italian fare and bargain prices on the Hill bring raves, but the no-reservations policy here causes a major debate among our surveyors, with "great pasta, terrible waits" a standard response; if a few find meals "overpriced" or "overrated", most cheer the pasta resoundingly.

DaBaldo's/S | 24 | 20 | 22 | $20 |
3518 Hampton Ave. (3 blocks north of Chippewa St.),
314-832-6660
M – This highly touted newcomer to the Hampton Avenue restaurant corridor has established a coterie of solid supporters who likes its "great Sicilian cuisine" and "excellent veal"; others coming with grand expectations call it "only fair" with "service not impressive."

Damon's/S | 19 | 14 | 17 | $14 |
1250 Graham Rd. (north of I-270), Berkeley,
314-838-3400
3811 S. Lindbergh Blvd. (south of Watson Rd.), Sunset Hills, 314-821-4040
M – Casual barbecue specialists with one place in North County, another in South; fans exclaim, "finally decent ribs in St. Louis" and laud the "a-ok" onion loaf; however, some surveyors react with "tasty but tiny" and "not bad for chain ribs."

ST. LOUIS | F | D | S | C |

Farotto's/SX | 24 | 7 | 16 | $11 |
9525 Manchester Rd. (west of Rock Hill Rd.), Rock Hill, 314-962-0048
U – When it comes to pizza, this bargain spot in Mid County gets highest marks for "excellent thin-crust pizza"; surveyors rate it the best in its class and also recommend its toasted ravioli; the menu and the seating have both been expanded recently.

Faust's Restaurant/S | 25 | 26 | 24 | $32 |
Adam's Mark Hotel, 4th & Chestnut Sts., 314-241-7400
U – The top hotel restaurant in every category, the Downtown Adam's Mark's elegant dining room earns curtain calls for its "excellent wine list", "creative food", "great view of the Arch" and "best sommelier"; you may feel they occasionally "overkill", but what a way to die!

Fio's La Fourchette Restaurant | 28 | 24 | 26 | $39 |
1153 St. Louis Galleria (Clayton Rd. & Brentwood Blvd.), Richmond Heights, 314-863-6866
U – Elegant in every respect, this French restaurant has overcome its mall location to take the lead as best for French cuisine; "most creative", "beyond incredible", "favorite for a splurge", are typical comments; not surprisingly, towering expectations leave some "very disappointed" by "tons of sauces on everything" and the "need for an improved wine list"; dinner only.

Gianpeppe's | 24 | 21 | 22 | $27 |
2126 Marconi Ave. (Bischoff Ave.), 314-772-3303
U – A solid legion of fans salutes this small, calm Italian restaurant on the Hill for "great food" and for being "consistently excellent", "warm and friendly"; a few claim, "Peppe's success has brought unpeppy service."

Giovanni's | 25 | 23 | 24 | $33 |
5201 Shaw Ave. (Marconi Ave.), 314-772-5958
M – One of the best on the Hill, this pricey Italian classic gets uniformly high ratings and elicits superlatives from local restaurant-goers, e.g. "the greatest", "fabulous", "superb", "most beautiful"; but a few grouse – "arrogant owner", "way, way overrated"; dinner only.

Giovanni's Little Place | 24 | 21 | 22 | $28 |
14560 Manchester Rd. (1 block west of Baxter Rd.), Ballwin, 314-227-7230
U – A strong majority votes this West County spin-off of the Hill original the "best Italian west of the Hill" and "best in West County" with "excellent food" and "superb service"; it may be on the expensive side, but for our reviewers, it's well worth the tab; dinner only.

ST. LOUIS

| F | D | S | C |

Giuseppe's/S | 22 | 16 | 21 | $17 |
4141 S. Grand Blvd. (Meramec St.), 314-832-3779
U – Once a Downtown landmark, now a South Side one, this homey, friendly Italian impresses most for "good value, good food", and is also noted for "superb chicken livers" and the "best salad in town"; if it has "a crowded feeling", that's because St. Louisans know a good thing when they taste it.

Hunter's Hollow/S | 22 | 23 | 19 | $26 |
Washington & Front Sts. (Hwy. T, 'Lewis & Clark Trail'), Labadie, 314-742-2279
M – This attractive, hunting lodge–style, Country French restaurant in Labadie (about an hour from Downtown) is "worth the drive"; most of our respondents praise the "great chef" for providing "gorgeous eating"; others complain: "too far", "disappointing", "overpriced" and "slow" service.

Kemoll's/S | 25 | 21 | 23 | $27 |
1 Metropolitan Sq. (Broadway & Pine St.), 314-421-0555
U – Foundations shook when this North Side Italian landmark restaurant recently moved Downtown; all's well, though – a solid coterie of fans still loves the "opulent" setting and outstanding food, e.g. "great fried artichokes"; a few people, perhaps due to impossibly high expectations, find it "disappointing."

Kreis' Restaurant & Bar/S | 23 | 16 | 20 | $23 |
535 S. Lindbergh Blvd. (bet. Hwy. 40 & Ladue Rd.), Frontenac, 314-993-0735
U – Getting a reservation is the main problem at this ever-popular West County landmark for beef; the surroundings haven't changed for generations, nor has the beef which continues to draw raves – for prime rib ("best and biggest in town"), steaks ("great porterhouse", "superb Vienna steak") and consistency ("hasn't disappointed yet"); dinner only.

La Patisserie – Cafe Jules/S | 21 | 14 | 14 | $10 |
6269 Delmar Blvd. (west of Skinker Blvd.), University City, 314-725-4902
M – Tiny French cafe that serves breakfast and lunch in a charming University City Loop storefront can be "cozy on a winter morning"; most sing of "fresh pastries", "great breakfast" and "quiche too good to be true", while a few decry "long waits and atrocious service"; not open for dinner.

ST. LOUIS

| F | D | S | C |

L'Auberge Bretonne | 23 | 20 | 21 | $30 |
200 S. Brentwood Blvd. (Bonhomme Ave.), Clayton, 314-721-0100
M – St. Louis's first haute cuisine restaurant, this elegant French, in a new Clayton location, still has an enthusiastic following of upscale customers who happily pay its steep prices and applaud its "great French cuisine", "super desserts" and "impeccable service"; detractors say "not as good as in years past", "food with no flair."

Lee's | 22 | 10 | 21 | $12 |
8610 Olive Blvd. (Woodson Rd.), University City, 314-997-1218
U – Highest food ranking among Chinese restaurants goes to this University City veteran Cantonese, still dealing from a plain, tiny storefront; "best Oriental cuisine in town", "great Chinese", "spicy, but great" is the chorus heard from a solid choir of fans who also like the owner.

Lorusso's | 24 | – | 22 | $15 |
3121 Watson Rd. (1/2 block south of Arsenal St.), 314-647-6222
12153 Manchester Rd. (east of Ballas Rd.), 314-965-8200
U – This excellent Hampton Avenue Italian favorite moved to a larger and far more attractive location just as our original Survey went to press, but ecstatic followers still consider it a terrific value – a home run.

Mai Lee/X | 23 | 5 | 14 | $11 |
8440 Delmar Blvd. (McKnight Rd.), University City, 314-993-3754
U – The highest-rated Vietnamese restaurant in St. Louis, and the second highest Oriental, this small bargain storefront may have "zero atmosphere", but still wins unanimous praise as the "best Vietnamese" with "fresh, interesting food" and "superb soups" – all in all, "a unique experience."

Malmaison/S | 25 | 26 | 24 | $30 |
St. Albans Rd. (off Hwy. T), St. Albans, 314-458-0131
M – "A little-known gem" is the general consensus on this lovely French restaurant reminiscent in its pastoral ambiance and decor of a French country inn, thanks to its setting in a 1920s country club; fans willingly drive about 45 minutes from Downtown for the "beautiful location", "excellent menu" and "an enchanted evening."

Mineo's | 24 | 22 | 22 | $27 |
13490 Clayton Rd. (Mason Rd.), 314-434-5244
U – "Quiet elegance" and some of the best Italian food in town distinguish this longtime West County Italian restaurant that also gets special notice as "very handicapped accessible"; it's a "lovely, gracious place" with "excellent" veal and pasta dishes, but "too much garlic" for a few.

ST. LOUIS

| F | D | S | C |

Nobu's | 24 | 12 | 19 | $17 |
8643 Olive Street Rd. (I-170), 314-997-2303
M – The highest-rated Japanese spot in St. Louis wins ecstatic, unanimous applause for the "best sushi in town" and "creative food", now in larger, more comfortable quarters.

O'Connell's Pub/L | 22 | 17 | 16 | $10 |
4652 Shaw Ave. (Kingshighway Blvd.), 314-773-6600
M – The best charcoal-grilled hamburger in the city, according to respondents and, what one surveyor at least, describes as "the best bar food in the world" is served at this busy, noisy bar/restaurant, once a Gaslight Square standby now on the edge of the Hill; some call service "indifferent", others say "surly but likable"; just count the crowd and you'll know it's a "favorite."

Pueblo Nuevo | 25 | 10 | 20 | $11 |
7401 N. Lindbergh (north of I-270), Hazelwood, 314-831-6885
U – The best Mexican food in St. Louis, according to our surveyors, is cooked in this small, North County storefront featuring bullfight posters; "authentic Mexican", "my favorite", "a bargain" and "salsa is muy caliente" are typical olés.

Seventh Inn | 25 | 24 | 25 | $30 |
100 Seven Trails Dr. (1½ miles west of Woods Mill Rd.), Ballwin, 314-227-6686
M – Continental food in a West County apartment complex gets raves from some – "lovely atmosphere", "always a good bet", "great dining" – while others see it as "pretentious", "gaudy", "all show"; still, it's hard to argue with the high ratings given by the restaurant's suburban neighbors who appear to be in seventh heaven; dinner only.

St. Louis Bread Company | 24 | 13 | 17 | $7 |
10312 Manchester Rd. (Woodlawn Ave.), Kirkwood, 314-965-8700
6309 Delmar Blvd. (Westgate Ave.), University City, 314-726-6644
14888 Clayton Rd. (Baxter Rd.), Ballwin, 314-391-3111
4651 Maryland Ave. (Euclid Ave.), 314-367-7636
10 S. Central Ave. (Forsyth Blvd.), Clayton, 314-725-9666
6655 Delmar Blvd. (Kingsland Ave.), University City, 314-721-8007
447 N. New Ballas Rd. (south of Olive Blvd.), Creve Coeur, 314-569-3031
St. Louis Galleria, Clayton Rd. (Brentwood Blvd.), Richmond Heights, 314-727-5300

ST. LOUIS | F | D | S | C |

St. Louis Bread Company (Cont.)
West County Ctr., I-270 (Manchester Rd.), Des Peres, 314-821-1123
U – Nothing fancy, but these bright, crisp bakeries and sandwich shops get universal cheers for lunch ("veggie sandwich on honey wheat bread fabulous", "marvelous sandwiches", "fantastic sourdough bread") and for the budget-conscious.

Tony's | 28 | 26 | 28 | $41 |
410 Market St. (bet. 4th St. & Broadway), 314-231-7007
U – The No.1 vote-getter in St. Louis for food, Vince Bommarito's truly elegant Italian-Continental began serving from new quarters in the spring of '92, which ended the problem of stairs for the disabled – and of watching the maitre d' climb up backward to seat guests; it's still the benchmark of St. Louis dining: "best of the best", "will never disappoint you", "incomparable", "consistently great" are oft-repeated comments; high expectations cause some to complain – "overrated", "too expensive" – but there's no gainsaying Tony's rating as St. Louis's most popular restaurant; dinner only.

Tornatore's | 23 | 22 | 22 | $24 |
12315 Natural Bridge Rd. (east of I-270), Bridgeton, 314-739-6644
U – A bit "expensive" for the West County, this upscale Italian restaurant gets very good ratings from supporters who call it "a hidden gem" and a "pleasant surprise", concluding that it is a "beautiful restaurant with delicious food."

Westerfield House, The/S | 24 | 27 | 24 | $32 |
Westerfield House, Jefferson Rd. (2 miles east of Rte. 15), Freeburg, IL, 618-539-5643
M – A phalanx of loyal fans calls this lovely, antique-filled bed-and-breakfast an hour away in Freeburg, a "romantic treat", citing its excellent American food, "colonial charm" and "gracious" service; critics say it's "too expensive", "too far" and "too cutesy."

TAMPA BAY/ ST. PETERSBURG

TOP 10 RESTAURANTS
(In order of food rating)

Restaurant	Cuisine Type
27 – Euphemia Haye	Eclectic
Armani's	Northern Italian
26 – Bern's Steak House	Steakhouse
Cafe L'Europe	Continental
Mis en Place	Amer. Contemp.
25 – Michael's on East	Amer. Contemp./Calif.
R.G.'s	Continental
Donatello	Northern Italian
Blue Heron	Eclectic
Lobster Pot	Seafood

OTHER TOP PLACES
(In alphabetical order)

Basta's	Northern Italian
Clearwater Beach Hotel	Continental
Colony	Amer. Trad./Continental
King Charles	Continental
La Poele d'Or	French Bistro
Le Bordeaux	French Bistro
Oystercatchers	Seafood
Sabals	Amer. Contemp.
Tio Pepe's	Spanish
Wine Cellar	Continental/German

| F | D | S | C |

Armani's | 27 | 28 | 25 | $38 |

Hyatt Regency, 6200 Courtney Campbell Causeway, Tampa, 813-874-1234

U – No. 2 for food in the area, this stylish Italian gets an assist from the "breathtaking sunsets" on Tampa Bay, visible most nights at this "first-class" hotel dining room; but there's much more here, from the "expansive antipasto bar" laden with "manna from heaven" to the "excellent" entrees; though the staff can be a tad "obsequious", the presentation is flawless, and the whole experience makes this, bar none, "the best restaurant in Tampa."

TAMPA BAY/ST. PETERSBURG | F | D | S | C |

Basta's | 23 | 19 | 23 | $27 |
1625 4th St. S. (16th St.), St. Petersburg, 813-894-7880
M – "An oasis of fine dining in a poor section of town", this "wonderful" Northen Italian's kitchen rates highly, as do the slightly snooty but very professional waiters; the real problems, say surveyors, are the too-close tables, too-long waits and too-shady neighborhood.

Bern's Steak House/S | 26 | 18 | 23 | $35 |
1208 S. Howard Ave. (bet. Marjorie & Watrous Sts.), Tampa, 813-251-2421
U – This "grande dame" "Tampa tradition", famous for its "great steaks" and "bordello" decor, may be "showing her age" a bit, but most surveyors love the hammy staff (imagine vermouth put into a martini with an eyedropper), "encyclopedic wine list" and, most of all, the "fabulous aged beef"; maybe it's a "circus", but it's an entertaining one that walks the highwire, year in and year out, without losing its balance.

Blue Heron | 25 | 20 | 23 | $26 |
3285 Tampa Rd. (Lake St. George), Palm Harbor, 813-789-5176
U – "Tampa Bay's newest hit" is an art deco storefront that takes a mix-and-match approach to the menu – French, Italian, South American, Thai and Vietnamese all have a place in the kitchen here; the results are "unpredictable, but they try hard" and usually succeed; the "stark" decor doesn't work for everyone, but the "very-special" staff attention does.

Cafe L'Europe/S | 26 | 25 | 23 | $32 |
431 St. Armands Circle, Sarasota, 813-388-4415
M – Located on tiny but exclusive St. Armands Key, this "jewel" of a Continental with its "très chic" setting featuring "flowers everywhere", "yummy" "Frenchy" fare and "pretentious" but pampering staff is a "longtime local favorite"; though there's some carping about noise and prices, most find it "unusually elegant for a Florida restaurant"; BYO.

Clearwater Beach Hotel Dining Room/S | 24 | 24 | 20 | $25 |
500 Mandalay Ave., Clearwater Beach, 813-441-2425
U – This "lovely dining room" in a "charming old hotel" is known for "gracious dining", Continental style, with results that are "never disappointing" and often "very good"; the "tasteful", "quiet and reserved" setting is "great for this area", and especially good for a leisurely lunch.

TAMPA BAY/ST. PETERSBURG | F | D | S | C |

Colony, The/S | 24 | 23 | 24 | $32 |
Colony Beach Resort, 1620 Gulf-of-Mexico Dr.,
Longboat Key, 813-383-5558
U – "Costly" but worth every penny, this airy dining room is so close to the Gulf that you can practically catch your own dinner; however, someone already has – the kitchen turns out very fresh, "imaginative" seafood specialties and excellent Continental-American food to boot; the "dressy dinner crowd" also praises the "large, well-appointed room" and "professional service."

Donatello/S | 25 | 21 | 22 | $34 |
232 N. Dale Mabry Hwy. (2 blocks north of Kennedy Blvd.), Tampa, 813-875-6660
M – This "Manhattanesque" Tampa Italian "overdoes the hand-kissing" and the "pink decor", but the "very dependable, professional" kitchen "makes up for any deficiencies"; though surveyors say it's been "slipping" lately, it's still "the place to impress a date or business partner."

Euphemia Haye/S | 27 | 23 | 25 | $33 |
5540 Gulf-of-Mexico Dr., Longboat Key, 813-383-3633
U – An Eclectic star housed in a cottage on posh Longboat Key, this "extraordinary" spot is "the place to celebrate something really special"; its "exquisite" setting is ideal for the "top-flight", highly inventive cooking of chef-owner Ray Arpke; quality is so high that it's immaterial that the staff's a bit "too impressed with itself" and the crowds can create a "harried atmosphere"; customers simply "wish we could get there more often."

King Charles/S | 23 | 25 | 23 | $36 |
Don Cesare Hotel, 3400 Gulf Blvd., St. Petersburg Beach, 813-360-1881
U – "Small portions" of "usually excellent" but pricey Continental food are served in a "romantic atmosphere" complete with harpist; you may "leave hungry and broke – but not unhappy" from what is surely one of St. Petersburg's best hotel dining rooms; P.S. "the sunsets are worth every penny."

La Poele d'Or* | 23 | 14 | 20 | $18 |
Plaza de Sunus, 7629 Ulmerton Rd. (Belcher Rd.), Largo, 813-531-4975
M – You "can't worry about cholesterol" (or decor) when you enter this outpost of "heavy but good" French bistro cooking that locals consider "a well-kept secret"; the dowdy surroundings won't distract you unduly from the fine food, and happily, the "pleasant" service and modest bill won't, either.

TAMPA BAY/ST. PETERSBURG | F | D | S | C |

Le Bordeaux/S | 24 | 19 | 21 | $23 |
1502 S. Howard Ave. (Hills Ave.), Tampa, 813-254-4387
U – Its simple, "classic" Provençal fare and attitude-free staff get nothing but praise from surveyors, though its "modest", if at times loud, atmosphere impresses less; still, the food's "good and down-to-earth" and prices are so fair one reviewer asks, "how can something so good cost so little?"

Lobster Pot/S | 25 | 17 | 21 | $28 |
17814 Gulf Blvd. (1 mile south of Park Blvd. Bridge), Reddington Shores, 813-391-8592
M – The decor is secondary to the food at this roadside spot that has the "best seafood on the Sun Coast", which inevitably means it's "crowded and loud"; naysayers complain there's "no innovation" on the "limited menu", but most say its "high standards are still achieved."

Michael's on East/S | 25 | 24 | 24 | $31 |
Midtown Plaza, 1212 East Ave. S. (US 41), Sarasota, 813-366-0007
U – This "chic", "trendy" "nouvelle" Californian-style American garners high marks for its "nice ambiance" and "delicious" food; though one critic sniffs that it's "pretentious", others compare it – favorably – to the best restaurants on either coast (presumably they're referring to U.S. coasts north of Florida).

Mise en Place | 26 | 15 | 22 | $26 |
1815 Platt W. (bet. Freemont & Packwood Moving 1091), Tampa, 813-254-5373
U – The "phenomenal" cookery at this "small, casual" storefront New American has made it the "new scene" in Tampa; however, the "unusual combinations" on the "marvelous" menu wear better than the "claustrophobic" setting, and the no-reservations policy means it's "sometimes not worth the wait" for a table; "excellent value" is an inducement to patience.

Oystercatchers/S | 23 | 26 | 21 | $27 |
Hyatt Regency, 6200 Courtney Campbell Causeway, Tampa, 813-874-1234
U – The "elegant Key West environment" of this Hyatt seafooder is "extraordinary" say surveyors, "and the food's just about as great"; the "wonderful and romantic" room includes expansive Tampa Bay views, and the popular, "leisurely" Sunday brunch offers "a wealth of wonderful food" choices; this is "where everyone in the area takes their object of desire."

TAMPA BAY/ST. PETERSBURG | F | D | S | C |

R.G.'s | 25 | 24 | 23 | $27 |

3 Tampa City Ctr., Ste. 20, 110 N. Franklin St., Tampa, 813-229-5536
3879 N. Dale Blvd. (Cross St.), Tampa, 813-963-2356
U – These "elegant special-occasion choices" "like to experiment and usually succeed", and as a result their Continental fare is highly popular; "top-flight, classy and sophisticated", both places make a "sincere effort" to please, though new ownership is a wild card; our surveyors tend to prefer the Dale Boulevard location.

Sabals/S | 24 | 19 | 21 | $27 |

315 Main St. (Alt. 19), Dunedin, 813-734-3463
M – Don't be put off by the storefront decor or "in-crowd atmosphere" of this suburban Tampa New American; its fans call it "a terrific, intimate dining experience", with "imaginative" if smallish dishes served in "very eclectic" surroundings; if it doesn't work, and if service can be slow and "a tad haughty", anyone with a sense of culinary adventure won't notice.

Tio Pepe's/S | 23 | 19 | 20 | $22 |

2930 Gulf-to-Bay Blvd. (5 blocks east of US 19), Clearwater, 813-799-3082
M – Most things don't vary at this "casual" Spaniard – the "excellent" food, the "colorful atmosphere", the crowds, the "confusion" and the "impossible noise level"; the "sustained quality" of the cooking, the festive air and the value (especially at lunch) make it a natural for families; BYO.

Wine Cellar/S | 22 | 19 | 20 | $27 |

17307 Gulf Blvd. (173rd Ave.), N. Reddington Beach, 813-393-3491
M – This "old-line" Continental with heavy German influences maintains "strict adherence to conventional European standards of preparation" – perhaps this is the reason some say it's "living on its laurels"; the "heavy-handed" if flavorful cooking, a room that some say is "too dark" and "indifferent service" notwithstanding, it remains "very popular" with an older crowd, who no doubt appreciate its formality, early-bird specials and sheer durability.

WASHINGTON, D.C.

TOP 28 RESTAURANTS
(In order of food rating)

Restaurant	Cuisine Type
29 – Inn/Little Washington	Amer. Contemp.
27 – Le Lion d'Or	French Classic
Jean-Louis	French Classic
L'Auberge Chez Francois	French Classic
26 – Yannick's	French Nouvelle
Prime Rib	Seafood/Steakhouse
Coeur de Lion	Amer. Contemp.
Obelisk	Northern Italian
Galileo	Northern Italian
25 – Imperial Hotel	Amer. Contemp.
Pizzeria Paradiso	Pizza
Morrison-Clark Inn	Amer. Tradition.
Morton's of Chicago	Steakhouse
Nicholas	Amer. Contemp.
Patisserie Cafe Didier	French Bistro
Le Caprice	French Bistro
Nora	Amer. Contemp.
Haandi	Indian
Colonnade	Amer. Contemp.
24 – Aux Beaux Champs	French Nouvelle
La Bergerie	French Classic
Peking Gourmet Inn	Chinese
I Ricchi	Northern Italian
Melrose	Amer. Contemp.
Lucie	Amer. Contemp.
Busara	Thai
Willard Room	Amer. Contemp.
Tivoli	Continental

OTHER TOP PLACES
(In alphabetical order)

Bice	Northern Italian
Duangrat's	Thai
Germaine's	SE Asian
Grill, Ritz/Pent. City	Amer. Tradition.
La Colline	French Bistro
Occidental Grill	Amer. Contemp.
Restaurant, Ritz/Tysons	Amer. Contemp.
Rio Grande Cafe	Tex-Mex
Sequoia	Amer. Tradition.

WASHINGTON, D.C.

| F | D | S | C |

Aux Beaux Champs/S | 24 | 26 | 25 | $50 |
Four Seasons Hotel, 2800 Pennsylvania Ave., NW (bet. 28th & 29th Sts.), 202-342-0810
U – This sophisticated hotel dining room overlooking a lush Georgetown canalscape provides an "elegant and polished" backdrop for "quiet conversation" over "beautiful" breakfasts and Contemporary French or spa lunches and dinners; every detail, from the award-winning wine list to the staff's steady professionalism, stamps it as a "place for adults" willing to pay for excellence; for less pricey pampering, insiders frequent the hotel's Garden Terrace for afternoon tea, informal meals, drinks or late-night dessert.

Bice/S | 24 | 24 | 20 | $43 |
601 Pennsylvania Ave., NW (entrance on Indiana Ave.), 202-638-2423
U – This Milanese import has been wowing the "high rollers", power brokers and people watchers, ever since it opened its splendid Downtown digs; by most accounts, the skillfully prepared, state-of-the-art pastas, risottos and main courses are simply "wonderful"; however, some warn that "arrogance" may have replaced the "individual attention" that was a key to its initial success; "food from Milan, attitude from NYC" – it's part of a burgeoning national chain.

Busara/S | 24 | 26 | 23 | $24 |
2340 Wisconsin Ave., NW (below Calvert St.), 202-337-2340
U – "Dazzling", "dramatic", this high-tech Thai opened shortly before this Survey, yet it zoomed to the top of the charts – hitting the top 10 for its visually spectacular, theatrically lit decor, and despite weak spots, edged out Duangrat's as top Siamese with a trendy menu of western-influenced dishes; as if that wasn't enough, this newcomer scores high on service and low on price, and has that Georgetown rarity, a lovely rear garden.

Coeur de Lion/S | 26 | 26 | 26 | $38 |
Henley Park Hotel, 926 Massachusetts Ave., NW (10th St.), 202-638-5200
U – "Most romantic", as "advertised", this snug English-style Downtown place near the Convention Center charms those who know it; their enthusiastic responses to its ambiance, chef Jon Lenchner's (ex McPherson Grill) Contemporary American creations and the "impeccable service" give it top-10 ratings across-the-board; try it for brunch when there's "wonderful music and champagne."

WASHINGTON, D.C.

| F | D | S | C |

Colonnade, The | 25 | 26 | 25 | $35 |
ANA Hotel Washington D.C., 24th & M Sts., NW,
202-457-5000
U – Set in an airy courtyard conservatory (seemingly miles from the West End bustle), this Contemporary American is justly considered "one of Washington's most beautiful restaurants" and an example of what fine "dining should be – elegant, refined"; it's "always great for business", a "civilized" brunch or for celebrations and "not as expensive as you would think."

Dining Room, The (CLOSED) | 26 | 27 | 26 | $56 |
Ritz-Carlton Pentagon City, 1250 S. Hayes St. (bet. Army Navy Dr. & 15th St.), Arlington, VA, 703-415-5000
U – This beautifully appointed hotel dining room near the Pentagon is a distinctive setting for an important meal that attracts so many powerful people, others come just to be seen here; the "intensely flavored" Contemporary French cuisine of its acclaimed Michelin two-star chef, Gerard Pangaud, and an assured staff make it one of Washington's "premier dining experiences"; seldom has a young restaurant achieved such high standing so fast; you pay top dollar, but, as the ratings suggest, you get real Ritz value.

Duangrat's/S | 24 | 22 | 21 | $23 |
5878 Leesburg Pike (near Glen Forest Rd.), Falls Church, VA, 703-820-5775
U – The top Thai, our reviewers call this sophisticated Siamese "very classy" with an "exciting menu" that has "lots of choices – all of them good" and well "worth the drive" to its modest Arlington shopping-strip location; "pricey for ethnic food" maybe, but not for comparable Italian or French fine dining.

Galileo/S | 26 | 23 | 23 | $46 |
1110 21st St., NW (bet. L & M Sts.), 202-293-7191
U – Few restaurants look and taste as authentically Italian as this Northern exemplar that many consider "the best of the best"; nationally acclaimed chef-owner Roberto Donna composes "exceptional" daily menus, fittingly displayed in smashing postmodern "L" Street digs; if a few diners feel "disappointed", that's because they come with maximal expectations and are paying top prices; P.S. look for Donna to revolutionize carry-out cuisine when he opens his Dupont Circle seafood outlet, Pesce, and Lafayette Center pizzeria.

WASHINGTON, D.C.

| F | D | S | C |

Germaine's/S
| 23 | 19 | 20 | $30 |

2400 Wisconsin Ave., NW (below Calvert St.),
202-965-1185
U – "Always good", this Southeast Asian standby in Upper Georgetown offers a collection of cuisines, attention to the customer and, most of all, the captivating personality of Germaine herself; those who wonder if the place is losing "some of its flair" should drop by on Sunday nights when "Washington heavies" check in and the place is "going strong."

Grill, The/S
| 23 | 25 | 24 | $40 |

The Ritz-Carlton at Pentagon City, 1250 South Hayes St. (bet. 15th & Army Navy Sts.), Arlington, VA, 703-415-5000
U – About as elegant as dining gets, yet you can reach this "country-club" hotel by Metro; its posh grill room gives everyone a chance to feel "pampered" over Chateaubriand or at Sunday brunch, when all the caviar one can eat and champagne one can drink costs a mere $32 (expensive for a meal but not for a once-in-a-lifetime experience); "how can you go wrong?"

Haandi/S
| 25 | 20 | 21 | $21 |

Falls Plaza Shopping Ctr., 1222 W. Broad St. (Rte. 7), Falls Church, VA, 703-533-3501
U – "Don't be discouraged" by the locale of this Indian; inside, soft pastels and crystal chandeliers set off "well-balanced", "agreeably-spiced" delicacies and perfectly textured breads; considering its "moderate prices" and the "best service, period", dining here is one of the best buys around; since there is no reserving on weekends, go early to avoid long lines.

Imperial Hotel
| 25 | 25 | 26 | $37 |

The Imperial Hotel, 208 High St. (Cross St.), Chestertown, MD, 410-778-5000
U – Ideal for a "romantic" out of D.C. weekend retreat is this "enticing" Victorian inn in a Colonial era Chesapeake Bay port; artfully restored by Al and Carla Missoni (whose credits include the Morrison-Clark Inn), with Daniel Turgeon, a talented young chef, turning perfect produce into a delicious Contemporary American cuisine, this inn gets top marks across the board: "a lovely experience", "stumbled onto a gem", "spend the night."

WASHINGTON, D.C. | F | D | S | C |

Inn at Little Washington/S | 29 | 29 | 28 | $71 |
Inn at Little Washington, Middle & Main Sts., Washington, VA, 703-675-3800
U – "Meal of a lifetime", "all it's cracked up to be", "an extravagant treat", "flawless" – people run out of superlatives to describe this glorious Virginia country getaway; chef-co-owner Patrick O'Connell constantly redefines New American cuisine; his "incomparable" food, the "romantic" setting and "impeccable service" are in complete harmony: in short, "money can buy happiness", especially if you "stay overnight" – a "wonderful weekend retreat."

I Ricchi | 24 | 22 | 22 | $41 |
1220 19th St., NW (bet. M & N Sts.), 202-835-0459
M – Reactions to this trendy Downtown trattoria depend on one's interest in robust Tuscan cuisine, which makes liberal use of olive oil and hefty grilled meats, and strains one's tolerance for "hauteur"; as high ratings and heavy traffic reflect, this "stimulating" place remains immensely popular, resulting in crowding, noise and waits.

Jean-Louis | 27 | 24 | 26 | $69 |
Watergate Hotel, 2650 Virginia Ave., NW (New Hampshire Ave.), 202-298-4488
U – A dinner prepared by Jean-Louis Palladin is "an experience you won't forget"; frequent diners are amazed by his "never ending originality" and an ambiance so intimate and attentive that "you feel like a house-guest" in his Watergate dining room; it is well "worth rearranging your life" to take advantage of his $43 pre-theater dinner (5:30-6:30 seating), a "must-splurge bargain" for food and service that at other times costs much more.

La Bergerie | 24 | 23 | 23 | $40 |
218 N. Lee St. (bet. King & Queen Sts.), Alexandria, VA, 703-683-1007
U – A very Old Town clientele "basques" in the warm glow of this special place, a romantic townhouse featuring outstanding exemplars of the regional cuisine of the Pyrenees and Perigord; perhaps it's a bit stuffy, with a leisurely (read "slow") pace, but its contented customers wouldn't change a thing – like old, slightly "tarnished silver", it's been burnished by time.

La Colline | 24 | 19 | 22 | $32 |
400 N. Capitol St., NW (bet. D & E Sts.), 202-737-0400
U – The premier Capitol Hill French bistro is one of those places where lobbyists "pay one bill to get another passed"; it's "fast and cheap" ($17.50 for a first-rate fixed price dinner), while offering "smooth-as-silk" service and "some of the best cooking in town"; typical comments include: "only place Senate staff will lunch", "lovely" private parties, "lobbyist dream"; its only blemish is the "Holiday Inn decor"; breakfast from 6 AM.

WASHINGTON, D.C.

| F | D | S | C |

L'Auberge Chez Francois/S | 27 | 27 | 26 | $44 |
332 Springvale Rd. (2 miles north of Georgetown Pike), Great Falls, VA, 703-759-3800
U – Some things never change and never should – most notably, our area's perennial favorite restaurant-cum-garden – a "stunningly understated French country inn" in Great Falls that "does everything right"; "words can't describe" its mystique: "always better than you expect", "fall in love all over again – with the restaurant and each other", "like being in another time and place"; apart from the two-weeks-in-advance reservation "hassle", there are no complaints.

Le Caprice/S | 25 | 19 | 22 | $38 |
2348 Wisconsin Ave., NW (1 block south of Calvert St.), 202-337-3394
M – This Parisian-feeling bistro is favored by Georgetown's old guard; its Alsatian patron, Edmond Foltzenlogel, keeps reinterpreting time-honored dishes with delectable results; his Gallic regard for good value is reflected in bargain prix fixe dinners ($18.50 and $23.50); less happily, service feels Parisian too.

Le Lion d'Or | 27 | 25 | 25 | $56 |
1150 Connecticut Ave., NW (18th & M Sts.), 202-296-7972
U – Respect for its solid virtues is reflected in the elevation of DC's leading exponent of French culinary classicism to second place for food; "year in, year out" master-chef Jean-Pierre Goyenvalle's lobster stew, pastry-wrapped fish, soufflés and superior wines set a standard that few restaurants in the country can meet; the "gilded" setting and formality (like a "White House state dinner") appeal to most, but not all, diners.

Lucie/S | 24 | 24 | 24 | $46 |
Embassy Row Hotel, 2015 Massachusetts Ave. (off Dupont Circle), 202-939-4250
U – Here is sumptuous Contemporary American dining in a refined hotel; surveyor comments include: "gifted chef", "creative cuisine, good wine list", "winemaster dinners are special value", "old-world service" ; "a favorite for treating out-of-town guests staying at nearby hotels or the Cosmos Club."

Melrose/S | 24 | 23 | 22 | $43 |
Park Hyatt Hotel, 24th & M Sts., NW, 202-955-3899
U – This elegant West End Contemporary American is wonderful at "any hour" – yet "no one seems to know"; its fare is "beautifully prepared and presented" and complemented by tranquil surroundings; for an affordable introduction, try its "ritzy" pre-theater dinner ($18.50); N.B. the Sunday brunch is also worth trying as is the "plush" afternoon tea.

WASHINGTON, D.C. | F | D | S | C |

Morrison-Clark Inn/S | 25 | 25 | 23 | $41 |
Morrison-Clark Inn, 1015 L St., NW (11th St. &
Massachusetts Ave.), 202-898-1200
U – This "ultracivilized" Downtown boutique is an ideal
place to take discriminating guests; its tasteful Victorian
dining room showcases American food at its best –
"sophisticated yet homey", "creative, fresh and well-
prepared", "satisfies body and soul" – we get very few
complaints (a tad too "prissy"); regulars find it most
delightful at lunch or brunch.

Morton's of Chicago/S | 25 | 20 | 22 | $45 |
3251 Prospect St., NW (Wisconsin Ave.), 202-342-6258
8075 Leesburg Pike (Gallows Rd.), Tysons Corner, VA,
703-883-0800
U – At these "Class A" meat houses, you get the best,
biggest, juiciest, most perfectly aged, slab of beef that
money can buy; "if you like steak", chances are you'll
love the "terribly loud", "suave", silk-shirt sleeved macho
milieu that accompanies it ("manly, wonderful for business
meals"); P.S. Morton's also serves lobster, fish and the
"best chocolate soufflé."

Nicholas/S | 25 | 25 | 24 | $45 |
Mayflower Hotel, 1127 Connecticut Ave., NW (bet. L &
DeSalles Sts.), 202-347-8900
U – This big sleeper – a Downtown hotel dining room
that some acclaim as the "best restaurant in DC" is
certainly one of the most elegant; the well-conceived,
Contemporary American menu is "truly inspired", with
"everything" else including "old-fashioned service" "done
well"; also the fixed price lunch and dinners are a "steal";
are there any warts? – maybe "a little pretentious."

Nora | 25 | 23 | 23 | $38 |
2132 Florida Ave., NW (bet. Connecticut &
Massachusetts Aves.), 202-462-5143
U – Nora's "philosophy" sounds simple – transforming
wholesome ingredients into "innovative, personal and
sophisticated Contemporary American food" served with
low-key panache "in a wonderful room" at a fair price;
bringing it off successfully is her trick, accomplished
with "better-than-ever" results this year.

Obelisk | 26 | 21 | 23 | $43 |
2029 P St., NW (between 20th & 21st Sts.), 202-872-1180
M – In a town that loves Italian food, this highly individual
boîte (off Dupont Circle) is the Numero Uno Italiano;
consistent excellence is the hallmark of chef-owner
Peter Pastan's daily-changing set-price Tuscan-inspired
dinners; complemented by well-priced wines, soft
surroundings and knowledgeable service, each meal
"never fails to surprise and delight"; the major flaw is it's
hard to get a table, a minor one that it may "take itself a
bit too seriously."

WASHINGTON, D.C.

| F | D | S | C |

Occidental Grill/LS | 22 | 23 | 21 | $35 |
The Willard Complex (Pennsylvania Ave. & 14th St.),
202-783-1475
U – A successful downscaling at this "very Washington" Pennsylvania Avenue address (by collapsing the nouveau, upstairs restaurant into the clubby downstairs grill room), capitalized on the Grill's best features – its "power atmosphere" and its relaxed menu featuring sandwiches, salads and regional American entrees; our surveyors report that the Grill "reduced prices, not quality", and that the celebs come in droves; still, some say it's "like eating in a law office."

Patisserie Cafe Didier/S | 25 | 16 | 17 | $13 |
3206 Grace St., NW (bet. M & K Sts.), 202-342-9083
U – This quiet cafe just off the canal is "like Paris" in Georgetown; it showcases Dieter Schoner's extraordinary breakfast croissants, wonderfully fresh soups, salads, soufflés and quiche for lunch, or his heavenly cakes and "best" crème brûlée as an afternoon treat; "the most incredibly, intricate, elegant and resplendent pastry at reasonable prices" doesn't overstate the case; "indifferent service" is the sole weakness.

Peking Gourmet Inn/S | 24 | 16 | 21 | $23 |
6029 Leesburg Pike, Falls Church, VA, 703-671-8088
M – Chinese food fanciers flock to this Falls Churcher for "superb" Peking duck and a host of Hong Kong delicacies; it's the tops in Chinese, yet almost everyone would "like it a lot more if I didn't have to wait in line to get in", if celebrity hadn't resulted in price inflation and if it weren't always expanding.

Pizzeria Paradiso/S | 25 | 19 | 17 | $18 |
2029 P St., NW (bet. 20th & 21st Sts.), 202-223-1245
U – At DC's top-rated pizzeria, maestro Peter Pastan eclipsed every other pie in town when he began creating crisp-crusted, brick-oven baked pies with extraordinary quality toppings plus panini (sandwiches), on homemade focaccia and garden-fresh salads; "everything is perfect but the wait" at this casual, modern Dupont Circle cafe.

Prime Rib, The | 26 | 25 | 24 | $42 |
2020 K St., NW (bet. 20th & 21st Sts.), 202-466-8811
U – Hundreds of heavy-hitters and hearty eaters say this "dark, grand", "tried-and-true", "clubby" K Street mainstay has the "best beef" and "the freshest seafood" in town; it remains the ultimate "place for heavy arm-twisting", is great to impress clients and is appreciated for black-lacquer decor ("the older you are, the better the darkness seems"); the unconverted call it "Baltimore South" or "NY in DC."

WASHINGTON, D.C.

| F | D | S | C |

Restaurant, The/S | 23 | 27 | 23 | $39 |
The Ritz-Carlton at Tysons II, 1700 Tysons Blvd. (at the Galleria, International Blvd.), McLean, VA, 703-506-4300
U – Everyone loves being treated with "attention" at this elegant "oasis" that shares near-the-top decor ratings with other spectacular dining rooms in Ritz-Carlton's top-flight groups; this lovely room in Tysons II showcases regional American cooking (even the fitness meals taste good); lunchtime buffets and a lavish Friday night seafood buffet for $25 bring luxury within normal budgets.

Rio Grande Cafe/S | 22 | 17 | 18 | $19 |
4919 Fairmont Ave. (off Old Georgetown Rd.), Bethesda, MD, 301-656-2981
4301 N. Fairfax Ave. (Glebe Rd.), Arlington, VA, 703-528-3131
Reston Town Ctr., 1827 Library St. (Reston Pkwy.), Reston, VA, 703-904-0703
U – Tex-Mex cantinas favored by politicos, and almost everyone else in town, including the kids; our reviewers debate whether the "amazingly good" shrimp, fajitas, quail and cabrito (goat), are worth the looong waits and noise so loud you "can't hear" the perky staff "drop plates"; chances are you'll be deciding for yourself – so "grab a margarita and stand in line."

Sequoia/LS | 17 | 24 | 16 | $28 |
3000 K St., NW (Washington Harbour), 202-944-4200
M – Sunset views over the Potomac from the spacious outdoor terrace ("glorious on a sunny" spring day), and inside, the feeling of being on a luxury ocean liner – this Washington Harbour megalith has undoubted physical charms; yet its ambitious, all-American food and chipper service could easily be better; it's best for a "meal of snacks" or a drink with tourists in tow; "lovely and empty for lunch", its bar is "a blast" on Friday nights.

Tivoli | 24 | 23 | 23 | $32 |
1700 N. Moore St. (N. 19th St. & Wilson Blvd.), Rosslyn, VA, 703-524-8900
U – A resurgence of old-fashioned values – which this highly professional Rosslyn Continental exemplifies – may be responsible for a rise in its ratings; the quiet, classic room "with service and cuisine to match" is both sophisticated and relaxing; it's "a great place for lunch" as well as for its pre-theater dinner.

WASHINGTON, D.C. | F | D | S | C |

Twenty-One Federal (CLOSED) | 25 | 22 | 23 | $43 |
1736 L St., NW (bet. 18th St. & Connecticut Ave.),
202-331-9771
U – *Hard-working and creative, chef Robert Kinkaid doesn't rest on his laurels; he has moved to lighten his "imaginative" Contemporary American fare (without sacrificing flavor or quality) and has introduced a pre-theater dinner that puts this handsome "major league" dining place within middle-class budgets; though some feel that Twenty-One is still not priced right, don't tell that to his prestigious clients.*

Willard Room/S | 24 | 28 | 25 | $49 |
Willard Hotel, 1401 Pennsylvania Ave., NW (bet. 14th & 15th Sts.), 202-637-7440
U – *"Luxury to the max", "totally first class", this opulent turn-of-the-century dining room is "the place to take the British Ambassador" or "have tea with your great-aunt"; also it's "a very, very good choice for a business meeting"; it has "rich classical American dining" and white-glove "pampering for when you need a lift"; if a place that makes people feel like they're in heaven has a flaw, it's being a bit "too formal to relax"; though pricey, it's premium.*

Yannick's/S | 26 | 23 | 24 | $61 |
Radisson Plaza Hotel, 5000 Seminary Rd. (Beauregard St.), Alexandria, VA, 703-845-1010
U – *Redoubtable Yannick Cam in his Suburban showcase has bounced back to the top ranks less than two years after his Le Pavillon folded; "exquisite" dinners (and lunches) redefine his French Nouvelle cuisine – full-flavored and more affordable, although still luxury class – but his real sleeper is a sumptuous "true bargain" brunch; the setting is tasteful, even "elegant"; however, some fans subtract points for being "aware its a hotel" and "10 miles outside the city."*

CITY ABBREVIATIONS

AC	Atlantic City	**NO**	New Orleans
AT	Atlanta	**NY**	New York City
BA	Baltimore	**OC**	Orange County, CA
BO	Boston	**OR**	Orlando
CH	Chicago	**PB**	Palm Beach
DA	Dallas	**PH**	Philadelphia
DC	Washington, DC	**PO**	Portland, OR
FL	Fort Lauderdale	**PS**	Phoenix–Scottsdale
FW	Fort Worth	**SA**	Santa Fe
HO	Honolulu	**SD**	San Diego
HS	Houston	**SE**	Seattle
KC	Kansas City	**SF**	San Francisco
LA	Los Angeles	**SL**	St. Louis
MI	Miami	**TS**	Tampa Bay/St. Pete
MK	Milwaukee		

TYPES OF CUISINE

Afghan
Helmand, SF

American (Contemporary)
Actuelle, DA
"a Mano", MI
Aragon Cafe, MI
Arcadia, NY
Atwater's, PO
Aureole, NY
Avner's, DA
Bishop's Lodge, SA
Brasserie Max, FL
Brickell Club, MI
Buckhead Diner, AT
By Word/Mouth, FL
Cafe, Ritz/Atlanta, AT
Cafe Arugula, FL
Cafe Aspen, FW
Cafe Chardonnay, PB
Cafe Max, FL
Cafe Renee, SL
Cafe Sport, SE
Campton Place, SF
Cardwell's, SL
Chaplin's, DA
Charlie Trotter's, CH
Checkers, LA
Chef Allen's, MI
Christopher's/Bistro, PS
City Cafe, DA
Coeur de Lion, DC
Colonnade, DC
Conservatory, DA
Cornucopia, BO
Cypress Room, FL
Dahlia Lounge, SE
Delectables, AT
Dining Room, AT
Dux, OR
Evermay on Del, PH
Explorers, PB
Gaspar's, DA
Gordon, CH
Gotham, NY
Hamptons, BA
Icarus, BO
Imperial Hotel, DC
Inn/Anasazi, SA
Inn/Little Wash. DC
Ivy, LA
Jake's, PH
Joe's Restaurant, PH
Lambert's, SA
Lark Creek Inn, SF
Latilla Room, PS
Laurels, DA
Le Mesquite, FL
Linwood's, BA
Lucie, DC
Mainland Inn, PH
March, NY
Mark, PB
Mark's Place, MI
Melrose, DC
Michael's, FW

Michael's, TS
Mis en Place, TS
Morada, PB
Nicholas, DC
Nora, DC
Occidental Grill, DC
Orchids, HO
Papa Haydn, PO
Partners, AT
Pavilion/Walters, BA
Pebbles, OR
Pierpoint, BA
Pleasant Peasant, AT
Printer's Row, CH
Puffin's, BA
Pump Room, CH
Quilted Giraffe, NY
Quilted Toque, HG
Rarities, BO
Reflections, FW
Restaurant, Ritz, DC
Ritz-Carlton D.R., SF
River Cafe, NY
River Oaks Grill, HG
Roller's, PH
Rotisserie Beef/Bird, HG
Roxsand, PS
Ruggles Grill, HG
Sabals, TS
Saddle Peak, LA
Sanford, MK
Silverado Cafe, FL
72 Market Street, LA
St. Cloud, BO
Twenty-One Fed., DC
Union Square Cafe, NY
Upperline, NO
Veranda, MI
Willard Room, DC
York Street, DA

Guadalupe Cafe, SA
Horny Toad, PS
Houston's, PS
Immigrant Room, MK
Jordan's Grove, OR
La Tertulia, SA
Lawry's, DA
Lawry's, LA
Le Picnique, KC
Locke-Ober Cafe, BO
Max's Grille, PB
Morrison-Clark Inn, DC
Mrs. Peter's, KC
Murphy's, AT
95th, CH
Oasis Cafe, BO
Pandl's, MK
Pano's/Paul's, AT
Parker's, BO
Peppercorn, KC
Prime Rib, BA
Pyramid Room, DA
Raindancer, FL
Rainwater's, SD
Ram's Head Inn, AC
Ringside, PO
Seasons, CH
Sequoia, DC
Stephenson's, KC
Stroud's, KC
Swann Lounge, PH
Taste of Texas, HG
T.C. Eggington's, PS
Thee Bungalow, SD
"21" Club, NY
Vincent Guerithault, PS
Walker Bros., CH
Waterside, BA
Westerfield House, SL
Zia Diner, SA

American (Traditional)

American Res, KC
Braddock's, PH
Cafe, Ritz/Buckhead, AT
Celebration, FW
Chatham's Pl., OR
Coach and Six, AT
Colony, TS
Cottage, CH
Dining Galleries, MI
English Room, MK
Forge, MI
Grill, Ritz, DC
Grill, Ritz, PS
Grill Room, NO

Austrian

Chimney, DA

Bar-B-Q

Angelo's Barbeque, FW
Bubbalou's BBQ, OR
Clark's BBQ, DA
Damon's, SL
East Coast Grill, BO
Green's BBQ, HG
Smoke Stack, KC
Sonny Bryan's, DA

Belgian

Belgian Lion, SD

Cajun/Creole

A Taste of N.O., AT
Bon Ton Cafe, NO
Brennan's, HG
Brigtsen's, NO
Clancy's, NO
Esplanade, PO
Greenery, CH
La Cuisine, NO
Lafitte's Landing, NO
Mosca's, NO
Pappadeaux, HG
Upperline, NO

Californian

Azalea, AT
Balaban's, SL
Bel-Air Hotel, LA
Bistro 201, OC
Cafe/Chez Panisse, SF
Cafe Pacifica, SD
Campanile, LA
Campton Place, SF
Chefs' Cafe, AT
Chez Panisse, SF
Citrus, LA
Cypress Club, SF
George's/Cove, SD
Granita, LA
Joe's, LA
La Coquina, OR
L'Avenue, SF
Le Chardonnay, LA
Max's Grille, PB
Michael's, LA
Michael's, TS
Mille Fleurs, SD
Parkway Grill, LA
Patina, LA
Postrio, SF
Rockenwagner, LA
Stars, SF
Spago, LA
Terra, SF
302 West, CH
WineSellar, SD

Cambodian

Elephant Walk, BO

Caribbean

East Coast Grill, BO
Green Street Grill, BO

Chinese

B.C. Chong, MI
Bird, CH
Cafe Katsu, LA
Chau Chow, BO
Chen's Dynasty, PO
China Blossom, NO
Chopstix, AT
Empress of China, HG
First China, AT
Flower Lounge, SF
Forbidden City, OR
Genghis Khan, NO
Golden Dragon, HO
Gourmet House, PS
Ho Ho, AT
Honto, AT
House of Chan, AT
House of Nanking, SF
Hsu's, AT
Hunan Empire, KC
Hunan, HG
Jasmine, DA
Lee's, SL
Mah Jong, AT
New Peking, KC
Peking Duck, AC
Peking Gourmet, DC
Princess Garden, KC
Red Dragon House, KC
Royal China, KC
Shun Lee Palace, NY
Su Shin, MI
Susanna Foo, PH
Tony Cheng's, BA
Trey Yuen, NO
Uncle Tai's, DA
Uncle Tai's, PB
Woks, KC
Yujean Kang's, LA

Coffee Houses

Dolce & Freddo, HG

Continental

Aujourd'hui, BO
Balcony, FW
Bali-By-The-Sea, HO
Bellucci's, KC
Bon Appetit, HO
Cafe L'Europe, PB
Cafe L'Europe, TS
Cafe Matthew, FW
Carbo's Cafe, AT
Carriage House, FW
Chapparal Room, PS
Charade, MI
Charley's 517, HG
Christo's, PS

Clancy's, NO
Clearwater Beach, TS
Colony, TS
Compound, SA
Cottage, CH
Different Pt./View, PS
Dominique's, MI
Empress Room, OR
Faust's, SL
Fleming, MI
Four Seasons, NY
Frenchtown Inn, PH
Fullers, SE
Georgian Room, SE
Grand Cafe, MI
Grant Grill, SD
Green Hills Inn, PH
Grenadier's, MK
Gustaf Anders, OC
Harrow Inne, PH
Hedgerose, AT
Hersh's Orchard, BA
House of Joy, PS
Ivana's, AC
Janousek's, AT
JW's, OC
King Charles, TS
Kings Contrivance, BA
Le Dome, FL
Le Jardin, NO
Le Palais, AC
Le Pavillon, MI
Maile, HO
Maison et Jardin, OR
Mancuso's, PS
Michel's, HO
Milton Inn, BA
Nick's, HO
Nikolai's Roof, AT
Old Swiss, FW
Old Warsaw, DA
103 West, AT
Palace, SA
Palm Court, PS
Park Plaza, OR
Peerce's, BA
Pink Adobe, SA
Plaza Dining, BO
Plum Room, FL
Pyramid Room, DA
Rainbow Room, NY
Reg. Bev. Wilshire, LA
Restaurant 210, PH
Restaurant, PS
R.G.'s, TS
Ritz-Carlton Hotel, HG
Ritz-Carlton, OC
Ritz Dining Room, BO
Ritz, OC
Rivoli Restaurant, HG
Rudys' 2900, BA
Sazerac, NO
Secret, HO
Seventh Inn, SL
Studio One Cafe, FL
Tavern/Green, NY
Tivoli, DC
Tony's, HG
Tony's, SL
Top/Cove, SD
Top/World, OR
Tours, FW
Willows, HO
Windows/World, NY
Wine Cellar, TS

Cuban

Casa Larios, MI
Havana Cafe, PS
Yuca, MI

Czech

Labuznik, SE

Delis

brusseau's, SE
Carnegie Deli, NY

Desserts

Dessert Place, AT
Dolce & Freddo, HG
Downtown Bakery, SF
Murray's, KC
Napoleon Cafe, PH
Patisserie Descours, HG
St. Louis Bread, SL

Diners

Cafe Haleiwa, HO

Eclectic

Azalea, AT
Bellucci's, KC
Biba, BO
Bijou Cafe, PO
Blue Heron, TS
Blue Room, BO
Cafe Allegro, KC
Classic Cup, KC
Euphemia Haye, TS
Flying Saucer, SF
Grand Street, KC
Hamersley's, BO
Harvard Street Grill, BO

Indigo, AT
Jordan's Grove, OR
L'Ecole, PS
Metropolis, KC
Mike's, NO
Parkway Market, KC
Pavilion, OC
Pavilion/Walters, BA
Peppercorn, KC
Reading Term. Mkt., PH
Rockenwagner, LA
Rozzelle Court, KC
Seasons, BO
Square One, SF
Venue, KC

Eurasian

Le Mikado, CH

Florida Regional

Ocean Grand, PB

Frankfurters

Jody Maroni's, LA

French Bistro

Addison Cafe, DA
Bistro Banlieue, CH
Bistro, MI
Cafe de France, OR
Cafe Provencal, CH
Cafe Renee, SL
Campagne, SE
Chanteclair, OC
Chez Georges, HG
Chez Gerard, DA
Chez Nous, HG
Cindy Black's, SD
Crozier's, NO
Dobson's, SD
French Side, SD
Gazebo Cafe, PB
Hamersley's, BO
Harvard Street Grill, BO
Hunter's Hollow, SL
Inn/Phillips Mill, PH
Jean Claude's, PS
La Bonne Crepe, FL
La Campagne, PH
La Colline, DC
La Ferme, FL
La Poele d'Or, TS
L'Auberge, PB
Le Bar Lyonnais, PH
Le Bordeaux, TS
Le Caprice, DC
Le Chardonnay, FW
Le Chardonnay, LA
L'Economie, NO
Le Coq au Vin, OR
Le Cordon Bleu, OR
Left Bank, FL
Le Vichyssois, CH
Martick's, BA
Montrachet, NY
Newman's, FL
Odeon, PH
Pascal, OC
Patisserie Cafe, DC
Pinot, LA
Saint-Emilion, FW
Tersiguel's, BA
Un Grand Cafe, CH

French Classic

Antoine, OC
Belgian Lion, SD
Bon Appetit, HO
Cacharel, FW
Cafe Chauveron, MI
Cafe de France, SL
Cafe des Amis, PO
Cafe des Artistes, NY
Cafe L'Europe, PB
Carlos', CH
Chanterelle, NY
Chefs de France, OR
Chez Louis, SL
Conservatory, BA
Coventry Forge, PH
Deux Cheminees, PH
Diaghilev, LA
Didier's, MI
Dining Room, CH
Dynasty Room, LA
El Bizcocho, SD
English Room, MK
Everest Room, CH
Fio's La Fourchette, SL
Fleur de Lys, SF
Fountain Court, SE
French Room, DA
Gerard's Relais, SE
Harrow Inne, PH
Jean-Louis, DC
Jean-Pierre's, PH
Jeannier's, BA
La Bergerie, DC
La Bonne Auberge, PH
La Caravelle, NY
La Colombe d'Or, HG
La Coquille, FL
La Cote Basque, NY
La Folie, SF

La Fourchette, PH
La Grenouille, NY
La Mediterranee, KC
La Mer, HO
La Normandie, OR
La Patisserie, SL
La Provence, NO
La Reserve, FL
La Reserve, HG
La Reserve, NY
La Tour, CH
La Truffe, PH
L'Auberge, BA
L'Auberge Bret., SL
L'Auberge Chez F., DC
L'Auberge, PO
La Vieille Maison, PB
Le Bec-Fin, PH
Le Bernardin, NY
Le Bocage, BO
Le Cirque, NY
Le Festival, MI
Le Francais, CH
Le Gourmand, SE
Le Lion d'Or, DC
L'Entrecote, DA
Le Perigord, NY
Le Regence, NY
L'Escargot, SF
Le Tastevin, SE
Le Titi de Paris, CH
Les Celebrites, NY
Lespinasse, NY
L'Orangerie, LA
Louis XVI, NO
Lutece, NY
Maison Robert, BO
Malmaison, SL
Meadows, AC
Michel's, HO
Montparnasse, CH
Restaurant, Ritz, AT
Riviera, DA
St. Honore, PB
Tatsu's, KC
Terrace, NY
231 Ellsworth, SF
Versailles, NO
Voltaire, PS

French Creole

French Quarter, FL

French/Japanese

Jimmy's Place, CH
Rodin, SF
Yoshi's Cafe, CH

French Nouvelle

Alisa Cafe, PH
Ambria, CH
Andre's Gourmet, SE
Aureole, NY
Aux Beaux, DC
Bel-Air Hotel, LA
Bouley, NY
Cafe Katsu, LA
Checkers, LA
Chez Nous, BO
Chez Robert, PH
Christopher's/Bistro, PS
Ciboulette, PH
Citrus, LA
City Grill, AT
Dining Room, DC
Domaine Chandon, SF
Elephant Walk, BO
Empress of China, HG
Enjolie, FW
Evermay on Del, PH
Fleur de Lys, SF
Fresh Cream, SF
Jackie's, CH
Julien, BO
La Coquina, OR
La Toque, LA
Le Mesquite, FL
Le Mouton Noir, SF
Le Provencal, SE
L'Espalier, BO
Marius, SD
Masa's, SF
Mille Fleurs, SD
Never on Sunday, FL
Patina, LA
Sanford, MK
Sherman House, SF
Tallgrass, CH
WineSellar, SD
Yannick's, DC

German

Berghoff, CH
Bevo Mill, SL
Haussner's, BA
Josef's, BA
Karl Ratzsch's, MK
Mader's German, MK
Wine Cellar, TS

Greek

Adriatica, SE
Athena on B'way, KC
Greekfest, PS

Ikaros, BA
Little Greek, NO

Hamburgers

Charles Kinkaid, FW
Kua Aina, HO
O'Connell's Pub, SL

Haute Creole

Antoine's, NO
Arnaud's, NO
Bacco, NO
Brennan's, NO
Christian's, NO
Commander's Pal., NO
Palace Cafe, NO

Haute New Orleans

Bayona, NO
Bistro/Maison, NO
Mr. B's, NO

Hawaiian

Ono Hawaiian, HO

Indian

Bombay Cafe, LA
Bombay Grill, BA
Haandi, DC
Haveli, AT
India Palace, DA
Indian Delhi, PS
Indian Delights, AT
Indigene, PO
Plainfield's Mayur, PQ
Taj Mahal, HG

International

Arthur's 27, OR
Cafe Sophie, SE
Fedora, KC
Fountain, PH
Quilted Toque, HG
Space Needle, SE

Italian (Northern)

Alessio's, DA
Andrea's, NO
Anthony's, HG
Antonello, OC
Armani's, TS
Arturo's, PB
Bacco, NO
Basta's, TS
Bice, DC
Brass Elephant, BA
Cafe Sistina, HO
Caffe Abbracci, MI
Caffe Piemonte, OC
Casa Rolandi, MI
Casa Vecchia, FL
Christo's, PS
Damian's, HG
Davide, BO
Da Umberto, NY
Donatello, TS
Enzo's, HG
Fio's, SD
Franco's Trattoria, PS
Gaetano's, PH
Galileo, DC
Genoa, PO
Giovanni's, SL
Giovannia's Little Pl., SL
Il Capriccio, BO
Il Mulino, NY
Il Tartuffo, FL
I Ricchi, DC
Il Verdi, AC
Jasper's, KC
Kemoll's, SL
La Bussola, MI
La Cena, OR
La Finestra, PB
La Grotta (Roswell), AT
La Grotta, AT
La Scala, OR
La Tavernetta, FL
La Traviata, SA
L'Originale, OR
Mimma's Cafe, MK
Monte Carlo, PH
Never on Sunday, FL
Newman's, FL
Obelisk, DC
Olives, BO
Paesano, FL
Pane e Vino, SF
Phillip Paolo's, HO
Prezzo, PB
Primavera, NY
Ristorante Toscano, BO
Ruggeri's, DA
Saleh al Lago, SE
Trattoria Alberto, BA
Tra Vigne, SF

Italian (Southern)

Adriatica, SE
Al Boccalino, SE

Cafe Macaroni, SF
Gianpeppe's, SL
Giuseppe's, SL
Grotto, HG
Il Terrazzo, SE
Portofino, AC
Sal & Judy's, NO

Italian
(North & South)

Abruzzi, AT
Agostino's, SL
Antonio's, OR
Benedetto's, SL
Botticelli Cafe, SE
By-The-Sea, AC
Ca'Brea, LA
Capriccio, AC
Caruso's, AC
Chiapparelli's, BA
Christini's, OR
Cunetto, SL
DaBaldo's, SL
Delphina's, PO
Dilullo Centro, PH
Drago, LA
Enzo's, OR
Farotto's, SL
Franco's, CH
Frenchie's, HG
Gene & Georgetti, CH
Giacomo's, BO
Il Bistro, SE
Il Tulipano, MI
La Famiglia, PH
La Riviera, NO
Locanda Veneta, LA
Lorusso's, SL
Mineo's, SL
Mosca's, NO
Nina L'Italiana, PS
Nino's, HG
Osteria del Teatro, MI
Osteria Romana, PH
Palma Maria, OR
Piccolo Mondo, FW
Pranzo Italian, SA
Pricci, AT
Renato's, PB
Rex Il Ristorante, LA
Ristorante Ecco, SF
Ristorante Savino, DA
Roberto's, AC
Saloon, PH
Spiaggia, CH
Tony Angello's, NO
Tony's, SL
Tornatore's, SL
Trattoria No. 10, CH
Tre Figlio, AC
Valentino, LA
Va Pensiero, CH
Veco's, KC
Veni Vidi Vici, AT
Vivande Porta Via, SF
Vivere, CH

Japanese

Ginza Japanese, HG
Gyuhama, BO
Hatsuhana, CH
Hatsuhana, NY
Hyakumi, AC
Kabuto Sushi, SF
Katsu, LA
Kawasaki, BA
Kitayami, OC
Kyo-Ya, SF
La Salle, HO
Little Tokyo, NO
Matsuhisa, LA
Mr. Sushi, DA
Nikko's, SE
Nobu's, SL
Obi, PO
Restaurant Suntory, HO
Sagami, PH
Sasaki, HG
Shogun, HO
Shogun, PS
Su Shin, FL
Sushi Nozawa, LA
Sushisay, NY
Takeshima, BO
Yamakasa, PS
Yanagi Sushi, HO

Jewish

Rascal House, MI

Mediterranean

Adelmo's, DA
Bay Wolf, SF
Campanile, LA
Casa Vecchia, FL
Dmitri's, PH
Mary Elaine's, PS
Olives, BO
Splashes, OC
Square One, SF
Tabrizi's, BA
Zov's Bistro, OC

Mexican/Tex-Mex

Cal. Taqueria, KC
El Puerco Lloron, SE
Fajitas, PS
Frontera Grill, CH
Javier's, DA
Joe T. Garcia's, FW
La Calle Doce, DA
La Casa Sena, SA
La Hacienda, PS
La Playa Maya, FW
Las Brisas, OC
La Taqueria, SF
Old Mexico Grill, SA
Pappasito's, HG
Pueblo Nuevo, SL
Quintero's, HO
Rio Grande Cafe, DC
Santa Fe, NO
Topolobampo, CH
Via Real, FW
Zarela, NY

Middle Eastern

Boulevard Cafe, KC
Byblos, FW
Nabil's, KC
West Side Cafe, KC

Moroccan

Hajjibaba's, HO

New Mexican

Rancho de Chimayo, SA
Shed, SA

Northwest Regional

Chez Shea, SE
Fountain Court, SE
Fullers, SE
Heathman, PO
McCormick, PO

Nouvelle Creole

Emeril's, NO
Galatoire's, NO
Gautreau's, NO

Nuova Cucina Italian

Acquerello, SF
Bruno's Little Italy, SL
Cafe Juanita, SE
Caffe Baci, MI
Carrabba's, HG
Davio's, BO
Il Fornaio, OC
Maxaluna, PB
Mezzanotte, MI
Michela's, BO
Primavera, FL
Tutto Mare, OC
Upstairs/Pudding, BO

Pacific New Wave

C'est Fan Fan, LA
Chaya Brasserie, LA
Chinois on Main, LA
Five Feet, OC
Matsuhisa, LA
Shiro, LA

Pacific Rim

Prince Court, HO
Roy's, HO

Pizza

Acapella, DA
Farotto's, SL
Patsy's Pizza (Bklyn), NY
Pizzeria Paradiso, DC
Pizzeria Uno, CH
Star Pizza, HG
Tacconelli's, PH

Russian

Diaghilev, LA
Russian Tea Rm., NY

Salvadoran

Eliana's, PS

Sandwiches/Fast Food

Central Grocery, NO
Kua Aina, HO
Patisserie Descours, HG
St. Louis Bread, SL
White House, AC

Seafood

Anthony's Star, SD
Aqua, SF
Aragon Cafe, MI
Boston's Fish, OR
Bristol, KC
Burt & Jack's, FL
Cafe Pacific, DA
Cafe Pacifica, SD
Casamento's, NO
Charley's Crab, PB

Couch Street, PO
Down Under, FL
Entre Nous, CH
Fish Market, MI
Fish Market, SD
Fleming, MI
George's/Cove, SD
Grill, LA
Harbor View, AC
Haussner's, BA
Hemingway's, OR
Jasper's, BO
Joe's Stone Crab, MI
John Dominis, HO
La Calle Doce, DA
Le Bernardin, NY
Legal Sea Foods, BO
Lobster Pot, TS
Lobster Shop, SE
Man. Ocean Cl., NY
McCormick's Fish, PO
Monty's, MI
Nick's, HO
Oaks, AC
Obrycki's, BA
Opus Too, PO
Oyster Bar, NY
Oystercatchers, TS
Pappadeaux, HG
Peerce's, BA
Pierpoint, BA
Pier 7 Restaurant, AC
Polo Grill, BA
Portobello, OR
Prime Rib, DC
Ray's Boathouse, SE
Savoy Grill, KC
Shaw's, CH
Steamer's, PS
Straub's, OR
Swan Oyster, SF
Uglesich, NO
Water Grill, LA
Winterborne, PO

SE Asian

Germaine's, DC
Wild Ginger, SE

Serbian

Three Brothers, MK

South American

Churrascos, HG

Southern/Soul Food

Burton's Grill, AT
Gennie's Bishop Grill, DA
Mrs. White's, PS
Ruby's, KC
Stroud's, KC
Tom's Place, PB

Southwestern

Arizona Kitchen, PS
Armadillo Cafe, FL
Baby Routh, DA
Cafe Annie, HG
Cafe Pasqual's, SA
Cardwell's, SL
Coyote Cafe, SA
DeVille, HG
Golden Swan, PS
Kachina, OC
Mansion, DA
Mesa Grill, NY
Nana Grill, DA
Pacifica Grill, SD
Paradise Diner, KC
Routh Street, DA
Ruggles Grill, HG
SantaCafe, SA
Scarlett Loco, SD
Staab House, SA
Top/Rock, PS
Vincent Guerithault, PS
Z'Tejas Grill, PS

Spanish

Cafe Seville, FL
Casa Juancho, MI
Dali, BO
El Farol, SA
Emilio's Tapas, CH
Marquesa, PS
Meson Sabika, CH
Ramiro's, MI
Tio Pepe, BA
Tio Pepe's, TS

Steakhouses

Al Baker's, SL
Al's Restaurant, SL
Andria's, SL
Bern's, TS
Bone's, AT
Brenner's, HG
Bristol, KC
Burt & Jack's, FL
Castle Stkhse., AC

Chops, AT
Christy's, MI
Churrascos, HG
Del Frisco's, DA
Down Under, FL
Gene & Georgetti, CH
Grill 23, BO
Grill, LA
Harris', SF
Hy's, HO
Kelly's, HG
Kreis', SL
Linda's La Cantina, OR
Lynn's, HG
Max's, AC
Metropolitan, SE
Mortons, BO
Mortons, CH
Mortons, DA
Mortons, DC
Mortons, PH
Nikko, KC
Oaks, AC
Palm, MI
Palm, NY
Peter Luger, NY
Plaza III, KC
Polo Grill, BA
Prime Place, AC
Prime Rib, DC
Raindancer, FL
Ruth's Chris, DA
Ruth's Chris, FL
Ruth's Chris, HO
Ruth's Chris, MI
Ruth's Chris, NO
Ruth's Chris, OR
Ruth's Chris, PB
Ruth's Chris, PS
Sally's, MK
Saloon, PH
Savoy Grill, KC
Smith & Wollensky, NY
Sparks, NY
Taste of Texas, HG
Young's, NO

Swiss

Andre's Confiserie, KC
Le Cordon Bleu, OR
Quail Hollow Inn, HG
Swiss Inn, HO

Thai

Alisa Cafe, PH
Arun's, CH
Bangkok IV, OC
Busara, DC
Celadon, SD
Duangrat's, DC
Keo's, HO
Keo's Thai, HO
Khan Toke, SF
Malee's, PS
Mekong Thai, HO
Nit Noi Thai, HG
Thai Orchid, MI
Thai Restaurant, SE
Thai Soon, DA

Vegetarian

(Almost all health
food spots, Chinese,
Indian, Thai and
other ethnics have
vegetarian meals,
as do the following)

Five Seasons, BO
Green's, SF
Unicorn Village, MI

Vietnamese

Andre's Gourmet, SE
Hy-Vong, MI
Mai Lee, SL
Vietnam, PH
Yen Ha, PO

ALPHABETICAL PAGE INDEX

Abruzzi Ristorante, AT	13	Bellucci's, KC	95
Acapella Cafe, DA	55	Benedetto's, SL	210
Acquerello, SF	189	Berghoff, CH	44
Actuelle, DA	55	Bern's, TS	218
Addison Cafe, DA	55	Bevo Mill, SL	210
Adelmo's, DA	55	Biba, BO	34
Adriatica, SE	202	Bice, DC	223
Agostino's, SL	209	Bijou Cafe, PO	179
Al Baker's, SL	209	Bird, CH	44
Al Boccalino, SE	202	Bishop's Lodge, SF	197
Alessio's, DA	55	Bistro, MI	114
Alisa Cafe, PH	162	Bistro Banlieue, CH	44
Al's Restaurant, SL	209	Bistro/Maison, NO	127
"a Mano", MI	114	Bistro 201, OC	145
Ambria, CH	44	Blue Heron, TS	218
American Rest., KC	95	Blue Room, BO	34
Andrea's, NO	126	Bombay Cafe, LA	104
Andre's, KC	95	Bombay Grill, BA	26
Andre's Gourmet, SE	202	Bon Appetit, HO	77
Andria's, SL	209	Bone's, AT	13
Angelo's BBQ, FW	71	Bon Ton Cafe, NO	127
Anthony's, HO	85	Boston's Fish, OR	150
Anthony's Star, SD	183	Botticelli Cafe, SE	202
Antoine, OC	144	Boulevard Cafe, KC	95
Antoine's, NO	126	Bouley, NY	136
Antonello, OC	144	Braddock's, PH	162
Antonio's, OR	150	Brass Elephant, BA	27
Aqua, SF	189	Brasserie Max, FL	64
Aragon Cafe, MI	114	Brennan's, HO	85
Arcadia, NY	136	Brennan's, NO	127
Arizona Kitchen, PS	171	Brenner's, HO	85
Armadillo Cafe, FL	64	Brickell Club, MI	114
Armani's, TS	217	Brigtsen's, NO	127
Arnaud's, NO	126	Bristol, KC	96
Arthur's 27, OR	150	Bruno's Little Italy, SL	210
Arturo's, PB	156	brusseau's, SE	202
Arun's, CH	44	Buckhead Diner, AT	13
A Taste of N.O., AT	13	Burt & Jack's, FL	64
Athena on B'way, KC	95	Burton's Grill, AT	14
Atwater's, PO	178	Busara, DC	223
Aujourd'Hui, BO	34	By-The-Sea, AC	21
Aureole, NY	136	By Word/Mouth, FL	64
Aux Beaux, DC	223	Byblos, FW	72
Avner's, DA	56	Ca'Brea, LA	104
Azalea, AT	13	Cacharel, FW	72
Baby Routh, DA	56	Cafe Allegro, KC	96
Bacco, NO	126	Cafe Annie, HO	85
Balaban's, SL	209	Cafe Arugula, FL	65
Balcony, The, FW	71	Cafe Aspen, FW	72
Bali-By-The-Sea, HO	76	Cafe Chardonnay, PB	156
Bangkok IV, OC	145	Cafe Chauveron, MI	115
Bubbalou's, OR	150	Cafe/Ch. Panisse, SF	189
Basta's, TS	218	Cafe de France, OR	150
Bay Wolf, SF	189	Cafe de France, SL	210
Bayona, NO	126	Cafe des Amis, PO	179
B.C. Chong, MI	114	Cafe des Artistes, NY	136
Bel-Air Hotel, LA	104	Cafe Haleiwa, HO	77
Belgian Lion, SD	183	Cafe Juanita, SE	203

Entry	Page	Entry	Page
Cafe Katsu, LA	104	Chez Louis, SL	211
Cafe L'Europe, PB	157	Chez Nous, BO	35
Cafe L'Europe, TS	218	Chez Nous, HO	86
Cafe Macaroni, SF	189	Chez Panisse, SF	190
Cafe Matthew, FW	72	Chez Robert, PH	162
Cafe Max, FL	65	Chez Shea, SE	203
Cafe Pacific, DA	56	Chiapparelli's, BA	27
Cafe Pacifica, SD	184	Chimmey, The, DA	57
Cafe Pasqual's, SF	197	China Blossom, NO	128
Cafe Provencal, CH	45	Chinois on Main, LA	105
Cafe Renee, SL	210	Chops, AT	15
Cafe Seville, FL	65	Chopstix, AT	15
Cafe Sistina, HO	77	Christian's, NO	128
Cafe Sophie, SE	203	Christini's, OR	151
Cafe Sport, SE	203	Christo's, PS	171
Cafe, AT	14	Christopher's/Bistro, PS	171
Cafe, AT	14	Christy's, MI	116
Caffe Abbracci, MI	115	Churrascos, HO	86
Caffe Baci, MI	115	Ciboulette, PH	162
Caffe Piemonte, OC	145	Cindy Black's, SD	184
Cal. Taqueria, KC	96	Citrus, LA	105
Campagne, SE	203	City Cafe, DA	57
Campanile, LA	104	City Grill, AT	15
Campton Place, SF	190	Clancy's, NO	128
Capriccio, AC	21	Clark's BBQ, DA	57
Carbo's Cafe, AT	14	Classic Cup, KC	96
Cardwell's, SL	211	Clearwater Beach, TS	218
Carlos', CH	45	Coach and Six, AT	15
Carnegie Deli, NY	136	Coeur de Lion, DC	223
Carrabba's, HO	86	Colonnade, DC	224
Carriage House, FW	73	Colony, TS	219
Caruso's, AC	22	Commander's Pal., NO	128
Casa Juancho, MI	116	Compound, SF	198
Casa Larios, MI	115	Conservatory, BA	27
Casamento's, NO	127	Conservatory, DA	57
Casa Rolandi, MI	115	Cornucopia, BO	35
Casa Vecchia, FL	65	Cottage, CH	45
Castle Stkhse., AC	22	Couch Street, PO	179
Celadon, SD	184	Coventry Forge, PH	162
Celebration, FW	73	Coyote Cafe, SF	198
Central Grocery, NO	128	Crozier's, NO	129
C'est Fan Fan, LA	105	Cunetto, SL	211
Chanteclair, OC	145	Cypress Club, SF	190
Chanterelle, NY	136	Cypress Room, FL	66
Chaplin's, DA	56	DaBaldo's, SL	211
Chapparal Room, PS	171	Dahlia Lounge, SE	204
Charade, MI	116	Dali, BO	35
Charles Kincaid, FW	73	Damian's, HO	87
Charlie Trotter's, CH	45	Damon's, SL	211
Charley's Crab, PB	157	Da Umberto, NY	137
Charley's 517, HO	86	Davide, BO	35
Chatham's Pl., OR	151	Davio's, BO	35
Chau Chow, BO	34	Delectables, AT	15
Chaya Brasserie, LA	105	Del Frisco's, DA	57
Checkers, LA	105	Delphina's, PO	179
Chef Allen's, MI	116	Dessert Place, AT	16
Chefs' Cafe, AT	14	Deux Cheminees, PH	163
Chefs de France, OR	151	Deville, HO	87
Chen's Dynasty, PO	179	Diaghilev, LA	106
Chez Georges, HO	86	Didier's, MI	116
Chez Gerard, DA	56	Different Pt./View, PS	171

DiIullo Centro, PH . . . 163
Dining Galleries, MI . . 117
Dining Room, AT . . . 16
Dining Room, CH . . . 46
Dining Room, DC . . . 224
Dmitri's, PH 163
Dobson's, SD 184
Dolce & Freddo, HO . . 87
Domaine Chandon, SF 190
Dominique's, MI 117
Donatello, TS 219
Downtown Bakery, SF 190
Down Under, FL 66
Drago, LA 106
Duangrat's, DC 224
Dux, OR 151
Dynasty Room, LA . . 106
East Coast Grill, BO . . 36
El Bizcocho, SD 184
Elephant Walk, BO . . 36
El Farol, SF 198
Eliana's, PS 172
El Puerco Lloron, SE . 204
Emeril's, NO 129
Emilio's, CH 46
Empress of China, HO 87
Empress Room, OR . . 151
English Room, MI . . . 122
Enjolie, FW 73
Entre Nous, CH 46
Enzo's, OR 152
Enzo's, HO 87
Esplanade, PO 180
Euphemia Haye, TS . . 219
Everest Room, CH . . 46
Evermay on Del., PH . 163
Explorers, PB 157
Fajitas, PS 172
Farotto's, SL 212
Faust's, SL 212
Fedora, KC 96
Fio's La Fourchette, SL 212
Fio's, SD 185
First China, AT 16
Fish Market, MI 117
Fish Market, SD 185
Five Feet, OC 145
Five Seasons, BO . . . 36
Fleming, MI 117
Fleur de Lys, SF 191
Flower Lounge, SF . . 191
Flying Saucer, SF . . . 191
Forbidden City, OR . . 152
Forge, MI 117
Fountain Court, SE . . 204
Fountain, PH 163
Four Seasons, NY . . . 137
Franco's, CH 46
Franco's Trattoria, PS . 172
French Quarter, FL . . 66
French Room, DA 58
French Side, SD 185
Frenchie's, HO 88
Frenchtown Inn, PH . 164
Fresh Cream, SF . . 191
Frontera Grill, CH . . . 47
Fullers, SE 204
Gaetano's, PH 164
Galatoire's, NO 129
Galileo, DC 224
Garrozzo's, KC 97
Gaspar's, DA 58
Gautreau's, NO 129
Gazebo Cafe, PB . . 157
Gene & Georgetti, CH . 47
Genghis Khan, NO . . 129
Gennie's Bishop, DA . . 58
Genoa, PO 180
George's/Cove, SD . 185
Georgian Room, SE . 204
Gerard's Relais, SE . 205
Germaine's, DC . . . 225
Giacomo's, BO 36
Gianpeppe's, SL . . . 212
Ginza Japanese, HO . 88
Giovanni's Little Pl., SL 212
Giovanni's, SL 212
Giuseppe's, SL . . . 213
Golden Dragon, HO . . 77
Golden Swan, PS . . 172
Gordon, CH 47
Gotham, NY 137
Gourmet House, PS . 172
Grand Cafe, MI . . . 118
Grand Street, KC . . . 97
Granita, LA 106
Grant Grill, SD 185
Greekfest, PS 173
Greenery, CH 47
Green Hills Inn, PH . 164
Green's, SF 191
Green's BBQ, HO . . . 88
Green Street, BO . . . 36
Grenadier's, MI . . . 122
Grill, Ritz, PS 173
Grill Room, NO . . . 130
Grill, DC 225
Grill, LA 106
Grill 23, BO 37
Grotto, HO 88
Guadalupe Cafe, SF . 198
Gustaf Anders, OC . 145
Gyuhama , BO 37
Haandi, DC 225
Hajjibaba's, HO 77
Hamersley's, BO 37
Hamptons, BA 27
Harbor View, AC 22
Harris', SF 192
Harrow Inne, PH . . . 164
Harvard Street, BO . . 37
Hatsuhana, CH 47

Entry	Page
Hatsuhana, NY	137
Haussner's, BA	27
Havana Cafe, PS	173
Haveli, AT	16
Heathman, PO	180
Hedgerose, AT	17
Helmand, SF	192
Hemingway's, OR	152
Hersh's Orchard, BA	28
Ho Ho, AT	17
Honto, AT	17
Horny Toad, PS	173
House of Chan, AT	17
House of Joy, PS	173
House of Nanking, SF	192
Houston's, PS	173
Hsu's, AT	17
Hunan Empire, KC	97
Hunan, HO	88
Hunter's Hollow, SL	213
Hyakumi, AC	22
Hy's, HO	78
Hy-Vong, MI	118
Icarus, BO	37
Ikaros, BA	28
Il Bistro, SE	205
Il Capriccio, BO	38
Il Fornaio, OC	146
Il Mulino, NY	137
Il Tartuffo, FL	66
Il Terrazzo, SE	205
Il Tulipano, MI	118
Il Verdi, AC	22
Immigrant Room, MI	122
Imperial Hotel, DC	225
Indian Delhi, PS	174
Indian Delights, AT	18
India Palace, DA	58
Indigene, PO	180
Indigo, AT	18
Inn/Little Wash., DC	226
Inn/Phillips Mill, PH	164
Inn/Anasazi, SF	198
I Ricchi, DC	226
Ivana's, AC	23
Ivy, LA	107
Jackie's, CH	48
Jake's, PH	164
Janousek's, AT	18
Jasmine, DA	58
Jasper's, BO	38
Jasper's, KC	97
Javier's, DA	58
Jean Claude's, PS	174
Jean-Louis, DC	226
Jeannier's, BA	28
Jean-Pierre's, PH	165
Jimmy's Place, CH	48
Jody Maroni's, LA	107
Joe's, LA	107
Joe's, PH	165
Joe's Stone Crab, MI	118
Joe T. Garcia's, FW	73
John Dominis, HO	78
Jordan's Grove, OR	152
Josef's, BA	28
Julien, BO	38
JW'S, OC	146
Kabuto Sushi, SF	192
Kachina, OC	146
Karl Ratzsch's, MI	123
Katsu, LA	107
Kawasaki, BA	28
Kelly's, HO	89
Kemoll's, SL	213
Keo's, HO	78
Keo's Thai, HO	78
Khan Toke, SF	192
King Charles, TS	219
Kings Contrivance, BA	29
Kitayama, OC	146
Kreis', SL	213
Kua Aina, HO	78
Kyo-Ya, SF	192
La Bergerie, DC	226
La Bonne Auberge, PH	165
La Bonne Crepe, FL	67
La Bussola, MI	118
Labuznik, SE	205
La Calle Doce, DA	59
La Campagne, PH	165
La Caravelle, NY	137
La Casa Sena, SF	198
La Cena, OR	152
La Colline, DC	226
La Colombe d'Or, HO	89
La Coquille, FL	67
La Coquina, OR	153
La Cote Basque, NY	138
La Cuisine, NO	130
La Famiglia, PH	165
La Ferme, FL	67
La Finestra, PB	157
La Folie, SF	193
La Fourchette, PH	166
La Grenouille, NY	138
La Grotta, AT	18
La Grotta, AT	18
La Hacienda, PS	174
Lambert's, SF	199
La Mediterranee, KC	97
La Mer, HO	79
La Normandie, OR	153
La Patisserie, SL	213
La Playa Maya, FW	74
La Poele d'Or, TS	219
La Provence, NO	130
La Reserve, FL	67
La Reserve, HO	89
La Reserve, NY	138
La Riviera, NO	130

Lark Creek Inn, SF	193	Linda's La Cantina, OR	154
La Salle, HO	79	Linwood's, BA	29
Las Brisas, OC	146	Little Greek, NO	131
La Scala, OR	153	Little Tokyo, NO	131
La Taqueria, SF	193	Lobster Pot, TS	220
La Tavernetta, FL	67	Lobster Shop, The, SE	206
La Tertulia, SF	199	Locanda Veneta, LA	108
Latilla Room, PS	174	Locke-Ober Cafe, BO	39
La Toque, LA	108	L'Orangerie, LA	108
La Tour, CH	48	L'Originale, OR	153
La Traviata, SF	199	Lorusso's, SL	214
La Truffe, PH	166	Louis XVI, NO	131
L'Auberge, BA	29	Lucie, DC	227
L'Auberge Bret., SL	214	Lutece, NY	139
L'Auberge Chez F., DC	227	Lynn's, HO	89
L'Auberge, PB	158	Mader's German, MI	123
L'Auberge, PO	180	Mah Jong, AT	19
Laurels, DA	59	Mai Lee, SL	214
L'Avenue, SF	193	Maile, HO	79
La Vieille Maison, PB	158	Mainland Inn, PH	166
Lawry's, LA	108	Maison et Jardin, OR	154
Lawry's, DA	59	Maison Robert, BO	39
Le Bar Lyonnais, PH	166	Malee's, PS	174
Le Bec-Fin, PH	166	Malmaison, SL	214
Le Bernardin, NY	138	Mancuso's, PS	174
Le Bocage, BO	38	Man. Ocean Cl., NY	139
Le Bordeaux, TS	220	Mansion, DA	59
Le Caprice, DC	227	March, NY	140
Le Chardonnay, FW	74	Marius, SD	186
Le Chardonnay, LA	108	Mark's Place, MI	119
Le Cirque, NY	138	Mark, The, PB	158
L'Ecole, PS	172	Marquesa, PS	175
L'Economie, NO	131	Martick's, BA	29
Le Coq au Vin, OR	153	Mary Elaine's, PS	175
Le Cordon Bleu, OR	154	Masa's, SF	194
Le Dome, FL	68	Matsuhisa, LA	109
Lee's, SL	214	Maxaluna, PB	158
Le Festival, MI	119	Max's	23
Le Francais, CH	48	Max's Grille, PB	158
Left Bank, FL	68	McCormick, PO	181
Legal Sea Foods, BO	38	McCormick's Fish, PO	181
Le Gourmand, SE	205	Meadows, AC	23
Le Jardin, NO	131	Mekong Thai, HO	79
Le Lion d'Or, DC	227	Melrose, DC	227
Le Mesquite, FL	68	Mesa Grill, NY	140
Le Mikado, CH	49	Meson Sabika, CH	49
Le Mouton Noir, SF	193	Metropolis, KC	98
L'Entrecote, DA	59	Metropolitan, SE	206
Le Palais, AC	23	Mezzanotte, MI	119
Le Pavillon, MI	119	Michael's, FW	74
Le Perigord, NY	139	Michael's, LA	109
Le Picnique, KC	97	Michael's, TS	220
Le Provencal, SE	206	Michel's, HO	80
Le Regence, NY	139	Michela's, BO	40
L'Escargot, SF	194	Mike's, NO	132
Les Celebrites, NY	139	Mille Fleurs, SD	186
L'Espalier, BO	39	Milton Inn, BA	29
Lespinasse, NY	139	Mimma's Cafe, MI	123
Le Tastevin, SE	206	Mineo's, SL	214
Le Titi de Paris, CH	49	Mise en Place, TS	220
Le Vichyssois, CH	49	Monte Carlo, PH	167

Name	Page	Name	Page
Montparnasse, CH	49	Palm Court, PS	175
Montrachet, NY	140	Palm Too, NY	140
Monty's, MI	119	Pandl's, MI	123
Morada, PB	159	Pane/Vino, SF	194
Morrison-Clark Inn, DC	228	Pano's and Paul's, AT	19
Morton's, BO	40	Papa Haydn, PO	181
Morton's, CH	50	Pappadeaux, HO	90
Morton's, DA	60	Pappasito's, HO	90
Morton's, DC	228	Paradise Diner, KC	99
Morton's, PH	167	Parker's, BO	40
Mosca's, NO	132	Park Plaza, OR	154
Mr. B's, NO	132	Parkway Grill, LA	109
Mrs. Peter's, KC	98	Parkway Market, KC	99
Mr. Sushi, DA	60	Partners, AT	20
Mrs. White's, PS	175	Pascal, OC	147
Murphy's, AT	19	Patina, LA	109
Murray's, KC	98	Patisserie Cafe, DC	229
Nabil's, KC	98	Patisserie Descours, HO	90
Nana Grill, DA	60	Patsy's Pizza, NY	140
Napoleon Cafe, PH	167	Pavilion, The, OC	147
Never on Sunday, FL	68	Pavilion/Walters, BA	30
New Peking, KC	98	Pebbles, OR	155
Newman's, FL	68	Peerce's, BA	30
Nicholas, DC	228	Peking Duck, AC	23
Nick's, HO	80	Peking Gourmet, DC	229
Nikko, KC	98	Pepper Corn, KC	99
Nikko's, SE	206	Peter Luger, NY	141
Nikolai's Roof, AT	19	Phillip Paolo's, HO	81
Nina L'Italiana, PS	175	Piccolo Mondo, FW	74
95th, CH	50	Pierpoint, BA	30
Nino's, HO	89	Pier 7 Restaurant, AC	24
Nit Noi Thai, HO	90	Pink Adobe, SF	199
Nobu's, SL	215	Pinot, LA	110
Nora, DC	228	Pizzeria Paradiso, DC	229
Oaks, AC	23	Pizzeria Uno, CH	50
Oasis Cafe, BO	40	Plainfield's Mayur, PO	182
Obelisk, DC	228	Plaza Dining Rm., BO	41
Obi, PO	181	Plaza III, KC	99
Obrycki's, BA	30	Pleasant Peasant, AT	20
Occidental Grill, DC	229	Plum Room, FL	69
Ocean Grand, PB	159	Polo Grill, BA	30
O'Connell's Pub, SL	215	Portobello, OR	155
Odeon, PH	167	Portofino, AC	24
Old Mexico Grill, SF	199	Postrio, SF	194
Old Swiss, FW	74	Pranzo Italian, SF	200
Old Warsaw, DA	60	Prezzo, PB	159
Olives, BO	40	Pricci, AT	20
103 West, AT	19	Primavera, FL	69
Ono Hawaiian, HO	80	Primavera, NY	141
Opus Too, PO	181	Prime Place, AC	24
Orchids, HO	80	Prime Rib, BA	31
Osteria del Teatro, MI	120	Prime Rib, DC	229
Osteria Romana, PH	167	Prince Court, HO	81
Oyster Bar, NY	140	Princess Garden, KC	99
Oystercatchers, TS	220	Printer's Row, CH	50
Pacifica Grill, SD	186	Pueblo Nuevo, SL	215
Paesano, FL	69	Puffin's, BA	31
Palace, SF	199	Pump Room, CH	51
Palma Maria, OR	154	Pyramid Room, DA	60
Palm, NY	140	Quail Hollow Inn, HO	91
Palm, MI	120	Quilted Giraffe, NY	141

Quilted Toque, HG	91	Saddle Peak, LA	110
Quintero's, HO	81	Sagami, PH	168
Rainbow Room, NY	141	Saint-Emilion, FW	75
Raindancer, FL	69	Sal & Judy's, NO	133
Rainwater's, SD	186	Saleh Al Lago, SE	207
Ramiro's, MI	120	Sally's, MI	123
Ram's Head, AC	24	Saloon, PH	168
Rancho de Chimayo, SF	200	Sanford, MI	124
Rarities, BO	41	SantaCafe, SF	200
Rascal House, MI	120	Santa Fe, NO	132
Ray's Boathouse, SE	207	Sasaki, HO	92
Reading Term., PH	168	Savoy Grill, KC	100
Red Dragon, KC	100	Sazerac, NO	133
Reflections, FW	75	Scarlett Loco, SD	186
Reg. Bev. Wilshire, LA	110	Seasons, BO	41
Renato's, PB	159	Seasons, CH	51
Restaurant Suntory, HO	81	Secret, HO	82
Restaurant 210, PH	168	Sequoia, DC	230
Restaurant, AT	20	Seventh Inn, SL	215
Restaurant, DC	230	72 Market Street, LA	111
Restaurant, PS	175	Shaw's, CH	51
Rex II, LA	110	Shed, SF	200
R.G.'s, TS	221	Sherman House, SF	195
Ringside, PO	182	Shiro, LA	111
Rio Grande Cafe, DC	230	Shogun, HO	82
Ristorante Ecco, SF	194	Shogun, PS	176
Ristorante Savino, DA	61	Shun Lee Palace, NY	142
Ristorante Toscano, BO	41	Silverado Cafe, FL	70
Ritz-Carlton D.R., SF	194	Smith & Wollensky, NY	142
Ritz-Carlton Hotel, HO	91	Smoke Stack, KC	100
Ritz-Carlton, OC	147	Sonny Bryan's, DA	62
Ritz, OC	147	Space Needle, SE	207
River Cafe, NY	141	Spago, LA	111
River Oaks, HO	91	Sparks, NY	142
Riviera, DA	61	Spiaggia, CH	51
Rivoli Restaurant, HO	91	Splashes, OC	147
Roberto's, AC	24	Square One, SF	195
Rockenwagner, LA	110	Staab House, SF	200
Rodin, SF	195	Stars, SF	195
Roka, BO	41	St. Cloud, BO	42
Roller's, PH	168	Star Pizza, HO	92
Rotisserie Beef/Bird, HO	92	Steamer's, PS	176
Routh Street, DA	61	Stephenson's, KC	101
Roxsand, PS	176	St. Honore, PB	160
Royal China, KC	100	St. Louis Bread, SL	215
Roy's, HO	82	Straub's, OR	155
Rozzelle Court, KC	100	Stroud's, KC	101
Ruby's, KC	100	Studio One Cafe, FL	70
Rudys' 2900, BA	31	Su Shin, FL	70
Ruggeri's, DA	61	Su Shin, MI	121
Ruggles Grill, HO	92	Susanna Foo, PH	169
Russian Tea Rm., NY	142	Sushi Nozawa, LA	111
Ruth's Chris, DA	61	Sushisay, NY	142
Ruth's Chris, FL	70	Swan Oyster, SF	195
Ruth's Chris, HO	82	Swann Lounge, PH	169
Ruth's Chris, MI	120	Swiss Inn, HO	82
Ruth's Chris, NO	132	Tabrizi's, BA	31
Ruth's Chris, OR	155	Tacconelli's, PH	169
Ruth's Chris, PB	159	Taj Mahal, HO	92
Ruth's Chris, PS	176	Takeshima, BO	42
Sabals, TS	221	Tallgrass, CH	51

Taste of Texas, HO	93	Upstairs/Pudding, BO	42
Tatsu's, KC	101	Valentino, LA	112
Tavern/Green, NY	142	Va Pensiero, CH	52
T. C. Eggington's, PS	176	Veco's, KC	101
Terra, SF	196	Veni Vidi Vici, AT	20
Terrace, NY	143	Venue, KC	102
Tersiguel's, BA	31	Veranda, MI	121
Thai Orchid, MI	121	Versailles, NO	134
Thai Restaurant, SE	207	Via Real, FW	75
Thai Soon, DA	62	Vietnam, PH	169
Thee Bungalow, SD	186	Vincent Guerithalt	177
Three Brothers, MI	124	Vivande Porta Via, SF	196
302 West, CH	52	Vivere, CH	52
Tio Pepe, BA	32	Voltaire, PS	177
Tio Pepe's, TS	221	Walker Bros., CH	53
Tivoli, DC	230	Water Grill, LA	112
Tom's Place, PB	160	Waterside, BA	32
Tony Angello's, NO	133	West Side Cafe, KC	102
Tony Cheng's, BA	32	Westerfield House, SL	216
Tony's, HO	93	White House, AC	25
Tony's, SL	216	Wild Ginger, SE	207
Top of Cove, SD	187	Willard Room, DC	231
Top of Rock, PS	177	Willows, The, HO	83
Top of World, OR	155	Windows/World, NY	143
Topolobampo, CH	52	Wine Cellar, TS	221
Tornatore's, SL	216	WineSellar, SD	187
Tours, FW	75	Winterborne, PO	182
Trattoria Alberto, BA	32	Woks, The, KC	102
Trattoria No. 10, CH	52	Yamakasa, PS	177
Tra Vigne, SF	196	Yanagi Sushi, HO	83
Tre Figlio, AC	25	Yannick's, DC	231
Trey Yuen, NO	133	Yen Ha, PO	182
Tutto Mare, OC	148	York Street, DA	62
Twenty-One, DC	231	Yoshi's Cafe, CH	53
"21" Club, NY	143	Young's, NO	134
231 Ellsworth, SF	196	Yuca, MI	121
Uglesich, NO	133	Yujean Kang's, LA	112
Uncle Tai's, DA	62	Zarela, NY	143
Uncle Tai's, PB	160	Zia Diner, SF	200
Un Grand Cafe, CH	52	Zov's Bistro, OC	148
Unicorn Village, MI	121	Z' Tejas Grill, PS	177
Union Square, NY	143		
Upperline, NO	134		

WINE VINTAGE CHART 1981-1991

These ratings are designed to help you select wine to go with your meal. They are on the same 0–to–30 scale used throughout this *Survey*. The ratings reflect both the quality of the vintage and the wine's readiness to drink. Thus if a wine is not fully mature or is over the hill, its rating has been reduced. The ratings were prepared principally by our friend Howard Stravitz, a law professor at the University of South Carolina.

WHITES	81	82	83	84	85	86	87	88	89	90	91
French:											
Burgundy	15	20	15	11	28	29	13	23	27	20	14
Loire Valley	—	—	—	—	17	18	14	19	25	24	15
Champagne	23	29	23	—	25	24	—	—	26	25	—
Sauternes	25	—	28	—	21	26	—	27	26	23	—
California:											
Chardonnay	—	—	—	18	22	25	19	26	22	28	25
REDS											
French:											
Bordeaux	23	29	25	14	28	24	22	24	26	24	19
Burgundy	—	18	25	—	28	13	22	24	24	26	23
Rhône	16	16	25	—	25	21	14	25	24	23	17
Beaujolais	—	—	—	—	18	17	18	22	25	23	24
California:											
Cabernet/ Merlot	22	23	16	27	26	25	25	17	20	24	23
Zinfandel	—	—	—	18	18	17	20	15	16	19	19
Italian:											
Chianti	14	16	13	—	25	15	—	23	—	24	—
Piedmont	13	25	—	—	25	12	17	20	25	22	11

Bargain sippers take note—some wines are reliable year in, year out, and are reasonably priced as well. These wines are best bought in the most recent vintages. They include: Alsatian Pinot Blancs, Côtes du Rhône, Muscadet, Bardolino, Valpolicella and inexpensive Spanish Rioja and California Zinfandel.